MOUNT RUSHMORE

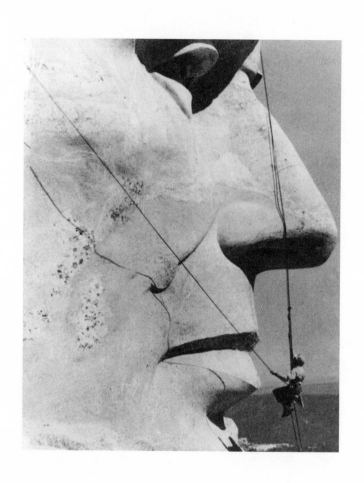

MOUNT RUSHMORE

AN ICON RECONSIDERED

JESSE LARNER

Thunder's Mouth Press/Nation Books

FOR ANN MARIE WOOD

CONTENTS

1

THE FACES

About three hours' fast driving west from Chicago, the straggling small towns of the city's umbra give out, and the great rolling plains begin. Taking the local roads—I was on Iowa 6, but it went for two hundred miles without an identifying sign—I could see cows, horses, and sheep; lots of silos; split-rail fences; farmhouses and barns, all under an enormous blue bowl of sky, from which, if one believes the radio evangelists, the All-Seeing Eye of God was watching my car pick its way across the landscape like an ant, like a speck, like the glowing pinprick of light that is a human soul. The eye misses nothing.

Halfway across South Dakota, on South Dakota 38 West this time, I saw water on the road ahead. I didn't slow down at first because I'd seen the optical illusion of water before.

There really was water on the road. I could see the place where water collects by the side of the road in wet years, and this was more

1

than a wet year. The two ellipses of pond beside the raised road kissed each other, meeting four or five inches deep over the tarmac.

I drove through, not wanting to get stuck but not expecting to, either. A hundred yards past the overflow I stopped, backed up, and parked on the shoulder. I got out and waded through the water on the road, still wearing my sandals.

It was a hot, sunny day, with fantastic shapes of clouds filling up that huge sky. The flatness of the land gave an extra dimension to the sky, and the clouds were great shapes with definition on all sides at once. The grass waved gently in the breeze. Blackbirds were singing in the rushes growing out of the pond, but aside from that it was so silent I could hear the faint humming of the telephone lines, sagging between roadside poles. My feet were cool beneath the water. A cow watched me from across the pond.

I felt alone in a pristine world, a world without other human presence, even as I realized that virtually everything I could see—the road, the telephone poles, the highly bred cows, the European plants all around me—had been shaped by the hand of man. I was certainly a long way from New York, where, about six months earlier, I had been in a bar explaining Mount Rushmore to a Slovak friend. It was an interesting exercise, talking about an icon of my culture to someone who did not share that culture, and her frame of reference for colossal sculpture was different from mine: Stalin, socialist realism, alien rule. This intrigued me.

In Indian Country the parallel is tempting, but even before I got to Rushmore I knew it was not exact. In America we are ruled at least as much by the market as by politics, and Rushmore, which people take seriously, is for sale in a way that Stalin's images would not be until no one took him seriously. Approaching Rapid City from the east, highway billboards advertise Mount Rushmore and its spinoff attractions as far back as Iowa: the waxwork Parade of Presidents; Bear Country, USA; Reptile Land; Black Hills Maze; Rushmore Cave; Sitting Bull's Crystal Cave. What the Hunkpapa Lakota holy man and warrior would have thought of his part in all this is unknowable, although we should not be too quick to assume he'd object: Sitting Bull certainly enjoyed the celebrity that was mixed with the bitterness of his post-Custer years.

Keystone, the town nearest the monument, is a minor amusement park, complete with cotton candy, tacky souvenirs, cowboy hats, and buffalo burgers. Buffalo tastes much like beef, a little stringier; at powwows Indians usually serve it well boiled. It's supposed to be healthier than beef, although the South Dakota Cattlemen's Association denies it.

Before I had ever seen the Black Hills I expected Rushmore to dominate the Rapid City skyline, but it does not. The town is on the edge of the plains in the southwest corner of South Dakota, surrounded by modest foothills, while the stone heads carved into the mountain are twenty miles away in the Black Hills, in an alpine landscape only recently subjected to ax, asphalt, and billboard. Late in the afternoon of my first day in South Dakota I rounded the final curve before the monument just as the sun was casting its fading light over Washington's cheek.

The faces, lithic ciphers five stories tall, stare out over the West that was the romantic muse of their creator. At any rate they're supposed to look west. I had read articles by the sculptor in which he wrote of the westward gaze and its significance. In fact, my army surplus compass surprised me by showing Jefferson looking home-ward to the east, Roosevelt to the northwest, and Washington and Lincoln to the southeast. They look to the west in romantic metaphor only.

Like most immigrants, the majority of the post-Indian settlers came west not out of romantic sentiment but because they were hungry and saw an opportunity. Gold and silver drew the prospectors first. It was only after the claims were staked and the early Hills towns had gone boom and sometimes bust, when the buffalo were on their way out and the Indians confined to the reservations, that cattle ranching on the plains of this drier, western half of the state began.

Towns like Rapid City sprang up first to supply the miners, then to supply the ranchers, railway workers, and such farmers as could make a living on this soil. Rapid—as people who live there call it— had some close calls in the early days. The original settlement of 1876 was illegal under the prevailing Indian treaty, and the govern-ment tried hard, for a while, to keep settlers out, blockading the trails from Sydney, Pierre, Cheyenne, and Bismarck, the towns the settlers passed through on their journey. Whatever the government chose to do, the Indians were quite capable of protecting their own lands by picking off careless or isolated settlers. When four were killed near Rapid on August 24, 1876, most settlers joined a mass exodus eastward to Pierre, on the banks of the Missouri river. A few brave souls decided to stay. They built a blockhouse for protection at the present intersection of Rapid and Fifth Streets—near where an elaborate parking structure stands today, whose walls, while they climb in an open and airy design, include a sort of lookout-tower staircase that lends a fortresslike effect.

The settlers dug a well inside the stockade, and retreating into the blockhouse, they held off Indian attacks for a terrifying, lonely month. Just when their food supply was about to give out, word came that the government had abandoned its policy of intercepting immigrants and, along with the policy, its treaty obligations. Rapid City quickly recovered from this low ebb in the fortunes of its white settlers.

Ranchers around Rapid City did better than farmers. South Dakota west of the Missouri has never been good land for cash crops, although many who wanted to farm a small bit of their own earth—immigrants from the eastern United States, from Germany, from Scandinavia—were lured here, after the profitable claims had been staked and the gold fever receded, by the railroad companies' promises of a bountiful land. Their abandoned homesteads dot the Badlands fifty miles to the east and south of Rapid, small lonely memorials to human hope and disappointment in the midst of some of the most dramatic and weirdly beautiful landscape I have ever seen. The view conveys a different sensation, but the same kind of sensation, as what I felt getting out of my car on the Great Salt Flats and facing away from the road: I could have been on a different planet. This illusion has not escaped calculation. Scenes from the science fiction movie *Starship Troopers* were filmed in the Badlands.

There is a connection between these pathetic, wind-twisted

shacks and the famous sculpture in the Black Hills. The carving on Mount Rushmore was originally conceived as a way to supplement the income of an agriculturally sparse land with some precious tourist dollars. By the time the planned sculpture took on a presidential cast it was no longer about money, or not only about money. Gutzon Borglum, the man who created the sculpture, took the original concept and added a thick layer of storytelling, rich with his idiosyncratic and mostly fantastical ideas about American identity and destiny. Although Rushmore invites comparisons to the monuments of the most extreme personality cults, and although personal power had an almost erotic quality for Borglum—he was certainly in love with the office of the presidency, and when a president failed to use power boldly, no betrayed lover felt deeper outrage—the monument is not meant to portray great presidents. Its official theme is territorial and political growth: "The Founding, Preservation and Expansion of the United States."

Washington was an obvious president to carve in the mountain— the unifier, father of his country, the man who represents the original territory of the nascent Union. Jefferson is there as much for his acquisition of the Louisiana Purchase as for his authorship of the Declaration of Independence. Lincoln held the Union together with blood; and Teddy Roosevelt—he was controversial.

Roosevelt had been dead only five years when Borglum first saw the mountain in 1924, and there were those who thought it too soon to put him in the national pantheon. Borglum wanted him there for building the Panama Canal and for his willingness to stand in the way of the turn-of-the-century monopolists, targets of populists both left and right—Borglum was a populist of the right. Give Teddy his due: it was an unusual president who would dare limit the ambitions of the monopolizing titans of American industry at the beginning of the century in the name of the public good.

Perhaps tying the continent together was a glorious task, but Roosevelt's pet project was not good for the economy of South Dakota. Faced with cheaper shipping through Panama, the railroads cut their rates where competition was direct, and increased rates on goods originating far from any seaport, such as the wheat and beef that South Dakota farmers and ranchers had to send to market. Some of the homesteads in the Badlands that had held on until the canal opened went bust then. Such details were not the concern of the sculptor, who said again and again that his work was national and not local and that the monument did not belong to the people of South Dakota.

There were other reasons Borglum wanted Roosevelt on the mountain. The two were good friends, had known each other since Roosevelt was New York City police commissioner in the 1890s. They had similar personalities. They were both virile, passionate, and impulsive; men of action, enormous energy, and self-belief. Roosevelt in his prime took morning exercise with sumo wrestlers; Borglum was a boxer and a mountain climber. Both loved the West, politics, horses, and warfare.

They also happened to look somewhat alike, a fact that did not go unnoticed at the time. Rushmore was, obviously, the project of a great egotist.

There was a lot more than ego at stake, however. Borglum wholeheartedly believed in the glory of territorial expansion justified by the democratic virtue of America and the vocation of the white races—Manifest Destiny—an idea that was not at all controversial in his time. Although the agenda predates the phrase by which it is known, the phrase has an interesting evolution.

Most accounts trace its origin to John O'Sullivan. O'Sullivan's father, John Thomas O'Sullivan, was an Irish-American merchant sea captain with strong ties to Latin America. He had fought with Bolivar for Venezuela's independence. One of his vessels, the *Dick*, was seized by U.S. authorities on suspicion of piracy while in port in Buenos Aires in 1823. John Thomas drowned in a shipwreck in 1824, but in 1836 his widow received a massive settlement for the confiscation of the *Dick*, something that was quite out of character for the administration of tight-fisted President Andrew Jackson. One explanation for the settlement is that Vice President Martin van Buren, an old friend of the O'Sullivan family and soon to be President, used his influence to secure the settlement—in exchange for the family's loyalty to the Democratic Party.[1]

The younger O'Sullivan used the settlement money to found the *United States Magazine and Democratic Review*, advocate of the Democratic Party and something of a pet project of van Buren. From the first issue the young editor, not yet twenty-four, saw a close identity between Christianity and democracy, an attitude that inevitably lent a sense of divine mission to American patriotism, serving as a major justification of expansionism. In the inaugural issue O'Sullivan developed a theory of democracy that is infused with a Jeffersonian distrust of government, and then wrote:

[Democracy is] written in letters of light on every page of the great bible of Nature. It contains the idea of full and fearless faith in the providence of the Creator. It is essentially involved in Christianity, of which it has been well said that its pervading spirit of democratic equality among men is its highest fact, and one of its most radiant internal evidences of the divinity of its origin.[2]

Later, in his newspaper *The New York Morning News*, O'Sullivan was to continue his proselytizing for Christian democracy and especially for the expansion of Christian democratic territory. In both publications he grew more militant according to circumstance. Where at first he had argued for Christian example and political voluntarism as the mechanisms of an inevitable expansion, in the mid-1840s, as war with Mexico loomed and tensions with Britain grew over the Oregon territory, he oversaw an ever-more aggressive line. Still, at least at first, and at least in the *Review*, O'Sullivan's policy was to appeal to reason, not emotion, and the *Review*'s enthusiasm for expansionism was usually grounded in very sophisticated discussions of international law: in June, 1845, it traced the American claim to the Oregon territory, through many twists and turns, back to the 1713 Treaty of Utrecht.

In the very next issue, however, in the context of the annexation of much of the west from Mexico, the expansionist orientation of the *Review* began to take on a decidedly racial cast, in terms claiming a higher standard of civilization rather than of government or religion.

California will, probably, next fall away from [Mexico] . . . .The Anglo-Saxon foot is already on its borders. Already the advance guard of the irresistible army of Anglo-Saxon emigration has begun to pour down upon it, armed with the plough and the rifle, and marking its trail with schools and colleges, courts and representative halls, mills and meeting houses.

In this editorial, westward expansion is tantalizingly called the "manifest design of Providence."[3] The more populist *New York Morning News* was always a bit less circumspect, and already in February 1845 exulted in a Manifest Destiny that was conveniently as noble as it was expansive.

Yes, more, more, more! Will be the unresting cry, till our national destiny is fulfilled, and—"The whole boundless continent is ours!"

Texas, Oregon, California, Canada, yes, all, all, are sooner or later to be embraced within the ever-widening circle . . . of our peaceful union of free and independent States . . . for this great destiny, purpose and necessity, we want . . . the whole, and nothing short of the whole; and wanting it, we shall have it, we must have it, we will have it . . . [4]

The phrase we know finally emerges in the *Morning News* of December 27, 1845, in an editorial making the case for America's claim to Oregon over that of Britain. As divine right and necessity take center stage, the legal argument fades away:

> Away, away with all these cobweb tissues of rights of discovery, exploration, settlement, continuity, &c. To state the truth at once in its naked simplicity . . . our claim to Oregon . . . is by the right of our Manifest Destiny to overspread and to possess the whole of the continent which Providence has given for the development of the great experiment of liberty and federative self-government entrusted to us . . . The God of nature and of nations has marked it for our own; and with His blessing we will firmly maintain the incontestable rights He has given, and fearlessly perform the high duties He has imposed.[5]

Manifest Destiny may be only a phrase, yet it allowed the American belief in American exceptionalism, American virtue, to coexist with the conquest of land occupied by others. Not that this wouldn't have happened without O'Sullivan, but he gave the notion a solid and poetic name. Armed with this name, a philosophy could eventually be expressed in something as bulky as Mount Rushmore without anyone really remarking on its essential contradictions. O'Sullivan had a real literary talent, a talent that was one more piece of bad news for those who stood in the way of the young nation's destiny.

Of course he didn't come up with what the times demanded in

isolation. In Judaeo-Christian civilization the idea of a popular mission linked to land acquisition goes back to God's promises to Moses in *Exodus*. American exceptionalism has been with us since the Pilgrims and John Winthrop's City on a Hill, and is with us still. The blessing of the Pilgrim ship *Speedwell* is an important mural in the U.S. Capitol, seat of our legitimacy as a nation.

No one believed in the special destiny of America more than Borglum. The idea of carving a mountain somewhere in the Rockies had been at the back of his mind before he ever saw Rushmore in 1924. At least ten years earlier he had been thinking and writing about something he called the Northern or National Memorial, in contrast to the work he had in hand at the time, a mountain sculpture dedicated to the soldier heroes of the Confederacy; it was typical of his romantic naïveté that he could idolize both Lincoln and Lee. He took very seriously his self-appointed task of "providing a formal rendering of the philosophy of our government into granite on a mountain peak."[6]

Yet I've stood many times on the crowded viewing terrace of Doane Mountain, where tourists have the most direct view of the sculpture, and I've never overheard anyone talking about the monument quite this solemnly. More often I've heard people express amazement that one man with a hammer and chisel could have done so much.

The visitors should know better. The orientation center goes into great detail about the crews of up to fifty men at a time, mostly out-of-work Depression-era miners, who took the measurements, drilled the blasting holes, and finished the surfaces with "bumper" drills. An exhibit also describes the pointing system that Borglum invented for transferring the relative dimensions of his model to the mountain. He used cranes and plumb lines to divide up three-dimensional space on the mountain and on his models, so that an inch on the one-twelfth scale model in his studio equaled a foot on the mountain. "Pointer" men on the mountain would work from the models, guiding drillers and blast planters suspended in harnesses below. The procedure was ingenious.

The technology, however, is the easiest part of the Rushmore story. What the monument says about the Black Hills, American history, and our common national life is more difficult.

From my first visit I was struck by how much the National Park Service, which administers the monument, uses the exhibits to concentrate on technique rather than on meaning, although exhibits do give the theme of the work and locate the tenure of each president on a time line that shows stages of our national development. There is some attempt to discuss the Black Hills in history and to cite the familiar pattern of Indian treaties. "In 1868, representatives of the United States government signed a treaty at Fort Laramie in Wyoming with the Lakota, Cheyenne and Arapaho nations of the Great Plains, by which a large area in Eastern Wyoming and Western Dakota Territory was designated Unceded Indian Country while much of present-day South Dakota was set aside as the Great Sioux Reservation. But in 1874, gold was discovered in the Black Hills, the heart of the new Indian reservation, and thousands of settlers swarmed into the region." The text goes on to describe the eventual ultimatum to the Indians to give up the Black Hills and wanders into a generality: "Many Battles would be fought before the Native Americans were forced to submit."[7] The lost treaty, the Indian wars, and the monument are not explicitly linked.

Although the historical text may be meager and confused, the Rushmore exhibits are not designed to stuff patriotism into the visitors. This ideological reticence is odd, almost as odd as the fact that visitors seldom ask the rangers anything about what the project was meant to represent. People miss the larger message of this large creation, which probably makes the ranger's job easier, for not too many Americans think like Borglum anymore. Once, sitting on a bench in the Rushmore amphitheater, I heard a mother coach her small daughter from a NPS quiz for children. "What is the theme of the monument?" The girl's answer: "It is very big . . . "

The Park Service does not conceive its mission as the preservation of the political thought of Gutzon Borglum. The modern exhibits are a service to the public and an estimate of its needs, which have changed over time. Borglum created the sculpture under a contract that was paid out almost entirely by the U.S. Treasury. Although he never claimed that his physical creation belonged to him, he took his proprietorship of its ideology very seriously; and a message that changed to accommodate the comfort level of later generations would have outraged him.

The interpretation of Rushmore wasn't always left to chance. Plans for an earlier visitors' center were far less shy about proselytizing. Back in 1957, near the height of the Cold War, a NPS proposal for a revised orientation center apparently had the goal of protecting the visitor from any unauthorized thoughts.

At a time when ideological forces within our nation are attempting to undermine our democratic form of government, while at the same time powerful totalitarian forces from without threaten us with harassment and a war of extinction, it is tremendously important that the United States Government take advantage of every opportunity to remind its citizens of the historic origin of their precious democratic rights and privileges. . . . [A] major [patriotic] theme should pervade all elements of the interpretive program. . . . The Presidential Hall of the Visitors' Center will be entirely concerned with it. . . . It is integrated in all parts of the historical handbooks, as well as deserving of a special section. Almost any presentation in any form of any aspect of Mount Rushmore can be an excuse to include an interpretation of the significance."[8]

The world was different then. Perhaps it is something of a saving grace that the sheer bigness that Borglum pursued as metaphor often strikes modern viewers as an element of kitsch, of novelty. To them the monument is often merely a larger and more durable version of the waxwork Hall of Presidents down the hill in Keystone.

The problem with a unified patriotic presentation is that, sixty years after work on the mountain stopped, the old single, simple story of the conquests that underlay the expansion of the American states is, if not exactly under siege, open to challenge. To their credit, former Superintendent Dan Wenk and former Chief of

Interpretation Jim Popovich, now Acting Superintendent, the two men most responsible for the present exhibits, seem to be aware of the delicacy of their task. As public servants, they must present a history they did not make in a culture that, for the most part, is little interested in old wounds. When I interviewed Wenk in 1998, he was quietly diplomatic as he parried my questions about the politics of interpretation. He explained that the public wasn't ready for an exhibit on Borglum's lifelong white supremacism but that he wouldn't rule it out for the future. "I understand how, from their perspective, Native Americans could feel uncomfortable with the idea of the Shrine of Democracy. Since I've been here I have certainly been educated to the issues that each of those four presidents carries with him for Native Americans."

Anyway Wenk and Popovich had more pressing matters on their minds than the politics of the sculptor when I spoke with them. They were in the middle of a massive preservation and renovation effort at the mountain, including an enormous new pay parking lot for the growing numbers of tourist cars, and for their trouble they had come under bitter attack from the South Dakota public. What started as an argument about good taste and the legality of a parking fee—the enabling Rushmore legislation forbade charging admission to view the monument—had by that time taken on a much larger dimension: Wenk and Popovich were getting death threats.

To many in the region, the changes at Rushmore ironically suggest the evils of government. Some see conspiracies in the parking fee, legacies of Bill Clinton's plans for a one-world socialist state. For those who look for hidden meanings, subtle details stand out with disturbing clarity. Do the new pillars lining the approach to the orientation center suggest a pagan temple? Is it true that the U.N. banner will grace the refurbished Avenue of Flags at the monument? (No.) One morning, while having breakfast in a local coffee shop, I read a letter to the *Rapid City Journal* that captured such dark fears.

The architectures of the new facilities at Mount Rush-more convey the concealed yet discernable encryption of those [sinister] plans. The Shrine of Democracy has been transmuted into an international shrine of worship, and the legal craftwork has been enacted to transfer con-trol to the New World Order in preparation of the ruler who will unite the nations under the umbrella of world democracy, the deceptive politic-religion of his new kingdom, a religion tracing its roots to the Greco-Roman pantheon and ultimately to the Lord of Darkness as its supreme being.

It will be at our beloved monument where this ruler will desecrate our constitutional republic, its sacred her-itage, its hollowed [*sic*] calling, and its one true God, by conducting abominable ceremonies of worship of democracy and self-adulation, with the ruinous approval of the deluded masses.[9]

Odd how "New World Order," a young phrase, has come to mean precisely the opposite of what it did when it first appeared in the national vocabulary. I first heard it right after the 1991 Gulf

War, when President Bush the Elder proposed it as the tagline for a revived U.S. world hegemony, and because I lived in Berkeley at the time, I remember the response of the loopy leftist Revolutionary Communist Party. There was a time in the early 1990s when they would paint their slogans in big red letters on walls or long barriers, and for a while one such slogan was BUSH: TO HELL WITH YOUR NEW WORLD ORDER!—RCP. How quickly the phrase has been appropriated by the militia "movement" and the far right to signify some sort of dilution of American political and social values by an alien world culture—rather than the other way around, as Bush intended.

The letter writer's reaction to Rushmore is hard to fathom and hard to relate to any actual work being done on the mountain, but it makes sense in an odd way: the Shrine of Democracy necessarily ignores a lot of history, so much so that even on a sunny day it takes on a slightly hallucinatory sheen. The letter may be an extreme example of fantasy, but it reminds us that there are other hallucinations lurking behind the gargantuan narrative of progress, some of them far less attractive than the idea of national expansion.

Call it a national hallucination, or take it at face value, Rushmore doesn't appeal to everyone. In my many visits I have very rarely seen black Americans on the viewing terrace, and I never, ever saw an American Indian—perhaps messages are understood most clearly by those who have good reason to be skeptical. Howard Shaff, the Borglum biographer who now lives on a ranch near the memorial, told me with some sadness, "It is a white memorial." Shaff is more perceptive than most of the visitors and staff, who nonchalantly assume a national relevance transcending all division and history.

The tourists who come generally don't remark on the oddness of such a sculpture in the midst of what is, legally and historically, Indian land. The last legally executed document pertaining to ownership of the Black Hills and what used to be known as the Great Sioux Reservation and hunting lands is the treaty that gets a brief mention in the interpretive center; in it the U.S. government cedes most rights to the Sioux and Arapaho.

Indians are rarely seen in the Hills today, and it is a perennial theme of South Dakota politics that the Lakota Sioux on the reservations are painfully aware of what they are missing. This isn't surprising. Beyond any historical ties, beyond any commercial value, the Black Hills of South Dakota and Wyoming are beautiful, and generations have sought spiritual as well as physical sustenance here. On a clear morning, high up on the Iron Mountain Road in the Peter Norbeck Wildlife Preserve, hearing the occasional rustle of a pheasant or rattle of a woodpecker and looking out over an incredible panorama that includes Mount Harney, the highest elevation east of the Rockies, watching hawks wheel in the updrafts, I found it easy to lose all sense of time, to be wholly in the moment. Slightly to the right of Mount Harney the four faces of Rushmore are reduced to miniature, humbled, dominating only their parking lot. Here a white boy can at least try to imagine the mind of a Sioux youth on a vision quest, in the days when the Sioux were a part of this landscape, not visitors, although the white boy probably gets it wrong. Unlikely that anyone now living, Indian or otherwise, gets it right.

At Rushmore, on a summer day at the height of the tourist season, there is none of that vision quest stuff, except in the most literal sense, with tourists looking for the best background shot. An occasional helicopter roars past to provide an aerial view.

Some may find inspiration here, but it will probably not be the sort of inspiration that Sioux on their vision quests felt before white men pushed them out of the Hills or that, earlier, the Kiowa and Crow felt before the westward-moving Sioux evicted them in the early nineteenth century. This is not a place for denial, for insights induced by hunger and exhaustion.

There are other resources, though. The Black Hills are seeded with gold, flakes and nuggets and microscopic specks of it. The gold is very important to our story. A way of life—a way of life no less beloved by its practitioners than the ideals of Washington, Jefferson, Lincoln, and Roosevelt were to the Americans of their times—was changed suddenly and irrevocably a little more than a century ago, changed because of the gold here and its role in a solidifying national economy. The destruction of this way of life is a big part of the Rushmore story and casts an ironic light on something that the sculptor included in almost everything he wrote about Rushmore or America: "Man has a right to be free and to be happy."

2

THE COLONIZED LAND

My first few days in Rapid City I noticed how the expansionist history that the faces at Rushmore represent remains a living presence in the geography and economy of the region. Settlement, colonization, immigration, annexation, can't be separated from life and habits of thought in Rapid City, the Black Hills, and the reservations.

Pennington County has a relatively diverse economy for a rural state. Rapid City folks are ranchers, factory hands, service workers. There is the big Federal Beef Processors packing plant by Rapid Creek and the regional educational magnet of the South Dakota School of Mines and Technology. The professional class is relatively large—this small town supports a great many lawyers. Rapid is a small but modern American town, and like the rest of the United States, it is a far cry from the Jeffersonian ideal of the "yeoman farmer" that Borglum believed in passionately. More than 15 per-

cent of the workforce are employed in federal, state, or local government, and only slightly more than 1 percent is in agriculture.[1]

There are Indians and non-Indians who are doing well here, but
Indians are overly represented among the sad and desperate people
who panhandle on the streets of Rapid, as they are among the people
who seek food and shelter at the Corner Stone Rescue Mission on
Main Street, across East Boulevard from the post office. Many of
them are up from the Rosebud and Pine Ridge reservations about a
hundred miles to the southeast, passing through, looking for work,
visiting friends.

The layout of Rapid mirrors the course of colonial settlement in
miniature, with the Indian areas left undisturbed so long as they
were not greatly coveted by white businessmen and developers. The
town was originally bounded by the tight square made up of North
and South Streets and East and West Boulevards, with a business
district along Main Street and Saint Joseph Streets, today a pleasant
and peaceful small-town strip; the ten-story Alex Johnson Hotel at
Sixth and Main, with its Sioux motif and elks carved into the lintels,
is the tallest building in town. In the town's early days Indians set up
a shantytown by the railroad tracks that bisect the town just north of
this business district. Their quarter was too close for the merchants'
comfort, and the Indians were removed a bit farther north, to less
desirable land on a rise where the Holiday Inn now stands, where
they continued to be undesirables as far as the rest of the town were
concerned. As late as the 1950s a Federal Writers' Project trave-
logue remarked upon their open cooking fires near the city center
and the squalor of their encampments, suggesting a modern town

with a vaguely frontier ambience: "Weathered ranchers, occasional prospectors, and students at the School of Mines and Technology mingle with townspeople and tourists, while Sioux Indian families cluster in front of store windows or watch from their parked cars."[2]

Indians were removed northward again as the town expanded and their quarter became more valuable. They went to an area called the Sioux Addition, which the rest of the town didn't want at the time. This is where most of the modern development of Rapid City has taken place, with a big shopping concourse—the Rushmore Mall— at the northern edge of town where Interstate 90 comes through, and several other shopping centers north of the older buildings on Saint Joseph. A subsidized housing development on the very northern perimeter, Lakota Homes, was built specifically to accommodate Indians who could be persuaded to get out of the way of new construction. To this day, the north side of the tracks is noticeably poorer, and the police do most of their work there.

Rapid City, the reservations, the Black Hills, are all part of the 1868 treaty lands; and that treaty itself was the culmination of a series of treaties that fenced in the Sioux with legal understandings, where before they had ridden as far as their horses and their conquering rifles would take them. Just 175 years ago the various bands of the Sioux ranged from Minnesota to Montana, from Nebraska to Saskatchewan, following the buffalo, visiting, making war.

Most of the Indians around here are poorer than their non-Indian neighbors, but Indian country outside the reservations, the lost land, is rich. The Black Hills area where Rushmore presides has enormous resources of timber, coal, tin, silver, and gold, all of which are being extracted. Although plenty of roads now cut through the area, the trout streams and hunting woods are still bountiful, and along with Rushmore, they sustain a major tourist industry in southwest South Dakota.

To several generations of Lakota it is literally a matter of faith that the Black Hills are central to their sense of themselves as a people, the locus of their fundamental narratives, the sacred land of the vision quest, the emergency hunting grounds of the Lakota plains empire. There is even what may be called an artificial tradition of recent origin, strongly upheld by some Lakota, that the Lakota people themselves arose sui generis in the Black Hills, separate from the rest of humanity. The belief confounds both Darwin and more traditional origin tales and is a matter of dispute among Lakota elders.

Like other national myths, this belief is problematic if it is read as history. The Lakota people arrived in the region near the end of the eighteenth century. Starting about fifty years earlier, they had been driven west from the woodlands of Minnesota by the muskets of their enemies the Chippewa, who had close contacts with French traders. The Lakota adapted quickly to life on the plains, especially the use of horses, which they captured from whites or other Indians or redomesticated from the feral descendants of the horses that came with the early French and Spanish explorers. They made the buffalo hunt their way of life. They were fast, resourceful, fearless, and they dispossessed the Crow, Arikara and Kiowa, who held the Hills before them.

Many of those who defend the conquest of the Lakota lands point out this parallel, and it is not a trivial one. Intertribal warfare on the plains could be brutal, and the rights of the victor complete. In Indian warfare the argument, however, was about who would use resources, not about the physical and cultural survival of a people. It is also true that the Lakota entered into a treaty with the United States regarding this land—a treaty they saw as negotiated between equal, sovereign parties.

Perhaps it makes sense that as relative newcomers, the Lakota developed a cosmology that rooted them in the Hills, just as Rushmore symbolically insists that only absorption into the corpus of the colonizers is possible for them or any other Americans. During my time in South Dakota, I found that a conversation with any Lakota who retained even a small sense of commitment to a Lakota identity would return to the subject of the Hills. Even when other thoughts, feelings, and priorities had been washed away by despair, by alcoholism, by hard living and anger, the focus on the Hills remained.

The Lakota Sioux were robbed piecemeal of their 1868 land, most importantly in 1877, when they lost the Hills, but also in 1889, when the Dawes Act chopped their territory into six smaller, isolated reservations and forced them to hold land as individuals, an idea quite alien to them and much resisted; and again in 1906, when the Burke Act expropriated more land and granted more private titles; and finally in 1942, when the war-pressed government took Sheep Mountain, on the Pine Ridge reservation, for a gunnery range. The last little piece of land to be alienated from the tribe was twenty thousand acres signed over by the Pine Ridge reservation tribal chair Dick Wilson in 1972. In addition to land lost outright, much of the reservation land is in long-term lease to non-Indian ranchers.

Many non-Indian visitors to reservations are struck only by the poverty and never see past it. Yet the reservations are not areas of unrelieved poverty and hopelessness. Lakota ranchers make good lives for themselves and their families on the reservations, and dynamic tribal initiatives are improving life for residents. The Cheyenne River reservation, north and east of Pine Ridge and Rosebud, home to Minneconjou, Itazipco, Hunkapapa, Oohenonpa, and Sihasapa Lakota, maintains a thriving tribal buffalo herd of three hundred head. Prosperous ranchers, merchants, and professionals live on the reservations, just as they do in towns all across the West and, indeed, in all the cities of the United States.

Yet any reservation will certainly delineate the legacy of conquest in the tumbledown shacks and trailers that often don't have running water, in the mission schools, in the statistics. Anytime a national newspaper publishes anything about the Pine Ridge reservation, home of the Oglala Lakota, the article must include a mention that Shannon County, where the reservation is located, consistently ranks among the poorest five counties in the country; some years it's the very poorest, depending on how poverty is measured. Where the statewide unemployment rate in 2000 was a low 2.3 percent,[3] unemployment on Pine Ridge and its Sicangu Lakota sister reservation, the Rosebud, is officially reported at 73 percent,[4] and unofficially approaches 85 percent,[5] for they are isolated and barren patches of ground devoid of natural resources and there is virtually no industry. All the predictable indicators of social dysfunction that go with this unemployment rate are found: extremely high rates of alcoholism, child abuse, and violent crime and a life expectancy that is among the lowest in the nation.

Patterns of violence on the South Dakota reservations mirror those on American reservations in general. A Justice Department study of 1999[6] found that American Indians are almost twice as likely as those in the next racial category—black Americans— most likely to be the victims of violence, at 124 violent victimizations per 1,000 population, compared to 64 for blacks (and 50 for whites). Interestingly, while victims of all races are most likely to be the same race as the perpetrators, American Indians are more likely than those in other racial groups to be victimized by people of a different race, and alcohol is more likely to be involved, whether the perpetrator is Indian or not. Perhaps this is because Indians, more than other Americans, are likely to live in poor, rural areas with high crime rates, and to interact with non-Indians in an environment in which drinking is, for all races, often a way of life.

None of this means that people can't get along, on or off the reservations. On the streets of Rapid I would occasionally be greeted by an Indian with a cheerful *"Hau, Kola!"*—"Hello, friend." Yes, the "How" of the Hollywood "How, Paleface!" comes from the Great Plains, from the Lakota, as does the long, feathered war bonnet of the film and tobacco-store Indian. Although the Lakota and their cousins on the plains were late to encounter the colonizers, they met them at a time when industrialization was taking hold of the country, when electricity was being harnessed to what Black Elk called the "voice that went everywhere," which meant that their raids on encroaching railroads and settlers were transmitted by telegraph and printed in the papers in New York, Saint Louis, and Chicago. Their warrior ferocity, skill with horses, feathered bonnets, and a few words of their language found a place in the larger culture as the archetype of the Indian.

Sometimes the friendly greeting has an added message. Panhandlers in Rapid City often approach tourists with the words, "This was our land. This is our land. But we feel like strangers here"—part reminder, part attempt to extract some token payment on a debt the tourist may not feel.

My third day in town I was in the Ace Hardware parking lot when a very drunk Indian with a Pawnee haircut stumbled up to me.

"I am Antelope Running Through Timber. I am Lakota. I'm a full-blood. Full-blood." He looked it, except for the haircut. "My other name is Ajax."[7]

He was going to the American Indian Heritage powwow out on the Rushmore road in the Black Hills foothills, where one can see out over the city, owned by white people, operated by Indians. I gave him a lift, and on our way out of Rapid City I asked if he was Oglala, one of the two largest groups of the Lakota Sioux. "Minneconjou. My people went with Big Foot's people. The ones that were shot, not so far from here. Why did the white people want to do that?"

He gazed off for a moment. "I was supposed to be on security at this powwow. But I got drunk."

When we pulled up at the powwow gate there was a big sign: NO DRUGS OR ALCOHOL. A very polite Indian security officer asked us if we were camping. I said no, that we might be there only a short time. He looked us over.

"I'm afraid you can't come in because you, sir, are intoxicated.

Why don't you pull over here until these cars go through, and then I'll talk to you about it."

We sat to the side until we realized that they were not going to let us in at all. So we headed back to Rapid.

"Look at that." Ajax pointed out an incredible sunset, peeking over the sharp edges of the Black Hills. "Isn't it beautiful? The sun is gone, but it's not gone. Look at that"—he pointed out a water slide in an amusement park, one of many attractions that line the Rushmore road. "The kids come. They play there. Then they forget where they are." He gazed off into the distance for a moment. "Why did they come and take our land? Why did they take it? We Indian people act like we don't care, but—we care."

He told me to take a cutoff to return to Rapid by the winding sky-line road rather than the main highway. We continued down a side road. "Down there is where the mine is, they're tearing the earth out down there. The white people say we came here. Our bones are here. Our *bones* are here."

I wondered how much he was playing up Indianness, maybe in order to put more of a touch on me. But everything he was doing—the touch, the confusion, the alcoholic sentimentality, the pain of history—were real, all happening at once. He reached up to pat my head. "This is where they would have scalped you."

He asked me to pull over. "Down here is where they killed some people. They thought no one would ever find them. There are bones down here."

"When did this happen?"

"Nineteen-ninety."

Perhaps he was somehow mentally transposing 1890, the year of Wounded Knee, and 1990, and for the first time—the feeling recurred often when talking about Indian and treaty matters in the Black Hills—I sensed that the past was not so far away and that for many here it is not past at all but a sort of ghostly overlay on the present. Or it could be that he was just very drunk.

Ajax told me of his friends in the American Indian Movement. When he mumbled something about "Dino," I asked him if he meant Dino Butler, a hero of the movement, arraigned for the 1975 murders of two FBI agents on the Pine Ridge reservation. Leonard Peltier was also tried in this case, but Peltier was convicted, Butler acquitted. Ajax looked up at me, suddenly focused, suspicious.

"You know Dino Butler?"

But he was not thinking of Butler. He was looking at "Dino," the rusting surplus British Petroleum dinosaur that gazes out from the top of a low hill over Rapid, a regional landmark like the stone faces of Rushmore or the mines of Lead (the town is named for the main ore outcropping and its name is pronounced like the verb, not the noun). This Dino has more in common with the mines than with the militant Indian. Like them, he represents the commercial aim of conquest, not its arguments and counterarguments.

The logic of Dino the dinosaur lives in the way the present white occupiers of the Hills talk about local history: as far away and unrelated to how life is lived now, as distant and impersonal, providing some colorful anecdotes with happy endings, rather than a matter of loss, death, and cultural disorientation for the displaced. Dino the dinosaur represents cheerful progress for many; others still take

Wounded Knee personally. The process of dispossession has been going on for several generations, and no one now living remembers what things were like before the civilization commemorated on Mount Rushmore arrived; but it hasn't taken so long in years.

Wounded Knee is one point on the hard bright triangle of meaning whose other points are the Little Bighorn battlefield, in Montana, and the Black Hills, where Rushmore now presides. On my trips to the Pine Ridge reservation, down Shannon County route 27 toward Pine Ridge Village, the Oglala capital, I often passed a green sign that says that half a mile away, Big Foot and his band surrendered in their flight from Cheyenne River to Pine Ridge on December 28, 1890. The marker, which is just north of the present-day village of Porcupine, was erected in the 1950s by the South Dakota Highway Department, a result of a campaign by the Chicago and Black Hills Highway Association to make the roads more attractive to tourist traffic. It is usually surrounded by garbage and old rags.

The Minneconjou Lakota chief Big Foot (he was also known as Spotted Elk) and his band were apprehended during the religious revival known as the Ghost Dance Troubles. The Ghost Dance, begun by Jack Wilson, or Wovoka, a Paiute from Nevada, soon spread to Indian communities all over the West. It combined elements of traditional Indian religions and of redemptive, messianic Christianity, brought relentlessly to the Indians by thousands of missionaries over many years. If the Indians would only believe strongly enough and dance a certain dance constantly, to the point of exhaustion, reality would be changed by sheer force of belief. A new layer of earth would be laid down over all the world, burying the whites, while Indians would be lifted up into the air and protected. The buffalo would all come back. All the Indians who had ever lived would live again in perpetual happiness.

In South Dakota, the Ghost Dance religion included a particularly unfortunate belief: that adherents who wore specially painted and blessed "ghost shirts" would be invulnerable to the bullets of the whites.

The attractive power of this movement on the Sioux reservations was a direct result of the loss of the Black Hills in 1877 and the partitioning of the shrunken reservation territory in 1889, followed closely by a season of drought and starvation. The movement drew in some of the traditional leaders, like Sitting Bull, who could not adjust to life under the authority of a federally appointed Indian agent. The religion certainly had its military aspects, and indeed, many of its adherents were not planning to passively await the new world. Things became much more tense after James McLaughlin, the agent on the Standing Rock reservation in northern South Dakota, sent Indian police to arrest Sitting Bull, whom McLaughlin saw as a major instigator of the unrest. The fearful collaborators panicked, shot and killed the old chief. In the hysterical violence that followed his face was battered into jelly. Later his cabin, uprooted, toured with Buffalo Bill's Wild West show. Local whites had some reason to fear a general Indian uprising, like that of the Minnesota Sioux in 1862.

Big Foot's band was made up mostly of Minneconjou Lakota, although there were some Hunkpapa and other Lakota and even some Cheyenne and a few visiting Cree. In December 1890, Big Foot and his people were being chased around the Badlands by Major Samuel Whitside of the Seventh U.S. Cavalry, George A. Custer's old outfit, because they were suspected, incorrectly, of being "hostiles."

The most militant of the Ghost Dancers were out in the Badlands, on an isolated and defensible plateau known as the Fortress, and the soldiers were afraid that Big Foot was on his way to join them in a major uprising. He was actually going to visit Red Cloud's village, to settle a dispute—the calm and reliable Big Foot was known as a mediator—and to seek protection from the soldiers who had been following him from his village on the Cheyenne River reservation.

When Whitside's troop encountered the band at Porcupine Butte, the Indians surrendered without any resistance and allowed themselves to be taken into custody. The day after the surrender, the soldiers' nervous attempt at disarming the encamped Indians led to a scuffle, which led to a shot. Powerful Hotchkiss guns then opened up on the Indians, firing down from the gentle slopes of the hill that is now the site of the Wounded Knee cemetery, with its mass grave. Somewhere between two and three hundred were killed, although it is hard to know the exact number because many of the dead were carried off the field before contractors came three days later to bury them.

Nowadays all Americans recognize the phrase "Wounded Knee," although probably few know what happened there. Wounded Knee is remembered as the last openly violent chapter of the Indian wars, although this is not quite true, and it continues to be a source of bitterness to the Lakota, continues to poison relations between Indians and non-Indians. Seventeen of the soldiers who took part, some of whom chased women and children miles through the snow before cutting them down, were awarded Congressional Medals of Honor. Starting in the 1930s and continuing up to the present, the Lakota have lobbied Congress to rescind these medals, to no avail.[8]

Wounded Knee seems as if it belongs to another age, but two of the characters involved in the battle give an eerie premonition of things to come. John J. Pershing, the U.S. commander in Europe in the Great War, was one of the officers at Wounded Knee. Erwin von Luttwitz, a Red Cross worker who treated the wounded, was destined to become the military governor of occupied Belgium in 1914.

Some of the Indians who survived Wounded Knee, born in a time before they were fenced in on reservations, lived long enough to act in a movie. At a strange moment of transition from the nineteenth century to the twentieth, the aging William Cody staged a movie reenactment of the event in 1913. Cody—"Buffalo Bill"—was always a bit of a con man, a frontiersman who became a showman peddling a mythical, romanticized, above all a denatured West. He had been at Standing Rock Reservation during the Ghost Dance crisis in 1890, trying to arrange the surrender of his old friend and employee in his Wild West show, Sitting Bull. Sensing that Cody's involvement would only lead to trouble, Agent McLaughlin sent men to keep him drinking all night.

The 1913 movie was sponsored by the War Department, which hoped to use it as a recruiting aid for what looked to be war with

Mexico. General Nelson Miles played himself and was an adviser to the film. Miles was the commanding officer of the forces at Wounded Knee and after the fighting he moved into the village to personally oversee the occupation of the reservation. Miles wanted the spectacle to recreate the event, to the point of using eleven thousand troops—because eleven thousand troops had been there in the winter of 1890, half the U.S. army at the time. There were many Indian extras who had been participants in the real Wounded Knee, and rumors circulated among them that they would be using live ammunition for the film. When Cody finally convinced the Indians to open fire, many broke into tears.

For better or worse, the film has completely disappeared. Not even its final title is known, if there was one. Working titles were *The Indian Wars Refought*; *The Last Indian Battles*; or *From the Warpath to the Peace Pipe*; *The Wars for Civilization in America*; and *Buffalo Bill's Indian Wars*.[9]

Gutzon Borglum, who lived into modern times, was twenty-three years old on the day Big Foot's people died. Less than forty years later, he was raising presidential images in the Black Hills, Wounded Knee a minor event against the backdrop of his larger historical narrative.

Rushmore is a kind of forgetting, a new chapter; and there are other kinds of forgetting around here. One kind was brought by the missionaries. The process of "civilizing" the Dakota Indians, that branch of the Sioux family that stayed in Minnesota, had begun before the Dakota Territory was even opened to white settlers: it began when the missionaries moved in. Typical was the work of

Stephen Riggs, who learned Dakota and translated the New Testament into that language (he was sharp enough to translate from the original Greek, not the King James version). He also translated *Pilgrim's Progress* into Dakota. What effect this had on converting the Indians is not known.

In addition to translating religious texts, Riggs wrote a primer on the Dakota language. Here he renders *tatanka* (bull buffalo) as "ox," *tipi* as "house" (he includes pictures of each object). He thoughtfully included Dakota words for "yoke" and "plow," which must have been newly minted for the civilizing mission. The association of the farming life with religious virtue was nothing new.[10]

Most of the Lakota Sioux in the more westerly lands were first Christianized by Catholics, led by Jesuits; the Baptists originally claimed lands farther south, in Creek territory. Various denominations fought for concession rights on the reservations—the exclusive religious charters granted by the government—as if souls were resources to be extracted; and the South Dakota reservations eventually came primarily under the guidance of the Catholic, Episcopal, and Presbyterian churches, although missionaries of all sorts have swarmed into the reservations to get in on the gold rush for souls: Mormons, Christian Scientists, Seventh-Day Adventists, you name it. Up until the early twentieth century the government often used mission schools on the reservations as its agents in carrying out treaty obligations to educate the Indians, paying a certain amount per student to the church and leaving the church to do the retail work. It was not uncommon for church workers to withhold food rations in the absence of sufficient evidence of religious devotion.

Among the teachers and missionaries there were, of course, many devout individuals who believed, with the best intentions in the world, that the Lakota language, culture, and religion were the biggest barriers to the Indians' spiritual salvation.

The Catholic church remains one of the biggest landowners on the Pine Ridge reservation.

It would be easy to consider this sort of cultural bullying a dim remnant of a dishonorable past. A Rapid City monsignor helped me to get over this idea. When I asked him if he would really like to see an entirely Catholic world, with of all other religious philosophies eliminated, he seemed almost irritated. "That's a loaded question. Of course I do. As Christians, that's what we work for."

Sitting Bull took a different view. "Our religion seems foolish to you," he once told a government school teacher. "But so does yours to me."[11] Since whites were crazy and irrational by definition, Sitting Bull had little interest in what they did in their spare time, and was willing to live and let live where religion was concerned.

This principle is illustrated in an incident recounted by Olivia Black Elk Pourier, granddaughter of the Lakota mystic Black Elk, later in life known as Nicholas Black Elk. Although in his youth he had received a tremendous Lakota vision, he spent much of his adult life trying to reconcile his traditional ways with the Catholic faith, an internal struggle that was sometimes mirrored by external events. In an interview in the mid-1990s, Pourier told Hilda Neihardt of a visit from a priest.

[Father Sialm] saw my grandfather with the pipe. Father

Sialm grabbed the pipe and said, "This is the work of the devil!" And he took it and threw it out the door on the ground.

My grandfather didn't say a word. He got up and took the priest's prayer book and threw it out on the ground. Then they both looked at each other, and nobody said one word that whole time.

And then they both went out, and I saw Father Sialm pick up the prayer book, and Grandfather picked up his pipe. Each one picked up his own.

Then they turned around, and they just smiled at each other and shook hands![12]

Accommodations were not always reached with so few consequences.

Sometimes little incidents in Rapid will tie together the nearness of the past and the ideological legacy of colonialism. One warm August evening in Rapid City I went out for a walk. I took a book along and cut through the alleyway behind my house. Two Indian women were sitting on a low cinder-block wall, an old woman and a young woman. I nodded as I passed by. The young woman called out, "Hello! Do you want to talk? Come on over and shake my hand."

I came over and she introduced herself. "I'm Jacky, and this is Grandma. She's adopted me."

Jacky asked me about the book I was carrying. A little embarrassed, I said, "It's about Wounded Knee."

Jacky said, "I don't know why people have to keep thinking about the past, letting things in the past get them all messed up nowadays. Why can't people just live in the present, live for the future? Take me, now; I'm three-quarters Indian, but I don't speak Indian, just understand a little from what Grandma's taught me. My parents spoke only Indian, but I went to the boarding school and I learned English. And I believe in the Bible, I know the Lord."

Grandma said, "You were given away."

"I was not! I was not at all given away! That is not true!"

Grandma was thumbing through my book. She came to a section on Sitting Bull and began reading it intently.

I said, "Tatanka Yotanka, right?"

"What?"

"Sitting Bull."

She stared at me for a second, trying to figure out what I'd said. Then, "TAKHtanka iYOtakhta! *I was there!* I was there, at Wounded Knee. I am seventy-three years old. He was my chief. I knew them, I knew them all: Sitting Bull, Big Foot . . . . I am from Standing Rock, you betcha!"

She wasn't really there. If she was seventy-three in 1997, she was born thirty-four years after Sitting Bull died, which was two weeks before Wounded Knee; the closeness of the dates is anything but coincidental. But I had sense enough to realize that the literal truth was not what was important here.

I said, "It's not really a good book. There are better books."

"Yeah. It's BULLSHIT!" and then, shy and embarrassed, "Oh, pardon my French. I am a real, true Indian woman. I used to wear my hair in braids, wear moccasins like this. Sitting Bull was a great leader, a great man. He worked for his people. They killed him because his brother, you know, he turned him in. From Standing Rock, near Fort Yates. My reservation."

"You are Hunkpapa?" I ask. Sitting Bull's people.

"Hunkpapa, you betcha."

When I was little I had a book about Sitting Bull and another one about Buffalo Bill. One of the things that amazed me about the life of Sitting Bull was how dramatically his world changed around him in a single generation. When he was a boy, his people hunted with bows and arrows as well as rifles; he rarely saw a white man or any white-made articles other than rifles, kettles, and beads until he was in his teens. The Sioux ruled an enormous grassland empire, from Canada to Missouri, from Minnesota to Montana. When he was an old man, his people were confined on ever-shrinking reservations, he himself was forced to become a farmer, a great humiliation, and the warrior friends of his youth had nothing to do but hang around the agencies and wait for their handouts.

When he had a scrap with a rival leader, it was the white agent who passed judgment on him, he who had once been proclaimed the principal leader of the Sioux in a great conclave at one of the Lakota sacred sites, Bear Butte—Mato Paha—near the present town of Sturgis, South Dakota.

Here in South Dakota, this not-so-very-old woman obviously venerated Sitting Bull, his name moved her deeply, but there's more to it than that. She felt she knew him, knew him intimately, that he personally protected her and watched over her. And maybe she did indeed know the man he was, although their lives did not overlap in time; maybe she knew him better than any white biographer ever could.

It is conceivable, barely, that people still alive saw him or were at Wounded Knee. The officially oldest person in the world died recently at 117. Sitting Bull was assassinated December 15, 1890, and the massacre at Wounded Knee took place on December 30, 1890. So much can a life span encompass.

"You going back to the mission?" Grandma asked Jacky.

"Yes, they'll come looking for me."

"You don't have to go! You don't have to go in their damn program!"

"I want to go back, eat some protein. I'm gonna cook some kidneys, kick back, watch some TV. It's OK. They'll come looking for me about 10:30." She sounded relaxed, complacent, almost dreamy.

"I will *never* go in that mission!" said Grandma, and she meant it.

As I walked away I was hearing some words of Sitting Bull in my head, words I had recently read. Powerful words, spoken during the days of war on the Bozeman Trail and its forts: "Look at me. See if I am poor, or my people either. The whites may get me at last, as you say, but I will have good times till then. You are fools to make yourselves slaves to a piece of fat bacon, some hard-tack, and a little sugar and coffee."[13]

When I spoke with members of the Mount Rushmore Historical Society or to administrators at the memorial, it wouldn't take long before they would talk about how the Hills were "stolen" from the Indians, which was generally followed by talk about how the theft was "inevitable." Maybe so; using force to take territory is predictable enough in human affairs. The Lakota expulsion of the Crow and Kiowa shows it just as well as the deluge of land-hungry prospectors and settlers flowing west in the 1870s.

The Rushmore orientation center has little to say about how the Indians lost the Black Hills, but that does not mean that there is little to say about it. The treaty of 1868 is as good a place as any to start.

3

TREATY MATTERS

Throughout the summer season of 1927 the *Rapid City Journal* was full of the doings of President Coolidge, who was staying at the state game lodge in the Black Hills for an unprecedented presidential vacation far from the White House. Telephone, telegraph, and airmail had made this possible, and everyone in the country, no less than the people of South Dakota, was a little amazed that a president could wander so far from the political nerve center. While in South Dakota, Coolidge gave a speech at a dedication of the Rushmore monument—its second dedication, although no actual work had yet begun—and became a sort of patron of the project.

On July 27 he attended the Gold Discovery Days Pageant in the Black Hills town of Custer. The *Journal* reported:

> A group of nearly 200 Indians from the Pine Ridge Agency depicted the region before the coming of the whites.

Brawny braves in colorful costumes, buxom squaws with papooses on their backs, were shown in possession of the virgin wilderness . . . .Discovery of gold by Horatio N. Ross, trooper with the Custer expedition, 53 years ago, was shown . . . .Theodore Shoemaker, state forester, took the part of General Custer, riding a white horse, not unlike the steed which the famous character rode shortly before he met his death in the Battle of the Little Bighorn.'"[1]

It is hard not to wonder what these "brawny braves" and "buxom squaws" felt about their part in this grotesquerie, sharing the stage with their nemesis while performing a reenactment of their former freedom for the enjoyment of their conquerors. A clue to their motivation can perhaps be found in the pageant notes for the 1997 production, in the section Highlights of Yesteryear: "Many Indian families spent a good share of the summer performing at special events in Black Hills communities. Part of their payment included meat."[2]

Custer rode a sorrel horse on the day of his death, not a white one, and, incidentally, his famous hair was cropped short for his final battle, as it usually was on military campaigns. He also wasn't really a general. That had been a Civil War brevet appointment, or temporary appointment on the battlefield, and when the war ended he fell all the way back to captain. At the time of his Black Hills expedition—and at the time of his death—he held the rank of lieutenant colonel, and when acting in his capacity as an officer of the Seventh Cavalry he was addressed as colonel. To insist on these points would be to hold the real man more important than his legend, which would be a mistake.

There are other interesting details. Theodore Shoemaker, who played Custer in this pageant, was the man who guided Borglum and his thirteen-year-old son, Lincoln, on their exploration of the Black Hills in 1925, when Borglum settled on the Rushmore site, and who, as early as January 6 of that year, had suggested that one of the peaks around Keystone would best serve for carving. In a novel it would seem mechanical artifice: The man who set in motion the conquest of the Hills was played by the man who had helped choose the site for the symbolic representation of that conquest, its absorption into the national story.

The roots of this pageant go back before Custer to Meriwether Lewis and William Clark, who came through the plains in the early years of the nineteenth century on their famous journey of exploration, commissioned by Thomas Jefferson—the second face on Mount Rushmore. Their report showed the way, and by the 1830s and 1840s prospectors were coming west along the Oregon Trail, disrupting the buffalo and other game and fomenting conflicts over resources between tribes that already didn't get along so well, like the Sioux and the Pawnee, the Cheyenne and the Crow. The Oregon Trail brought a new element into the struggle for resources: Smallpox was a common companion of whites when they came to new lands. It struck the tribes along the Missouri in the tragic winter of 1837.

The disease came to the plains with an infected deckhand on the *Saint Peters*, an American Fur Company steamboat up from Saint

Louis to supply the trading posts along the river. When it broke out among traders at Fort Union, they tried to stem the disease with an inoculation of the smallpox virus, which was what they had on hand, rather than the harmless cowpox vaccine, which conferred protection from smallpox. The dose was available in the person of Mr. J. Halsey, assigned to take charge of the traders at the fort that summer, who was very ill. A small dose of the smallpox itself sometimes protected whites but was disastrous in unexposed populations with no natural resistance. As Indians and some whites died, the traders in desperation locked up the fort, survivors trapped inside with the stinking corpses. When Indians pressed against the gate, anxious to trade and demanding entrance, the traders held up an infected Indian boy and displayed his suppurating face as a warning of the infection inside.[3]

Three infected Arikara women disembarked from the *Saint Peters* at the busy post of Fort Clark and went to a Mandan village. From that point the disease raged out of control, helped on by the dense populations and unsanitary conditions around the trading posts and by a particularly badly timed attack of the Skidi Pawnee on the Oglala Sioux. The Pawnee went home with infected prisoners and regretted it. Over the next year perhaps seventeen thousand people died, among them a quarter of the Pawnee, half the Assiniboine and Arikara, and three-quarters of the Blackfeet; the Mandan and Hidatsa were practically wiped out.

A word about the Sioux, and then one about smallpox.

Sioux is an English corruption of a French corruption of an ethnic slur the Chippewa—or Ojibwa—used for their enemies, whom they called Nadoue-is-iw, or "little snakes." The word is very broad, artificially defining a large category of people who never used it to describe themselves as a group until the twentieth century. What they called themselves was Dakota, Nakota, or Lakota, depending on the dialect of a mutually comprehensible language. The word means "allies," "friends."

At the time of the greatest expanse of the Sioux plains empire, around 1825, the Lakota people were the westernmost group, inhabiting what are now North Dakota and South Dakota, and Nebraska west of the Missouri River, the Powder River country in Montana, and parts of Wyoming, on up to the Canadian prairies. The Nakota ranged over North Dakota and South Dakota east of the Missouri, and the western parts of Minnesota. The Dakota, or Santee, the "Woodland Sioux," were found in most of the rest of Minnesota. When the Chippewa, armed with weapons acquired through close contact with French settlers, drove the rest of the Sioux tribes out of Minnesota in the seventeenth and eighteenth centuries, the Dakota had remained.

The Lakota, or Teton Sioux, are by far the largest group, and they are in turn divided into various subtribes: the Hunkpapa, or Those Who Camp by the Village Entrance. The Itazipco, or Sans-Arcs, on a diviner's bad advice, once put their bows out of reach just before they were surprised by enemies. The Minneconjou, unusually for the Lakota, once practiced agriculture to some extent. *Mni*, sometimes written as *minne* or *mini*, is the Siouan word for water. Minnesota means, very poetically, "the fog that rises off the river in the morning." Minneapolis is a synthesis of the old world and the new, a Greek root with a Sioux modifier: "Watertown."

The name of the Oglala subtribe may refer to a gesture of flicking dirt off the fingertips, an expression of contempt for an enemy, or it may refer to a widely scattered people. The Oohenonpa, or "two-kettle," were known to brag that their hunters could provide twice as much food as necessary. The Sicangu, also known as the Brulé in French and occasionally as "burnt-thigh people" in English, were caught in a devastating prairie fire in the eighteenth century, and some of them received bad burns to their legs.

The Sihasapa are the Lakota Blackfeet, not to be confused with the Assiniboian Blackfeet. The largest and most powerful Lakota subgroups are the Oglala and the Sicangu.

These subtribal identities were rather informal and permeable, and their crystallization as hard-and-fast categories is to some extent a later development. There has always been much intermarriage and intersettlement. In addition, smaller bands within these subgroups often coalesced around charismatic spiritual or war leaders or around *tiyospaye* (extended family groups)—thus "Sitting Bull's Hunkpapa," "Red Cloud's Ogala." To this day, the Lakota people on the reservations to which they were confined after 1877 refer to the inhabitants of the Pine Ridge reservation as "Crazy Horse's people" (Oglala) and to those of the Rosebud reservation as "Spotted Tail's people" (Sicangu).

Smallpox. The one-way mortality of the encounter between the worlds was not arbitrary; it could not just as easily have gone the other way. This was, of course, a major factor in the colonization of the Americas, perhaps the decisive factor. Smallpox followed Cortés to Mexico, Pizarro to Peru, de Soto through the Mississippi Valley, Smith to the Chesapeake. Mortality in previously unexposed populations was sometimes as high as 95 percent, a rate that chokes off resistance and cultural continuity. The early English colonists at Jamestown took their epidemiological effect on the inhabitants as a sign of God's favor for their endeavor and their race, which was a natural enough reaction to something unseen, not understood, and enormously powerful.

Death flowed mostly in one direction because Europeans, with their domesticated plants and animals whose pedigrees went back to the Mesopotamian Fertile Crescent of eight thousand years ago, had experienced a "Neolithic revolution" in farming that had two major cultural effects: close daily contact with domestic animals and surplus food stocks, which in turn led to crowded cities. With a much denser disease environment, Europeans developed specialized immune systems that responded to the implications of this new way of life. Disease vectors between humans, domestic animals (and domestic pests, like rats), and their parasites played a very important role; smallpox was originally a disease of cattle, as influenza was of birds. Humans in the Americas, with less intensive agriculture and lower population densities, and with far fewer domesticated animals than the Europeans, never developed the diseases or the resistance to the diseases that were endemic in Europe.[4]

It took almost two hundred years for English-speaking whites to get from proto-Virginia to the North American plains in any numbers. Conflict with Indians resulted in a repeated ritual of treaty making that started as far back as 1825, a ritual deriving authority from the Northwest Ordinance of 1787. While the assumptions of its framers might nowadays be called patronizing, the relative power of the whites and Indians was more in balance in 1787 than it was later to be, and because of this fact we have no reason to believe them insincere:

> The utmost good faith shall always be observed towards the Indians; their lands and property shall never be taken from them without their consent; and, in their property, rights, and liberty, they shall never be invaded or disturbed, unless in just and lawful wars authorized by Congress; but laws founded in justice and humanity, shall from time to time be made for preventing wrongs being done to them, and for preserving peace and friendship with them.[5]

These treaties never really satisfied either party. To secure periods of relative peace, the government held parleys and gave out presents of food, blankets and rifles, as well as assistance to any tribes that might wish to settle down and take up farming. This was something of a forlorn hope on the part of the white negotiators. Some Indians did take up the vocation of hang-around-the-fort, depending on government handouts or scouting jobs or what they could negotiate with the traders, but there were few converts to farming. Annuities and rations were promised and given to the Indians to keep them quiet and were withdrawn or suspended when they misbehaved.

Such diplomatic offerings were tried at a major gathering of the tribes at Fort Laramie, a former fur trading post, in 1851. Here the Indians promised to stop harassing travelers on the Oregon Trail and accepted a large reservation and hunting territory. This treaty was only intermittently successful. Spells of peace were punctuated by periods of skirmishing, during which the rifles distributed by government agents as treaty presents were often turned on westward-bound trekkers and the soldiers who came to protect them.

There were never enough soldiers to definitively resolve the conflict. The army was reluctant to send soldiers to secure a land that it believed could never be settled. Right up until the 1850s the idea persisted in the East that the trans-Missouri regions west of the hundreth meridian were the "Great American Desert." Writing as late as the late 1860s, two generations after Lewis and Clark, Custer felt obliged to debunk this myth.

Although soldiers did some fighting in the West, the whites did not win the West with soldiers but with settlers—after enough adventurers had come through looking for gold and furs to see that the plains were not a desert; with railroads; and with the commercial buffalo hunt, which wiped out the Indians' means of subsistence.

Although the effect of the extermination of the buffalo was not unknown to policymakers and not outside their calculations, the demise of the great herds owed as much to markets as to policy. The commodification of the buffalo that came west with early traders created an American and European market in tongues, meat, and hides that both white professional hunters and Indians participated in. By 1800 most of the plains tribes were involved in trading buffalo products for European goods and for horses. By 1867, when rail-roads began to cut through the buffalo's range, disrupting their migrations and providing easy transport back to the Eastern meat markets and tanning factories (buffalo chamois was particularly prized), although the end was near, there were still tens of millions of buffalo on the plains.

By 1883 there were not enough to justify a commercial hunt. The last organized chase took place in 1882, on the Standing Rock reservation. It required the approval of Agent James McLaughlin, who gave permission, though with some misgivings about encouraging the old, uncivilized ways.

Tradition had more poignant vestiges. Up until the late 1880s the government beef ration at Pine Ridge, part of the Black Hills payment, was distributed "on the hoof," and the former buffalo hunters chased down the cattle rather than slaughtering them right away, sometimes for several miles. Later the agents put a stop to this and set up slaughterhouses on the reservations.

The commercial value of the buffalo persisted even after the buffalo themselves were gone. In a sad coda to the demise of the original herds of perhaps sixty to a hundred million buffalo, their bones followed their flesh and their hides to the factories; they were useful in industrial sugar-refining processes, and could be crushed into phosphate-rich fertilizer. The intense slaughter of the last fifteen years of the commercial hunt had left the plains littered with these bones, which speculators soon collected, by the tens of millions of pounds, and loaded into eastbound boxcars.

The commercial trade was the main cause of the destruction of the huge buffalo herds of the West, but Indian hunting outside this trade may have contributed. It is very likely that the newly introduced rifles and horses led to unsustainable Indian kill rates. Horses probably made a greater difference than rifles since they allowed Indians not only to hunt more effectively but to carry many more and heavier possessions than when dogs were their only draft animals. Indians began to make much larger tipis, which required many more buffalo hides. Horses also put pressure on buffalo populations by competing with them for grass.

Indian overhunting is an idea that many Indians resent and many whites are uncomfortable with, accustomed as we all are to the notion that Indians were stewards of the earth, who never took more than they needed, and used everything they took. In fact, Indians, like other human beings, approached resources with both wisdom and folly, both knowledge and superstition. There is much contemporary testimony to the effect that particular Indians in particular times and places did practice resource conservation, and others in other times and places did not. Sometimes the same action could indicate profound knowledge of the environment, economic good sense, or simple recklessness, depending on the circumstances. For example, plains Indians sometimes set the grasslands on fire out of a sophisticated understanding of the regenerative role that fire plays in the plains ecology, and sometimes they did it to manipulate buffalo grazing grounds for human convenience. Sometimes they did it to dismay their enemies, to cut them off, to destroy the pasturage of the buffalo they hunted.

Certain Indian preferences—like a taste for the meat of cows rather than bulls and for fetal buffalo—did not represent optimum conservation practices. Lakota buffalo hunters probably used the products of everything they killed when they needed to and when the net cost of doing so did not overwhelm the net benefit. Although the testimony of white observers arguably describes a culture penetrated by such alien cultural values as the trade of hides and tongues for liquor and guns, there is evidence that this formula had held since long before any contact with whites.

Certain hunting techniques, such as stampeding a herd off a cliff, made buffalo products difficult or impossible to use fully. Excavations of an ancient buffalo jump at Olsen-Chubbock, Colorado, show that eight thousand years ago, aboriginal hunters drove about two hundred buffalo of all ages and both sexes off a cliff into a narrow ravine. The huge pile of carcasses meant that those underneath were nearly inaccessible; those who ended up on top were fully butchered, but the hunters took only the tongues or other choice parts of those more deeply buried, and hardly touched the ones on the bottom, leaving at least forty whole or nearly whole buffalo to rot.

The anthropologist Shepard Krech III, writing on the cultural and economic relationship of Plains Indians and buffalo, points out that an animistic spiritual view of the world may have led hunters at buffalo jumps or other mass hunts to kill more than they actually had need for—because of the danger that if one escaped, he could tell all the other buffalo about the jump or slaughtering pound, making it useless.[6]

The disappearance of the buffalo altered the lives of plains Indians. It meant the end of their hunting culture and the narrowing of their options to alien agriculture, dependence on alien government, or death. This fate was well understood by the army, the government, and the railroads and much applauded by many whites. General ("Little Phil") Sheridan, who led many expeditions against Indians, once suggested that a medal be struck to commemorate their passing: a buffalo on one side, a sad-eyed Indian on the other.

From the 1830s to the 1870s, Indians were confronted more and more frequently with white technology and with white traders, soldiers, and railway surveyors; Indian lives were changing, but the whites were not yet strong enough to take possession of the land. During this time of tension and uncertainty there were a few massacres in the West, sometimes of Indians, sometimes of travelers or settlers. These events kept the idea of the dangerous and unconquered frontier alive in the minds of policymakers and would-be emigrants and made mutual trust and understanding almost impossible. The bloodshed involved not just whites and Lakota Sioux but sometimes tribes whose traditional disputes and competitions were exacerbated by contacts with whites and tactical alliances with them.

Sicangu and Minneconjou Lakota wiped out Lieutenant John Grattan and his men near Fort Laramie in 1854, in a dispute that began when a Mormon following the Bozeman Trail noticed that his lame cow had been liberated by Indians. The confrontation was escalated by a bellicose, drunken Métis translator and the stubbornness of the righteous Mormon, who would accept nothing less than the arrest of the Indian and the return of his exact cow, as if he were around the corner from a police station in Saint Louis.

Grattan was just the man to back him on this. He refused all offers of reasonable compensation from the band's spokesman, Conquering Bear. He did not know and would not have believed that Conquering Bear did not have the authority to arrest anyone; Lakota chieftainship didn't work that way. Attempting to demonstrate his power and urged on by his translator, Grattan fired a cannon. The shot killed Conquering Bear, whereupon Grattan and his men were efficiently wiped out by the infuriated Indians.

Before railroads connected East to West, consequences came in slow motion, but they did come. The next year soldiers came looking for Indians to chastise, and General William Harney—who gave his name to a Black Hills peak and to Harney National Forest—wiped out an entire village of Little Thunder's Sicangu on the Bluewater River. Harney had been dragged back from leave in Paris to punish the Indians for the Mormon cow incident, and going from the banks of the Seine to the banks of the Bluewater must have been an interesting contrast. He took six hundred men on the expedition. This was one of the first opportunities the Lakota had to see the full impact of the whites' technology of warfare up close, and it made a big impression. Harney won the Lakota name Mad Bear for his tactics.

After the battle Harney demanded the surrender of men who had attacked a mail wagon the year before. Spotted Tail, who would later become an important chief, stepped forward. He and several others spent four months in captivity at Fort Leavenworth, Kansas, where they were under a loose confinement. Spotted Tail got a good look at the numbers and technology of the whites, an experience that was to make a profound impression on him and on his beliefs about how best to maintain his people's independence.

There were strange interpenetrations of love and violence on the plains. Settlers and Indians sometimes captured and adopted each others' children, poignantly refusing to part with them when negotiated agreements called on them to do so.

Soldiers, settlers, and Indians were also known to kill children in war and to mutilate their victims whatever their age. Tribes had their trademark cuts, slashings, and severings intended to announce their chastisement of an enemy and strike fear into survivors. In this they were very practical. Sitting Bull at war once spared a young Assiniboine captive who called him Grandfather, much to the amusement and disgust of his companions. He adopted the boy and raised him as a Lakota; years later, Little Assiniboine made war on his former people.

It could easily have gone the other way with Little Assiniboine on the day his life was spared. The pendulum of Plains life swung quickly from generosity to violence, and it makes sense that two of the primary Lakota virtues are open-handedness and stoic tolerance of pain. Indians, when fighting each other, seldom attacked a large village, as Harney and Custer did. Casualties seldom reached the level of what might be called a massacre, although individuals could expect no mercy if they wandered into the wrong territory. Game on the plains was most plentiful where the tribal hunting boundaries were most ambiguous, for few hunters cared to venture into a borderland where they might be ambushed by strangers claiming exclusive rights.

Indians did massacre whites, usually when the Indians had been pushed to the limit. The Minnesota Sioux Uprising of 1862, for example, was the response of the Dakota, the eastern Sioux, to broken treaties and starvation. The Dakota had given up most of their lands through treaties and had been forced to depend on the annuities promised in exchange for those lands. The annuities were paid through the system of government stores. When they were late and the crops were bad, as in 1862, the Indians went hungry, even if the storehouses were full. When Little Crow, chief of the Mdewkanton Dakotas, demanded an explanation from the Indian agent and the traders at the agency at Redwood, one of the traders, Andrew Myrick—himself married to an Indian woman—told the agent that so far as he was concerned, "they would eat grass or their own dung."[7]

This attitude provoked the starving Mdewkantons to attack. A few days later Myrick was dead on the grounds of the agency, grass stuffed in his mouth, and the fighting was spreading. Before the Mdewkantons were overwhelmed by the superior government forces, more than six hundred white settlers and soldiers died. A large party of warriors led by Little Crow fled west onto the plains, into Lakota territory. Many of the remainder faced a military trial before General Henry Sibley, who believed the Indians had revolted without cause, and offered them no legal counsel in a system they did not understand. Sibley's court sentenced three hundred and three to death; when informed of this, President Lincoln ordered a review that sought to distinguish between those who had fought in battle and those who had murdered defenseless settlers.

Eventually thirty-eight of those deemed guilty were hanged in

Mankato, Minnesota, in 1863. The investigation into the uprising seems to have been greatly influenced by missionaries on the scene, who interceded on behalf of those Indians they considered good Christians. Maybe they missed a few, or maybe desperate moments will provoke desperate reactions. Many of the Indians who were hung went to the scaffold with a Presbyterian hymn on their lips.

Lincoln's limited clemency excited the anger and disgust of General Sibley, Governor Alexander Ramsey, and much of the white population of Minnesota. Sibley, with Ramsey's help, had in fact embezzled many of the annuities due the Indians under the treaties and thus bore as much responsibility as anyone for the uprising; but this does not seem to have weighed on his conscience.

The Dakota, conquered a generation earlier than the Lakota to the west and already confined to reservations, had been considered by the whites to be past such outbreaks.

Two other attacks in which soldiers wiped out Indians loomed large in the conflict that was developing in the West. One was so vicious as to prove a deep embarrassment to the government in Washington, D.C., despite the heightened anxiety about Indians among settlers in the West, government officials, and the army and militia in the wake of the unexpected Minnesota Uprising, which was the most wrenching event of that period of Western settlement.

Colonel John Chivington was a fanatical Indian-hater commanding the Colorado First and Third Militia. Chivington, a Methodist preacher and a one-time missionary to the Wyandot Indians, was called the "Fighting Parson" by his contemporaries, a name which expressed the confluence of zealotry and violence that marked his life.

The unit he commanded had been recruited in an atmosphere of hysteria brought about by an escalating history of Indian raids on settlements around Denver, culminating in a particularly nasty attack on a ranch in which the foreman, his wife and two children had been killed, scalped, and mutilated by Arapahoes. Territorial Governor John Evans called the tribes to a parley at which he planned to threaten them with destruction if such attacks did not cease; when there was no response he issued a proclamation in August 1864 empowering any citizen of Colorado to destroy Indians and to take and use their property, thus appealing simultaneously to the fear, greed, and bloodlust of the settlers. When this still didn't work—when the Indians cut the Overland Trail to Denver and continued to take captives—Governor Evans got permission from the War Department to raise a volunteer militia, the Third Colorado Cavalry, which operated with the First.

By the winter of 1864 Chivington was tired of hearing that he commanded the "bloodless Third." Governor Evans and Major Edward Wynkoop, with Chivington's reluctant participation, had been involved in some delicate negotiations with Black Kettle and his Cheyenne in regard to an exchange of captives that might lead to peace talks, negotiations in which Black Kettle and his people had been quite helpful. In November Chivington's troops ambushed Black Kettle's peaceful village at Sand Creek, Colorado. The village was under formal promises of protection from Wynkoop.

Chivington's men killed mostly women and children since the men were out hunting. They burned about 150 lodges, along with much of the band's winter food stocks, and captured several hundred horses and valuable buffalo robes.

Black Kettle was flying an American flag over his village at the time of the attack. It was a present from the commissioner of Indian affairs himself, who had told him that it would always protect him in his dealings with whites. It didn't. The excesses of battle were the familiar ones, the ancient atrocities with us in the wars of Alexander, Genghis Khan, Lyndon Johnson. Chivington's militia rode back to Denver with scalps, genitals, ears, and fingers dangling from their pommels, vulvae stretched for use as hatbands.[8] Chivington displayed his scalps at a victory rally at a theater in Denver.[9]

Testimony at an ensuing Commission of Inquiry revealed something of Chivington's character and motivation. Second Lieutenant Joseph Cramer of the First Colorado:

> To Colonel Chivington I know I stated . . . that I felt it was placing us in very embarrassing circumstances to fight the same Indians that had saved our lives, as we all felt they had. Colonel Chivington's reply was, that he believed it to be right or honorable to use any means under God's heaven to kill Indians that would kill women and children, and "Damn any man that was in sympathy with Indians."[10]

James M. Combs, a civilian who met Chivington on his way to Sand Creek:

> There was a promiscuous conversation about scalps, where they were going to arrange them, &c. He (Chiv-

ington) spoke up and said that "Scalps are what we are after." I told him that I thought he could get, any way, some four hundred or five hundred of them within one day's march of Fort Lyon; that I thought there was about that number, warriors, squaws and papooses . . . that they had given up their arms to Major Anthony, and were unarmed now . . . He (Chivington) . . . made the remark: "Well, I long to be wading in gore."[11]

Black Kettle escaped Chivington's massacre at Sand Creek and somewhat inexplicably remained friendly to whites until the ambitious and flamboyant Custer came to finish the job in 1868. The Battle of the Washita, at which Black Kettle was killed and his village wiped out for the second time, contributed greatly to Custer's reputation, and he wrote of it in some detail. His commander, General Sheridan, was impressed—until it turned out that Custer had abandoned a detachment of eighteen men, led by Major Joel Elliott, who had been pinned down under hostile fire away from the main engagement. Custer seems to have made some attempt to find out what happened to them but, with the fading light and the possibility of Indian reinforcements, left them to their fate. This was a piece of unprofessionalism that Sheridan never quite forgot, and the relations between the two men suffered. Still, and importantly for our story, Sheridan called on Custer's services again.

In 1862, the same year as the Minnesota Uprising, gold was discovered in Montana. Wagon trains of whites began coming through

Indian territory on the Bozeman Trail, a shortcut on the Oregon Trail from Fort Laramie to Bozeman.

The route was a serious matter. It was disrupting the buffalo migrations that were a matter of life and death to the Plains Indians. The Sioux, Cheyenne, and Arapaho took to attacking these travelers from the East; and to protect them the army built a chain of forts: Fort Phil Kearny near Story, in present-day Wyoming, in sight of the Bighorn Mountains; Fort Reno, near Kaycee, Wyoming, and Fort C. F. Smith, near Hardin, Montana. Fort Phil Kearny was the anchor of the system.

The Indians attacked these forts when they could. In strategic terms this was fine with the government, although perhaps not with the hapless soldiers who manned the forts or with the travelers who took refuge in them. If the Indians stayed busy harassing these soldiers and travelers, perhaps they wouldn't notice that the Union Pacific railroad, heralding their apocalypse, was creeping across their domain to the south.

By 1866 the Oglala chief Red Cloud was one of many Indian leaders warring on the Bozeman Trail against the U.S. army and its forts. Red Cloud had first learned of plans for the forts while at Fort Laramie for another round of treaty making, and no modern diplomat stalking out of a U.N. special session in boycott of debate could match him for the effect of his exit. The end of the year found Oglala harassing woodcutters in the vicinity of Fort Phil Kearny, in a series of skirmishes that started in early December.

The men of Fort Phil Kearny had been going a little stir crazy locked up behind the high wooden stakes of their stockade with their fellow soldiers, their wives and children, and a few other civilians. They were not getting along well. Ever since the attacks had begun, it had been too dangerous to venture casually outside the stockade. Almost every day a woodcutter was killed. When a young Army wife named Frances Grummond arrived at the fort in early 1866, the first thing she saw when she approached the gates was a wagon bearing the scalped and naked body of a woodcutter, killed within sight of the stockade walls. It was not a good omen.

Many of the career officers had come out to the Indian frontier because, with the Civil War recently ended, it was the only place they could expect to make a name and win promotion. Throughout that fall, as the small force hunkered down in the fort or drew protective duty for the woodcutting parties, they could see Indians outside the walls signaling to each other using hand-mirror messages sent at the speed of light, whose meaning the soldiers could guess did not bode well for them. There was increasing bitterness between two factions, one urging defensive actions, one offensive. The fort commander, Colonel Henry Carrington, knew that the soldiers were outnumbered, poorly equipped and trained. He preferred to rely on defensive measures like his powerful mountain howitzers to keep attackers away until requested reinforcements could arrive. Captain William Fetterman with his friends Lieutenant George Grummond—Frances' husband—and Captain Frederick Brown wanted very much to bring the fight to the Indians.

When Indians again attacked the wood-train on the 21st, Fetterman begged Carrington for a chance to take them on. As a brevet

Lieutenant Colonel he was the senior Captain at the post, he pointed out. All he needed was eighty men, and he could whip the entire Sioux Nation.

Carrington was cautious. He and Fetterman had led an expedition from the fort on the sixth, meant to strike fear into the Indians. They had badly miscalculated. Drawn into an ambush, the officers and their men had been lucky to escape with their lives on that occasion. Now Fetterman was eager to try it again. Captain Brown pleaded for another shot at Red Cloud's scalp. Grummond volunteered to lead a cavalry detachment.

Carrington gave Fetterman his party of eighty and let him out of the fort to protect the woodcutters and punish the Sioux. Carrington, who had recently been commanded by the Department of the Interior to be more aggressive with the Indian raiders, seems to have sent Fetterman out against his own better judgment. He insisted that Fetterman not go beyond Lodge Trail Ridge, which would put him out of the line of sight of the fort. He gave this order three times: to Fetterman in person, on the parade ground, and from the sentry walk as the column was leaving the fort.

Wise counsel means nothing to a certain kind of man, and Fetterman fell for the oldest trick in the book. Lured on by a young warrior on a horse that appeared to be lame but somehow managed to keep just out of rifle range, he and his troops passed over the ridge and . . . were surrounded by the Sioux and Cheyenne forces, armed, angry, and effective. Inside the fort, the women listened to rifle shots for half an hour or so, coming from exactly the place that Carrington had told Fetterman not to go. Then there was silence.

Maybe Fetterman believed the Indians incapable of any planned strategy, or maybe he was just stupid. There were no survivors. It is possible that the decoy was Crazy Horse, who would have been around twenty-six at the time.

Today Interstate 90 parallels the old wagon track of the Bozeman Trail: traffic still moves in more or less the same path. The battle-field oversees an immense landscape of what is now peaceful cow country, with the beautiful Bighorn Mountains shading off into atmospheric perspective to the northwest. What was it like in the winter of 1866? Were the soldiers struck by the beauty of life just before they were struck by Sioux arrows?

The Fetterman massacre was a shock to the army and led to its demand that the Indian Bureau, then, as now, under the control of the Department of the Interior, revert to the War Department, which had originally held jurisdiction. Military men could solve this problem, they said, if the bureau, responsible for the distribution of treaty goods, such as rifles, would only stop coddling the Indians. General William T. Sherman wrote to General Ulysses S. Grant: "Just arrived in time to attend the funeral of my adjutant-general, Sawyer. . . . I do not yet understand how the massacre of Colonel Fetterman's party could have been so complete. We must act with vindictive earnestness against the Sioux, even to their extermination, men, women and children. Nothing less will reach the root of the case." Evan S. Connell, in his book on Custer, *Son of the Morning Star*, notes that "if one word of this extraordinary telegram is altered it reads like a message from Eichmann to Hitler."[12]

Sherman's plan was impossible to carry through, and he was

pragmatic enough to know it. There were a lot of hostile Indians in the West. The country was not eager for conflict after the carnage of the Civil War; besides, when soldiers went out to fight Indians, they usually just got lost on the vast plains. If they could surprise a village, they might kill a few, as Custer and Chivington had done; and if they got overconfident, the Indians might kill a few of them, as Conquering Bear's Minneconjou and Red Cloud's Oglala had done. Faced with a situation that had no easy immediate solution— but certain that time was on the side of the immigrants from the East, with their numbers and their railroads—the government was willing to talk to the Indians and even to beat a strategic retreat. The Union Pacific was advancing to the south, the Northern Pacific to the north, two inexorable ribbons of track that would destroy the free life of the open plains forever.

Sherman himself carried the new invitation to parley. Already in 1867, with Fetterman dead less than a year, he was all over the plains, talking to Lakota leaders along almost the full north-south extent of their range, meeting Sitting Bull's Hunkpapa on the northern Missouri, Spotted Tail's Sicangu in Nebraska, and many other tribes besides, some of them allied with the Lakota, some of them not: Kiowa, Comanche, Apache, Arapaho. His plan was to bring them all back to Fort Laramie again and have them sign a treaty of perpetual peace with each other and the government. On this trip Sherman talked a lot about the benefits of settling down and farming the earth, a plan that was not received by the Indians with enthusiasm. But he was authorized to make some real concessions.

As always, the army men focused on the Indians they believed were the great chiefs, looking for a locus of power from which they could expect and demand enforcement of the rules. This focus arose from a deep misunderstanding of the nature of Lakota society, one that was at the root of much confusion and frustration among the whites. A chief of the Lakota or other Great Plains tribe did not wield the executive power, whether delegated or otherwise, that those of European cultural background took for granted. In developing a negotiating position the Lakota would strive hard for consensus, and if they could not reach it they were comfortable with leaving the matter unresolved, a habit which frequently drove the white commissioners appointed to treat with them right out of their skulls. Once an acceptable position had been found, a chief could persuade, cajole, advise, set an example, but he could not order his young men not to attack the local white settlement, and if he had tried to do so, they would have laughed at him, seriously diminishing his power. The messengers of democracy were not used to this sort of individualist social structure, and because they saw Red Cloud as a great chief, they assumed that his signature was indispensable on any treaty. They didn't know it, but in setting up Red Cloud as a paramount leader they weakened his power with his people and incidentally caused some irritation among his rivals—Old Man Afraid of His Horses, Spotted Tail, American Horse, Sitting Bull—who could claim as much influence. But it was Red Cloud's signature that mattered to the soldiers and their government. To them, it was "Red Cloud's War."

Emissaries began arriving at Fort Laramie in April 1868. Red Cloud kept them waiting and guessing. In the end he signed only after the forts were abandoned, a nonnegotiable item, and he didn't come to Fort Laramie until November. He'd chased some buffalo on his way to the parley, causing a detour. By the time he was ready to sign, Sherman and his party had given up and gone home, so he made his mark on the papers they'd left behind.

So there was a treaty. Ratified and signed by the new President, Ulysses S. Grant, early the next year, it was one of the few ever offered to Indians from a government position of weakness. It recognized the Black Hills as a "great Sioux reservation" in perpetuity or until the Indians should freely choose to give it up according to a specific formula, an aspect of the treaty that would prove important. The treaty granted more than just the Black Hills, in fact: all of present-day South Dakota west of the Missouri, a small chunk east of the river that now forms the Crow Creek reservation, and large pieces of Nebraska, Montana, Wyoming, and Colorado were set aside as hunting lands or "unceded Indian territory." Most important to the free hunting way of life were the lands in the areas of the Powder, Tongue, Bighorn, and Yellowstone Rivers.

White folks were not supposed to enter the reservation lands without an express invitation from their treaty partners, "except such officers, agents, and employes of the Government as may be authorized to enter upon Indian reservations in discharge of duties enjoined by law." In return for this legal concession, war with white settlers and with hostile tribes was to cease.

The treaty also specified that the government would assist in "civilizing" the Indians after the hunting grounds became so depleted of game that they could no longer support the hunting culture, an outcome eagerly anticipated by General Sherman, the commander in the West, who saw in the sport hunters who were decimating the plains buffalo herds the ultimate solution to the Indian problem.

The part of the treaty that dealt with renegotiation was Article 12. It provided that no future treaty or amendment would be valid unless it carried the signatures of three-fourths of the adult male Indians. This was designed to guard against the white negotiators' practice of designating Indian leaders and negotiating with them against the wishes of their putative constituencies.

The Lakota believed that they had won their land and their hunting rights, the whites that the Indians had agreed to settle down as farmers and to stay under the cultural, military, and economic influence of Indian agencies near the Missouri River. These differences in interpretation caused problems later.

Not too much later. By the early 1870s the buffalo herds were being destroyed in earnest as the railways advanced across the plains, and the Indians were increasingly dependent on trade and treaty goods. The government, almost immediately after the ratification of the treaty, began attempts to reinterpret it so as to disallow the use of the hunting grounds to the Indians, to confine them permanently to the specified reservations, and to oblige them to collect treaty goods at agencies on the Missouri River. On a trip to Washington, D. C. in the summer of 1870, and later in a public address at Cooper Union in New York, Red Cloud flatly denied that he had understood the treaty to require him to go to the Missouri.

Red Cloud would not cooperate. He knew that on the Missouri easy access to whiskey, and the government's easy access to the

Lakota, would corrupt his people and erode his own traditional authority.

Spotted Tail and his Sicangu had the same problem. Evicted from their Platte River hunting grounds by military threats, they were sent to the Whetstone agency on the Missouri, under the military command of General Harney, the chief's old opponent. At Whetstone the government had prepared a special location for the Sicangu, even hopefully turning some soil in preparation for arriving Indians ready to take up the farming life. Sophisticated modern farming machinery was waiting for the Indians. Like Red Cloud, Spotted Tail would have none of it. Too unhealthy, too restricted, too close to white settlements. He feared what the whiskey runners would do to his people. He moved west to the White River, about forty miles away.

Over the next few years Red Cloud and Spotted Tail found themselves trying to work out acceptable interpretations of the treaty in an ever-shrinking physical and political space, as game became scarce, government agents cheated on disbursement, and the Northern Pacific railroad crept up on recognized Sioux lands south of the Yellowstone, triggering a minor war with Sitting Bull. As the government continued to nibble at their lands, their own people grew increasingly skeptical of their chiefs' ability to hold the U.S. government to the terms of the treaty, even as many of them grew more resigned to an inevitable rapprochement with the power of the whites. War with the Arikara, Crow and Pawnee went on as it always had, punctuated by occasional atrocities perpetrated by Indians on settlers, and vice versa.

This tense situation was occasionally interrupted by odd proposals from the world of the whites. The editor of the *Sioux City Times*, Charles Collins, one of the most persistent advocates of white settlement in the reservation, eventually sponsored the first well-organized civilian expedition to enter the Black Hills, the Gordon party, which included the pioneer woman and chronicler of pioneer life Annie Tallent. Before that, Collins came up with a scheme that complemented his championship of gold fever. He proposed at the 1869 Saint Louis Fenian Convention that land be distributed to the Irish in western Dakota Territory. These settlers, after they prospected and prospered and accumulated the necessary supplies and capital, would use the resources gained in the Black Hills to conquer Canada. They would then hold the huge northern territory and use it to bargain with Queen Victoria for the freedom of Ireland.

What might the Lakota have made of such a crackpot nationalism, played out so far from the Anglo-Irish struggle? It would surely have taken a keen sense of irony to appreciate the role of the Black Hills in a different colonialism than the one they were themselves encountering.

Gold, not Irish nationalism and its politics, brought whites into the Black Hills. If the Black Hills really had gold, could such a vast, rich, and beautiful territory stay off-limits, just because some Indians wanted it and considered it theirs? Secretary of the Interior Columbus Delano, who oversaw the administration of Indian treaties, had been thinking about this possibility several years before the fact of gold was confirmed:

I am inclined to think that the occupation of this region

of the country is not necessary to the happiness and prosperity of the Indians, and as it is supposed to be rich in minerals and lumber it is deemed important to have it freed as early as possible from Indian occupancy.

I shall, therefore, not oppose any policy which looks first to a careful examination of the subject. . . . If such an examination leads to the conclusion that country is not necessary or useful to Indians, I should then deem it advisable . . . to extinguish the claim of the Indians and open the territory to the occupation of the whites.[13]

By arguing that the Indians did not "need" the land, the proscription of the Northwest Ordinance against seizure of land and the articles of the 1868 treaty itself could be neutralized for the greater national good.

Secretary Delano and many others had reason to suppose that the Hills were rich in timber and minerals. Anyone could see the trees, and intrepid travelers had reported gold as long as white people had been coming through the Hills, since the 1830s. Usually such adventures ended badly. One early white adventurer is remembered by a message scratched in sandstone:

Came to these hills in 1833 seven of us De Lacompt Ezra Kind G. W. Wood T. Brown R Kent Wm King Indian Crow all ded but me Ezra Kind—killed by Inds beyond the high hills got our gold June 1834

Got all the gold we could carry our ponys all got by

the Indians I hav lost my gun and nothing to eat and
Indians hunting me[14]

There's a kind of desperate poetry to this that lends authority, but it
may be a fake—it seems unlikely that a man running for his life would
bother. Annie Tallent of the Gordon party presents as evidence a
story that the gold collected by Kind and his friends was sold to the
Hudson Bay Company by its Indian appropriators for eighteen thousand dollars ("or probably its equivalent in fire water, beads, and other
gewgaws so dear to the hearts of savages"[15]—the practical Tallent
hated frivolity). True or not, Kind's lament was known in the East by
the 1870s, and his gold strike was supported by the reports of many
other mountain men and prospectors who had braved the Hills.

One didn't have to meet Indians to find gold and die: a convicted
murderer, Toussaint Kensler, emerged from the Hills with some
quills and a skull packed with gold dust, and was hanged on his return
to civilization when he tried to cash in. What became of his haul is
not reported. What was important was that people had seen it.

Indians did not like trespassers, and although they did not particularly value gold, they had some understanding of what a gold rush
by whites might mean for them. In 1852 eight returning prospectors
reported a strike and lots of Indians; the remaining twenty-two
members of their party were never seen again, and it is not hard to
guess their fate.

By 1874 the time was ripe for gold fever to spur a dash into the
Black Hills. The economy was in crisis, triggered in part by the collapse of financier Jay Cooke's banking and railway empire—which was

overextended in Western railroads, especially the Northern Pacific, the track so objectionable to Sitting Bull just a year before—and by Jay Gould's attempt to corner the gold market in 1869. The Panic of 1873 had become the worst depression the nation would know before the Great Depression. The Black Hills were rumored to be full of gold. That gold was the hope of armies of unemployed men and their families.

The government found itself squeezed between a plan and a constituency. On the plan side there was President Grant's Indian Peace Policy, based on confining Indians to reservations and cleaning up the Indian Service (as an antidote to the famous corruption of this institution, administrators who oversaw reservation life were drawn from the ranks of the clergy—Grant favored Quakers.) Indians off reservations were subject to the discipline of the army.

On the constituency side, Grant had a problem with the Great Sioux Reservation treaty. The American voting public didn't like it.

Custer, at Sheridan's request, rode through the Black Hills in the summer of 1874 with twelve hundred men and a military band mounted on white horses. His official mission was reconnaissance and the construction of a fort at the base of the Hills to discourage Indian raids south of the reservation into the Nebraska Territory, a symptom of the ineffectiveness of the treaty. Taken strictly as a military reconnaissance mission, Custer's trip did not violate the letter of the treaty, although plans to build a fort were of questionable legality and highly provocative to boot. The Lakota had not gone to war in the 1860s to see more forts on their land.

The expedition, however, was more than a military matter.

Whatever else he was supposed to be doing, Custer was looking for gold. A gentleman scholar who keenly enjoyed adventure and discovery, Custer brought along a paleontologist, a zoologist, a botanist, three journalists, and a photographer. In a capacity perhaps more ornamental than scientific or military, Colonel Fred Grant, the president's son, tagged along.

Custer also had a geologist and two miners with him, and some Arikara scouts. The scouts were a necessity, but the geologist and miners were pure calculation. The state of Minnesota paid for the geologist, Newton Winchell, sparing the federal government the need to explain his presence on the mission. The miners, Horatio Nelson Ross and William McKay, had no official sponsors; they were just there. Rumor had it that Custer had personally paid their expenses.

The Black Hills expedition was of great interest to settlers in the west. In spite of its potential for disrupting delicate relations with the Indians, there is no doubt that at least some whites saw it as an opportunity to redefine the relationship. It was clear what was coming, even before any gold had officially been found. In one of the most blatant—and often-quoted—statements of Manifest Destiny, the *Bismarck Tribune* wrote:

> . . . as the wild grasses disappear when the white clover gains a footing, so the Indian disappears before the advances of the white man . . . Humanitarians may weep for poor Lo [a word for Indians] and tell the wrongs he has suffered, but he is passing away . . . The American people need the country the Indians now occupy; many

of our people are now out of employment; the masses need some new excitement . . . An Indian war would do no harm, for it must come, sooner or later . . . [16]

The men of the Custer party thoroughly enjoyed themselves in the Black Hills. The only Indians they met with were a small band led by an elderly chief, One Stab, whom they took hostage for a short time but did not allow the Arikara scouts to kill, much to the scouts' disgust. They played baseball and picked the abundant wildflowers in the valleys, and they looked for gold. On July 30, Ross found some, about ten cents' worth. Custer immediately sent his favorite scout, "Lonesome Charley" Reynolds, riding off alone to Fort Laramie, through the territory of Indians who were very angry at the expedition's intrusion into their lands. Reynolds made it to the telegraph station.

William Eleroy Curtis rode with the expedition as a journalist. His reports had been appearing in the *Chicago Inter-Ocean* since the middle of August. With the delay inherent in nineteenth century communications from the wilderness, it wasn't until August 27— nearly a month after the discovery—that the paper got the big news. A huge headline in the first column blared

GOLD!

Followed by no less than ten subheads, describing the strike in the most excited terms—"A Belt of Gold Territory Thirty Miles Wide."[17] The *Inter-Ocean* reported on the prophets of gold in the region, like Charles Collins; on the gold country and how to get there; on the soldiers turning into miners; and of course on Custer, the modest hero of the moment.

The *Inter-Ocean*, for all its hyperbole, had been beaten out by the local Dakota Territory papers. The *Yankton Press & Dakotaian* matched the enthusiasm of Chicago.

STRUCK IT AT LAST!

Rich Mines of Gold and Silver Reported Found by

Custer

PREPARE FOR LIVELY TIMES!

Gold Expected to Fall Ten per cent.

—Spades and Picks Rising—

The National Debt to be Paid when Custer Returns

. . . Rich mines of gold and silver, in a beautiful, well-watered and timbered region, is the general purport of the welcome news that electrifies the whole country. . . . The sealed book has been opened and peeped into by a thousand intelligent men, some of whom stand in the front rank of science. It will never again be closed with the seal of our government, but will remain open and we will all take a look.[18]

This *Yankton Press and Dakotaian* edition includes a great many advertisements for outfitters and for the railroad route to the point bragged on as most convenient to the Black Hills—Yankton, cross-roads of the Dakota territory east of the Missouri.

At this point events began to move quickly in the Hills. The morning after the first strike the men and officers of Custer's party, abandoning such sense of restraint as nineteenth-century soldiers might know, were crowding around the site at French Creek with any implements that came to hand. Such industriousness was a fore-taste of the well-known effect of gold upon the great masses of white men, and there were great masses of white men in New York, in Denver, in Saint Louis and Chicago, who were anxious to make their fortunes. They came to French Creek, and they moved on to Spring Creek, in July of 1875, then to Rapid Creek, on and on through the Hills.

The first small-time placer miners did not find the mother lode, the source of the riverine deposits; but the town of Custer soon formed on the site of the French Creek strike. General George Crook was sent round to inform the fortune seekers that they had to be out of the Hills by August 15. Crook evicted most of them, although he gave them a verbal wink: "Boys, I must obey orders, but no doubt you will come back."[19] With Crook's consent, the prospectors elected aldermen, formally surveyed the town, and drew up town lots against the day when they would be allowed to reclaim their property.

Annie Tallent felt that Crook had no taste for the work of restricting intruders and did only the bare minimum necessary to carry out his orders. She had harsh words for his subordinate, Major Pollock, whom she found entirely too enthusiastic in enforcing policy.

The government did know the consequence—war—of allowing white men to violate the Great Sioux Treaty, and it did make some good-faith efforts to keep the flood of prospectors out of the Hills. Tallent, describing the Gordon party's journey to investigate the first gold strike at Custer, writes of their fear of Indians and also their fear of interdiction by soldiers. The group used what it thought to be elaborate evasive measures to avoid both, from advertising a false destination on signs hung on its wagons to doubling back in wide circles to confuse any tracking soldiers.

The soldiers had their orders. On September 3, 1874, the hard-headed General Sheridan, commander of the Division of the Missouri, gave clear instructions, based on government policy, to his subordinate General Alfred Terry. "Should companies now organizing at Sioux City and Yankton trespass on the Sioux Indian reservation, you are hereby directed to use the force at your command to burn the wagon trains, destroy the outfit and arrest the leaders, confining them at the nearest military post in the Indian country. Should they succeed in reaching the interior, you are directed to send such a force of cavalry in pursuit as will accomplish the purposes above named." He left Terry, the prospectors, and himself an out, in the form of a prediction for which we need assume no special prescience on his part: "Should congress open the country to settlement by extinguishing the treaty rights of the Indians, the undersigned will give cordial support to the settlement of the Black Hills."[20]

The Yankton Press and Dakotaian commented: "It is a great pity . . . that Gen. Sheridan cannot set about some more humane and

useful mode of employing his troops than that of defending the
Sioux Reserve from the invading foot of peacefully disposed miners.
No doubt the oft-violated treaty will some time be disposed of, and
then the Indian will have to come down to a level with white men,
though at present he is held by the government as a person entitled
to rights and immunities which white men never had the arrogance
to claim."21

Some of the groundwork for ignoring the treaty had already been
laid. In 1871, Congress had officially and unilaterally revoked the
status of Indian tribes as independent nations that could claim treaty
relationships with the government. This meant that Indians were to
be treated as other citizens under the law, as individuals with no specially recognized historic rights as members of independent nations;
yet they were not American citizens and could not claim citizenship
as a group until 1924, and citizenship was anyway a status that many
would resist when it was offered.

In obtaining the Black Hills the U.S. government clung to a cloak
of legality, but it was threadbare cover. In September 1875 a commission led by Senator William Allison came to the Hills, authorized to negotiate with the natives. Discussion wasn't on the Indians'
agenda: they thought they had already made a deal. This time they
didn't show up as they had at Fort Laramie in 1851 and 1868, to
smoke and talk and receive presents. They came to the conference
on the White River near the Red Cloud agency to show their military strength, firing guns into the air and galloping their horses
around the terrified commissioners. Little Big Man, standing in for
Crazy Horse, who never came to parleys with whites or anyone else,

approached the whites with a rifle in one hand, cartridges in the other, wearing a long war bonnet that came down to the ground behind him and nothing else. He threatened to kill the first Indian who suggested selling the Black Hills.

The Sioux who had never "come in" to the agencies were adamant. Their leaders were Sitting Bull, who was camped in Hunkpapa territory to the north of the Hills, and Crazy Horse, who stayed with his people on the Powder River hunting grounds in present-day Montana. They would fight for the land.

Bands who had been subsisting on rations and occasional hunting near the agencies, led by Red Cloud and Spotted Tail, were more fatalistic. Red Cloud knew how strong the *wasichus* were. He knew how the Hills had supported his people, and if he was now to be forced to give them up, he wanted to exchange them for some other means of support. He asked for seven generations of sustenance for his people—to put a price on it, between fifty and seventy million dollars' worth of goods and cash. And although Annie Tallent thought Indians reckoned in terms of "gewgaws," Red Cloud was far more sophisticated. He wanted the old ways, the hunting life, very much. If he could not have that, he wanted to get enough so that his people could live on the amount. Red Cloud understood compound interest.

The commissioners felt they could responsibly offer four hundred thousand dollars a year for mineral leases and the right to use the land for stockbreeding and agriculture or a flat purchase price of six million dollars.

This offer was not acceptable to any of the Indians. By this time

Grant, along with the Indian agents in the Powder River territory, had lost patience with the idea that the Indians would ever be "civilized." On November 3, 1875, he secretly—and in violation of the treaty—ordered that the army should no longer attempt to hinder the incursions of prospectors. The evidence survives in a letter from Sheridan to Terry: "The President decided that while the orders heretofore issued forbidding the occupation of the Black Hills country, by miners, should not be rescinded, still no further resistance by the military should be made to the miners going in."[22] And because the army was no longer going to keep them out of the Hills, it would soon have to protect them.

Something had to be done about the more militant holdouts in the unceded Powder River country, who in the winter were joined by many of the "agency Indians" who had obtained their agents' consent to hunt in these treaty lands. The government produced a transparent strategy. If these bands could be provoked into war, a new arrangement might be in place when the dust settled. On December 6, 1875, the government ordered them to report to the agencies on the reservations by January 31, 1876—or be considered "hostile" and face the consequences. It was a bitterly cold winter. Complying with this order, which had no legal basis under the treaty of 1868, would have meant starvation or death by exposure for many of the men, women, and children in these bands. Even if they had arrived at the agencies, they would have starved; the agents did not have enough food for so many people.

In December, before many bands could have complied or even been notified of the order and before the final deadline, the trader at the Standing Rock agency was ordered to stop selling ammunition to the Indians. On January 17 the commissioner of Indian affairs telegraphed the same order to the agents at the Red Cloud, Spotted Tail, Crow Creek, White River, Cheyenne River, Fort Peck, and Fort Berthold agencies. These orders meant that not only the hostile Powder River bands but also those already on the reservations could not hunt effectively. In the absence of adequate agency supplies, this amounted to condemnation to starvation—that is, to leverage for negotiating peace in a war that had not yet been declared.

By this time fifteen thousand miners were ripping up the Black Hills, the spiritual center of Lakota life, the emergency hunting grounds.

The plains campaign of the summer of 1876 was called to drive the Indians hunting along the Powder River back onto the reservations—Sitting Bull, Crazy Horse, Gall, and many of their friends and relatives who had come out from the agencies to enjoy what they may have realized were the last days of the free Indian life. Custer was part of a three-column strategy designed by Sheridan: a Montana column led by Colonel John Gibbon, a Dakota column led by General Alfred Terry, and a Wyoming column led by General George Crook. Custer was part of Terry's column. He had originally been slated to lead the column, but he was having political problems.

Custer had been called as a witness in a congressional investigation into a scandal at the War Department that involved the sale of licenses for post sutlers, the merchants who sold necessities on army bases. His testimony had implicated Secretary of War William Belknap and also President Grant's own brother Orvil. Grant was furious. He denied Custer the Dakota command and saw that it went to General Terry instead. Grant didn't want Custer going on the expedition at all—being in the field was a chance to win honor and promotion. Once again Sheridan intervened on his behalf, and with Sheridan's patronage Custer led the Seventh, though not the whole column, onto that dusty plain in Montana.

Crook's column was to march north along the old Bozeman Trail, the scene of that original unpleasantness with Red Cloud back in 1866. He was supposed to attack and harass "hostiles" he found off the reservation and drive them north into the other two columns. Crook, however, was delayed at the Battle of the Rosebud on June 17, 1876, when Lakota and Cheyenne fought his men to a standstill while wild rose petals fell among the desperate fighters. Needing to regroup, short of supplies, and not knowing how many Indians were on his route, Crook then headed off toward Wyoming. This gave the Lakota and Cheyenne he had fought with time to join the major encampment on the Little Bighorn.

At the Rosebud and at the Little Bighorn, the Lakota were fighting because to relinquish the Black Hills and go on the reservations was to give up their freedom. They chose to resist.

On June 25, on the dry rolling plain near the present town of Crow Agency, Montana, Custer rode to his fate against one of the largest groups of Indian warriors ever assembled. There are no reliable reports of Custer's last words, but according to his trumpeter, John Martin—aka Giovanni Martini, a twenty-three-year-old

Italian who had already seen action with Garibaldi and who survived Battle of the Little Bighorn because Custer sent him off with a message for Colonel Benteen's detachment—Custer rallied his troops with "Courage, boys, we've got them!" The words are poignant, and true or not, somehow they are what we expect. Nowadays we feel a chill for the recklessness of the boy general, so long protected by "Custer's luck"—he'd had a dozen horses shot out from under him during the Civil War—his final bid for grandeur as bitterly ironic as any other part of this unfolding American tragedy.

Custer's modern apologists say that he was merely defending a policy made by others, as was his duty; but it was a policy to which his own actions had greatly contributed. The Lakota mystic Black Elk, made famous in a different world and much later in life by his interlocutor John Neihardt, was thirteen at the time. He remembered miners flooding into the Black Hills after the Custer expedition. Although Custer buffs are able to separate cause and effect, Black Elk was never in doubt: "We heard that some *Wasichus* had come from the Missouri river to dig in the Black Hills for the yellow metal, because *Pahuska* [Long Hair—Custer] had told about it with a voice that went everywhere. Later he got rubbed out for doing that."[23] When battle came, the first in which Black Elk fought as a man, he was glad of the outcome. "I was not sorry at all. I was a happy boy. Those *Wasichus* had come to kill our mothers and fathers and us, and it was our country."[24]

The Indian victory only delayed the inevitable. Custer's defeat was the Alamo, the *Maine*, the Pearl Harbor, the World Trade Center of his day. Militias formed and army units mobilized all over the country to punish the Sioux for the death of a national hero; schoolboys around the country solemnly pledged to kill Sitting Bull on sight.

The great company of warriors split up days after the battle. Sitting Bull fled to Canada. Crazy Horse, his people starving and pursued by cavalry, surrendered at Fort Robinson, Nebraska, in the winter of 1877, where he was arrested and soon after bayoneted by a soldier while his old associate Little Big Man, transformed into an Indian policeman under the new order of things, held him for the blow.

With the surrender of Crazy Horse there were no longer any militants alive and at large and with any significant numbers of followers to fight for the treaty. In August 1876, Congress cut off all support to the bands of Lakota who had stayed near the agencies, almost none of whom had participated in the battle. They, too, paid the price and were held hostage to a new agreement. The aid that the government had forced the Indians to depend on would not continue until the Lakota gave up the Black Hills. This message was delivered by a new commission, led by former Commissioner of Indian Affairs George Manypenny, in September 1876, at the Red Cloud agency.

Manypenny offered a treaty that took the Black Hills for the United States and promised more aid for those Indians who wanted to become white farmers and more education for their children. It also required the Indians to come to the Missouri agency for their rations, keeping them far from their traditional hunting grounds, which they would now have to cede. The commissioners hinted that at some point in the future they might be relocated to the Oklahoma Indian Territory—a nightmare land of starvation and pestilence to which Indians from all over the country had been deported.

There was no way out. The commissioners explained that without an agreement, the Hills would be taken without compensation. A company of soldiers stood behind the negotiators with fixed bayonets. Cannon were prominently displayed.

The commission did not even seriously attempt to collect signatures from three-fourths of the adult males in each band as required to amend the 1868 treaty, so in legal terms the treaty was not valid, but that hardly mattered. The Indian representatives signed a document they could not read. Congress went right ahead and in February 1877 ratified the "agreement" that it would no longer call a treaty. The Lakota had lost the Black Hills.

Thus did the mountain that Gutzon Borglum would shape into the "Shrine of Democracy" become part of the territory of the United States.

4

BORGLUM'S MOUNTAIN

The Lakota called it The Six Grandfathers, aspects of the four directions, the earth, and the sky; but Mount Rushmore got its English name from a New York lawyer. Visiting the Black Hills of the Dakota Territory in 1885 to work out the legal details of tin-mining claims, Charles Rushmore asked a local prospector for the name of the rock he could see from the peak of nearby Bob Ingersoll mountain. Whites called the rock Slaughterhouse Peak—a name that could not have survived its fate in the next century—but according to local legend, the reply was, "Hereafter we'll call her Mount Rushmore!" There are several different versions, but the accounts agree on the main points. The mountain ended up with the name of the young lawyer. Charles Rushmore felt irrationally flattered by this abrupt truncation of history and carried his proprietary pride into old age. More than forty years later he contributed five thousand dollars to help turn the mountain into a monument, as much as any Black Hills railroad or mining company gave.

By the time the monument was being built, the world was very different than it had been in 1885. In 1925, South Dakota was part of the United States, which had recently played a decisive role in a world war and become a world power. The nation not only claimed all the land between its coasts, but had connected the coasts with railways and then connected them again by cutting through Panama. While Europe was choking on the bitterness of dismantled, chaotic empires, the American economy—youthful, exuberant— roared ahead, expanding as quickly as the nation had. It was the right time to begin a project that would announce the special American experience, the national character, and celebrate the American story.

So when the sculptor Gutzon Borglum held a pageant to dedicate Mount Rushmore in preparation for carving an enormous monument to "the foundation, preservation and expansion of the United States of America," some people found the project odd, and some criticized it from an aesthetic point of view; but the memorial impulse itself seemed perfectly natural.

The idea of carving a mountain in the Black Hills originated in 1923 with Doane Robinson, the South Dakota state historian. He didn't have Rushmore in mind, but rather the beautiful and unique geological features called the Needles, spires of hard granite weathered out of softer rock. Although Borglum, characteristically, later said that Robinson had been "pricked with a desire to immortalize the spirit that made America what it is,"[1] the original idea was not particularly patriotic. What mostly pricked Robinson was the thought that it would be a great thing to carve heroic figures of the Old West on these columns as a way of bringing a permanent gold rush of tourist dollars to the state. "I can vision Custer with his first gold discovering cavalcade winding through the Needles, with Redcloud and a band of Sioux scouts, resentful and suspicious, spying upon it through the rifts in the pinnacles of the opposite wall. . . . Commercially such an enterprise would be of tremendous value to the Black Hills and might within a few years bring you more money than does the precious mineral wealth of your section."[2]

Invited by Robinson and chosen because of his ongoing work at the Confederate Memorial at Stone Mountain, in Georgia, Borglum came to South Dakota and spoke to the Rapid City Commercial Club in 1924. The Needles turned out to be too soft for carving, and anyway that concept reminded Borglum of the totem poles of the tribes of the Pacific Northwest, a form he considered both primitive and parochial. He had his own well-developed ideas about what American monumental art should be, and bringing him into the project changed the concept—it had to be presidents and the achievement of national, not local, consolidation and identity—but not, from the point of view of the local businessmen, the goal of creating a profitable attraction.

The commercial club liked the idea. In 1925 state and federal laws were passed permitting "colossal sculpture" on the public lands in question, and the club, and all the associated commercial clubs of the Black Hills, took up fund-raising in earnest.

Much to the members' surprise, they had a very hard time finding even ten thousand dollars for a preliminary geological survey. People of the Black Hills region are very proud of Rushmore nowadays, but it began as a project of the business elite—a small part of that elite—who saw it as a long-term money-maker. Throughout his Black Hills career Borglum complained of the short-sightedness and indifference of the people of South Dakota, who would reap the benefits of what he was doing but contributed little toward its financing. He was disappointed in other ways, too. The federal enabling legislation for Rushmore that was passed in 1929 included an executive committee to oversee finances and operations. Borglum and his sponsor, Senator Peter Norbeck, managed to have rich people appointed to it, like the Texas oil king J. S. Cullinan, the railroad magnate Fred Sargent, and Julius Rosenwald, president of Sears Roebuck, in the hope that they would prove generous. They didn't.

The commercial clubs eventually proved Robinson right. Tourism is now South Dakota's second largest industry after agriculture. Every year almost three million people come to the state to see Rushmore. While they are here they visit the other attractions, stay in motels all over the southwest corner of the state, go to pow-wows and rodeos, and buy postcards, ice cream, and crafts, bringing almost half a billion dollars into the South Dakota economy, a measure of the harmony between Robinson's boosterism and Borglum's patriotism.

Borglum's patriotism was a complicated thing, and his views were at the core of the project. When he came west to build a message about the power and history of a conquering nation, he was not an unlikely messenger. He had won early renown as a painter of

Western themes, and had lived the Western conquest in more than just imagination. Part of the last generation of westward-moving immigrants who could truly be called pioneers, he was born in a log cabin at Ovid, Idaho, in 1867, only four years after Idaho became a U.S. territory and still twenty-three years before statehood.

His parents, James and Christina Borglum, were Danish Mormon converts who had escaped a life of poverty, war, and persecution in the old country when their church called them to the new religious community taking shape in the American West.

Jens Borglum—he became James in America—had two wives. He was married to the first, Ida Mikklesen (Michelson), in Liverpool in 1864, in a shipboard wedding before departure for America, a practice encouraged by the steamship company because married couples could share quarters and thereby relieve cabin crowding. On arrival in New York, the couple traveled west by train and boat and then walked from the railhead in the town of Wyoming, Nebraska, to the church in Salt Lake City, a distance of eleven hundred miles. Early the next year, Ida's younger sister Christina, arriving separately, entered into the marriage under the law of the Mormon church. The church then called the new family farther north and west, from the center of the Mormon world into the Idaho wilderness. The family, which eventually included nine children, wandered the frontier, settling for a few years each in Ogden, Utah; Omaha, Nebraska; and Los Angeles by the time Gutzon Borglum was seventeen. James Borglum lived a frontier life somewhat at odds with his philosophical turn of mind, working as a carpenter, farmer, railroad worker, and later as a country doctor.

In 1871, under threat of legal action for polygamy outside Mormon territory and with his two wives unable to get along with each other, James sent young Gutzon's mother, Christina, away. Within the marriage her position relative to that of her older sister may not have been pleasant; to hide the family's marital status from the 1870 federal census takers, Christina had been listed as a domestic.

When she left, James and Ida Borglum demanded that the children never talk about her. Ida's children seem to have had little trouble with this. For the young Gutzon, there were consequences. He was a restless and rebellious child who frequently ran away from home, going off alone across those broad Western plains. Secrecy about his mother was only partially maintained throughout his well-scrutinized adult life, and strange hints and inconsistencies in his later writings point to a fundamental sense of loss and betrayal. In his autobiographical sketches his mother was sometimes Ida, sometimes Christina.

The historian Simon Schama[3] and the art historian Albert Boime[4] have made much of a presumed mother complex. They draw the obvious conclusion about his first marriage, at twenty-two, to his patron and teacher Lisa Jaynes Putnam, who was forty, the same age as the vanished Christina. Schama sees in his conflicted feelings for his mother the roots of a misogyny that led him to dismiss the idea of putting a woman's face on Mount Rushmore, and Boime interprets his drive to make huge works as a desire to obliterate his own unhappy past. While these thoughts are interesting, psychological insight at a distance is a tricky subject.

The family story has an interesting place—or nonplace—in commentary on Rushmore. The loss of a mother is a profound event, one that must shape a man. Yet Christina is oddly absent in most of the biographies of Borglum. Those who were intent on writing patriotic iconography have delighted in the picture of the pioneer family fleeing persecution and walking across the West. They have been less comfortable with the plural marriage. Tom Griffith, a Rapid City journalist and booster closely associated with the Mount Rushmore Historical Society, highlights the Borglum family's pioneer values in his book *America's Shrine to Democracy*. The book has a patriotic introduction by President Ronald Reagan, another man associated with rough Western virtues; but although Griffith milks the frontier and the trek west for all they're worth, he never mentions the marriage.

June Culp Zeitner, writing with Lincoln Borglum, the sculptor's son, who certainly knew better, is vague and misleading on the topic: "[Christina] either died, or disappeared quite unexpectedly . . . records are not clear on this . . . the young immigrant father knew that his sons needed a mother, so he soon married Ida, his wife's sister. . . . [5]

Willadene Price, in her 1962 book *Gutzon Borglum: Artist and Patriot*, mentions Ida as a figure in Borglum's childhood but, like Zeitner and Lincoln Borglum, calls her his stepmother and strongly implies that his real mother died some time before James and Ida met. Zeitner, Lincoln Borglum, and Price all confuse the facts and the chronology, since Ida and James were married first, in Liverpool, and Christina, the junior wife, joined them later in America.

Robert Casey, who coauthored the Borglum biography *Give the*

Man Room, identifies the sculptor's mother as Ida and quotes two ambiguous paragraphs from Borglum's own writing: "Not many years after Solon was born, Gutzon recalls, 'She left us. I was five. She turned to me as she lay ill. There were tears in her eyes and she was trembling as she took my hand. . . . And she told me to take care of little Solon.

'I never forgot it, but I wondered why. I thought she was going to stay with us. She and Father had always been with us. I could not understand.'"[6]

Casey—and Borglum himself—never tells us that this mother was not in fact dying; but Casey could not have been blind to Borglum's deception. The other author of the autobiography was Mary Borglum, Gutzon Borglum's second wife and widow. Casey and Mary Borglum were writing after the artist's death. Mary Borglum wanted Casey to tell the real story, but their publisher, Bobbs-Merrill, did not think that a family history of polygamy was suitable for the sculptor of Mount Rushmore.[7] Mary Borglum also encountered great opposition from Ida's surviving children, who seem to have wanted to rationalize the break. Gutzon's younger brother August, Ida's son, wrote: "Whether Christine died or went out of our lives seems to have been about the same thing. I don't mean to belittle the sentiment that both Gutzon and Solon had for their mother. It is a sacred and holy feeling. I met her and knew her personally. She was a sweet personality and artistic. But she was not 'driven from the home and husband she had loved,' etc. It was a mutual separation of a second wife who did not really belong in that family, giving place to the rightful first wife Ida."[8]

Protests and threats of legal action from Ida's children meant that Casey had to do what Borglum had done throughout his life: be vague about relationships, births, the sequence of events, and dates. For Borglum, trying to keep the secret must have required much vigilance. Perhaps it contributed to an evident paranoid streak in his character. At any rate, the story can be confusing for those who don't already know it.

Would the real story have somehow tarnished Rushmore or Borglum's personal legacy? Apparently the many Borglum biographers who fudge the facts or avoid the subject entirely thought that it would. Their gloss on his early life should be seen as an urge to manage the history of Rushmore and its creator, an urge that has obscured much more important points than the details of the sculptor's family.

The present Rushmore orientation center, which reopened in August 1998 after extensive renovations, now displays a small panel with a note on the family and photographs of James, Ida, and Christina.

The story of Mount Rushmore involves Indian history, and Indians were not strangers to Borglum. Raised on the frontier, he may have had some sentimental sense of a destiny intermingled with Indians. In a radio address in the 1930s, Borglum told a tale of meeting the Sicangu Lakota medicine man Crow Dog when he, Borglum, was seven. The story is probably invented. Borglum had a tendency to get carried away, and he also claimed that his father knew Red Cloud of the Oglala Lakota and Chief Joseph of the Nez Percé personally, which is extremely unlikely. If true, the meeting with Crow Dog might have occurred in 1874, when Borglum was actually seven, or in 1878, reckoning from his preferred birth year of 1871.⁹

Crow Dog's legend resonated with Western history in a special way when Borglum told the story, and Borglum was using the connection to reinforce his image as a man of the West, a living reminder of a time when Indians and settlers had met on more equal terms. This legend embodied European ideas of chivalry and honor for many Americans, although its meaning may have been quite different to Crow Dog himself.

In 1881, on the Rosebud reservation, where the Sicangu Lakota had settled, Crow Dog shot and killed the great Sicangu chief Spotted Tail. Spotted Tail had chosen the path of diplomacy and conciliation rather than warfare. By the early 1880s, with conciliation having led to dispossession and the treaty of 1868 just a bitter memory, Spotted Tail was no longer a universal hero to his people. Crow Dog, a traditionalist, medicine man, and a deposed former chief of the Indian police on the Rosebud reservation, probably killed him for reasons that combined disapproval of Spotted Tail's ways with women, suspicion of personal gain in his business dealings with white ranchers, and anger at his course of appeasement of the white colonials. Crow Dog was arrested and taken to Deadwood to be hanged, but asked the judge for a month to go home to the Rosebud reservation to set his affairs in order. The judge asked, "How do I know you'll come back?" "Because I'm telling you. I am Crow Dog."¹⁰

A month later he kept his word and came back voluntarily to be hanged, his wife beside him in the wagon. By that time the Supreme Court had ruled that the white authorities had no jurisdiction in a matter between Indians on an Indian reservation. Crow Dog was free, but Spotted Tail had been popular with the whites. The national protest was so great that Congress was forced to reclaim federal jurisdiction over major crimes[11] committed on Indian reservations. This was one of the most important developments in American Indian law, and it is a fundamental aspect of the relationship between Indian tribes and the U.S. government to this day.

While the romance of the west was an important part of Borglum's public persona, there are other clues to the evolution of Borglum's ideas about the singular fate and role of the United States. Schama suggests that Borglum was greatly influenced by the thought of William Gilpin, an influential publicist of the west and philosopher of Manifest Destiny.[12] I found no direct evidence that this was so, but there are good reasons to believe it. Borglum would have known of Gilpin for many reasons; any man of the time who was moderately well-read and moderately interested in the west would have known of him, and Borglum was more than moderately well-read and more than moderately interested in the west. He also would have come to Gilpin's work through western patriarch John Charles Frémont and his wife, Jessie Benton Frémont, who were close friends of both Borglum and Gilpin.

The Frémonts were patrons of Borglum when he was a young man in Los Angeles. They were intrigued by his early western-themed paintings of horses and stagecoaches, and commissioned him to paint a portrait of the old man. John Frémont died in 1890, but his wife for many years thereafter was a powerful influence on the artist and helped him greatly in his career.

The Frémonts were a remarkable couple. John Frémont, of course, was the famed pioneer, the explorer of the Oregon Trail in the 1840s who did so much to popularize the idea of westward expansion. He was a leader of the Monterey Bear Flag Rebellion of 1846 that was a factor in the annexation of California from Mexico. Frémont would eventually be one of California's first two senators and the first Republican candidate for President in 1856. Jessie Benton Frémont was the daughter of Thomas Hart Benton, one of Missouri's first two senators and a lifelong evangelist for westward expansion, cheap land, and hard currency. William Gilpin accompanied John Frémont on his 1843 Oregon Trail exploration, and wrote about it voluminously.

The early 1840s were pivotal years in the course of the movement west. By an understanding of 1818, Britain and the United States were joint occupiers of the Oregon territory, but the agreement was vague in its details and it was clear that there would eventually have to be a reckoning. In the meantime both parties were trying to establish *de facto* claims, the British acting mainly through settlements sponsored by the Hudson's Bay Company and the Americans through their own settlements and through missionary projects. The missions usually lacked official sanction since the government was anxious to avoid provoking conflict with the British, and was for a long time unenthusiastic about further pioneering. Gilpin would often accuse Washington, under the influence of "Atlantic Monopolists," of transporting eastern Indians to the west as a barricade to white expansion.

By 1843, however, with the settlement of Missouri firmly established and filling up with a land-hungry population, there was great pressure to open the territory. The reports of men like Frémont and Gilpin played an important role in convincing the public that the lands to the west were fertile, full of gold—and the rightful territory of the American people.

Gilpin, scion of a wealthy and powerful Pennsylvania manufacturing family, had quite an adventurous life. As a youth he came west and south to fight in the Florida Seminole wars, later settling in Missouri, at that time the frontier. He was to spend much of his life wandering around the west: with Frémont, fighting in the Mexican war of 1846, as the first governor of the Colorado Territory. Although he struggled financially for much of his career, in his fifties he acquired an enormous tract of land in southern Colorado, originally granted to private ownership through a pre-war Mexican patent. This made him very rich, the proprietor of an empire of his own.

Throughout his life he was a passionate evangelist for the wealth of the west and the "Untransacted Destiny" of the American people that was to be realized in its settlement. He was extremely influential, and his work and speeches found their way into many Congressional reports as well as into newspapers and popular publications all over the country, both directly and as incorporated into the work of others. His idiosyncratic prose style is easy to spot; when the phrases "great calcareous plain," "vast auriferous region," or "isothermal zodiac" appear in contemporary works, it's a pretty safe bet that the piece owes something to Gilpin.

In his time Gilpin was seen as perhaps slightly eccentric, but a brilliant scientist nonetheless. Nowadays it is not so. Gilpin came from a long European habit of thought that located the source of cultural differences in climate or geography. Much of this thought was more imaginative than rigorous—see, for example, an experiment performed by Montesquieu, in which the French *philosophe* froze half a sheep's tongue and concluded on the evidence not only that the constriction of "nervous glands" in a cold environment effects the character of the entire organism, but that this has a profound explanatory power in understanding the varying courses of civilization in cold and in warm climates.[13] To Gilpin the determining factor in the advance of the great European and Asian empires—and of the nascent "American Republican Empire"—was the "isothermal zodiac," a temperate climatic belt spanning the world around 40 degrees of latitude.

There was more to it than that, though. Gilpin also believed that the "concave" structure of North America, with its mountain ranges on the coasts and its rivers draining into the central basin of the Mississippi, naturally threw its peoples together and forced them to collaborate as brothers rather than to compete as rivals; whereas the benighted Europeans, on their "convex" continent with its central Alps and its rivers flowing out to the sea in all directions, had to constantly struggle against the petty chaos of division. For Gilpin, no further proof was needed of the great destiny of the North American People. In his zeal to express the state of harmony that the North American environment must impose, he used rhetoric that

he—a man who lived most of his life in the west—must have known
was absurd:

> Of this [natural tendency toward unity] we have . . . illus-
> trations now under our eye. . . . The *aboriginal* Indian
> race, amongst whom, from Darien to the Esquimaux,
> and from Florida to Vancouver's Island, exists a perfect
> identity in hair, complexion, features, religion, stature,
> and language . . . [14]

His most famous and influential book, published in 1860 and
going through many printings, is a reworking of his earlier *The Central Gold Region*, unsubtly retitled *The Mission of the North American
People*. It develops his ideas about climate and geography and explores
their multitudinous implications for the happiness and prosperity of
the North American people and their inevitable spread across the
continent. The *Mission* reads in sections like a geography textbook,
but every few pages it veers off wildly in all directions, following its
author's enthusiasms as to civilizations, statesmen, railroads,
mythology, and the "infinite" supply of gold to be found in the
western cordilleras (Gilpin never seems to have considered that if he
were right about this, gold would be worthless). His prose is out of
control, even by nineteenth century standards, and he seems to have
suffered from more than a touch of literary attention deficit disorder.

Although this is clearly the stuff of Manifest Destiny, Gilpin was
no racialist. He never posits any inherent virtue of white Christians

beyond their luck in having developed their culture in a temperate zone, and he is a great admirer of the Asian empires—in fact one of the many reasons that North America is to grow rich beyond imagining is that it will serve as the conduit for the trade of East and West, China and Europe. Although the *Mission* is an undisciplined mass of repeated facts and bizarre fancies, Gilpin does occasionally try to tie all his ideas about mountains, climates, and civilizations together, with startling results:

> These ancient masses of population [Europe and Asia], then, *back to back*, and descending these contrasted slopes, both front America—they face one another across America. The short line of mutual approach is the axis of isothermal warmth, penetrating four-fifths of the land, and nine-tenths of the population of the globe!
>
> *This is the line of way-travel of all the white races, of the commercial activity and industry of the zodiac of civilization!*
>
> As, then, this interval of *North America* is filled up, the affiliation of all mankind will be accomplished: proximity recognized: the distractions of intervening oceans and equatorial heats cease: the remotest nations be grouped together and fused into one universal and harmonious system of fraternal relations.[15]

Gilpin might be read as an early prophet of globalization, but his ideas about causality in the context of his own time are the purest gibberish. Thomas L. Karnes, in his excellent 1970 biography of Gilpin, suggests that while he was an eccentric with some odd ideas, he was not entirely wrong about the west. This is certainly true; there is a lot of wealth in the west. However, the usually careful Karnes errs in asking "Who will wager today that the land between the Alleghenies and the Rockies will not support Gilpin's estimated 180,000,000 people?"[16] Unfortunately for Karnes, and for sweet reason, his question is off by a factor of ten. The number Gilpin actually suggests is eighteen hundred million.[17]

How much of this actually found its way into Borglum's thoughts? The sculptor of Mount Rushmore was not so inclined as Gilpin to put his faith in geography over individual and racial will, nor was he so taken with the accomplishments of non-white civilizations. In his boundless enthusiasm for exploration and for the nation's moral, physical, and political development, however, he shares a great deal with Gilpin.

Borglum may also have absorbed some of Gilpin's ideas about monumentality. Here is Gilpin on commemorating Washington:

> Where the summit-crest of our continent is found; the focal source of its rivers and its sierras; where the cloud-compelling Cordillera culminates over the "Gateway of empires;" let these commemorate this *name* immortally, while the grass shall grow and the waters run, as firm and enduring as the loftiest mountain. Let the children of the world be taught to say: Behold the Pass and the Pillars of WASHINGTON![18]

How did Borglum describe his own project?

> I want somewhere in America, in or near the Rockies,
> the backbone of the continent, so far removed from suc-
> ceeding, selfish, coveting civilization, a few feet of stone
> that carries the likeness, the dates, and a word or two of
> the great things we have accomplished as a nation,
> placed so high that it won't pay to pull it down for lesser
> purposes . . . Carved as close to heaven as we can, to
> show posterity what manner of men they were . . . [19]

The similarity is almost certainly not conscious, but if there is a connection it sheds light on the origin of Borglum's ideas about the American nation. Borglum and Gilpin had much in common in the degree of their intellectual eccentricity.

It was Jessie Benton Frémont who insisted that Borglum study in Europe. He worked for several years as a painter in Britain and France and learned sculpture in the studio of Auguste Rodin. When he came east in 1890 on his way to Europe with his first wife, Lisa Jaynes Putnam Borglum, he was in search of a success that would polish his rusticity, although he eventually returned to live many years of his life in the West, in Texas and in South Dakota.

He did find success, and much fame, after serving a lonely apprenticeship in Europe. Observing Borglum's progress through the early twentieth century is to watch a rococo epic of conflict unfolding, full of innovation and impulsive romanticism. Nowadays he would be called a dilettante; in his own time the boundaries of endeavor for an energetic man were less clearly defined.

He was one of the most prolific sculptors of his day. In addition to his work at Rushmore and Stone Mountain, he made the head of Lincoln in the Capitol rotunda, a casting of which is at Lincoln's grave. He contributed more pieces to the Capitol's Statuary Hall than any other artist. He made the North Carolina memorial at Gettysburg, three important pieces in Newark, New Jersey—his *Seated Lincoln*, the *Pilgrims and Indians Memorial*, and *Wars of America*, the last the largest bronze casting in the country—and two equestrian statues of General Sheridan, one in Chicago and one at Sheridan Circle in Washington, D.C. He had hundreds of other public and private commissions, even though from an early point in his career he refused to participate in contests for commissions, considering them degrading and politicized. Although he did employ assistants, he did much of the finishing work on his pieces himself, contrary to common practice.

He did not limit himself to sculpture. He was passionate about urban design and sat on the committee that planned New York City's Central Park. He made plans for an opera house and a waterfront promenade for Corpus Christi, Texas. He corresponded with Frank Lloyd Wright about architecture, modernism, and the layout of factories. He designed public fountains, coins, buildings, airplanes and parts for airplanes, bridges, and educational curricula. He painted, although early in his career he decided to concentrate on sculpture professionally, and he sketched and wrote constantly. He gave speeches on art and politics and the meaning of art and politics in America, both to paying audiences and on the radio. He was inde-fatigable, a one-man industry.

Politics was among his chief passions, but he was a strange and inconsistent political eccentric. He hated socialism but for a time loved Robert La Follette, leader of the Winconsin-based Progres-sive movement and the farmers' revolt against Eastern plutocrats. A Republican who supported both Roosevelts, he loved capitalism but hated the businessmen, bankers, and railroad men, whom he believed were killing democracy in the name of profit. Briefly a leader of the Ku Klux Klan, he wanted to form it into the instrument of a white, Christian farmers' revolt. He wrote of Jews in the most vicious terms but was quite friendly with many of them, including Felix Frank-furter and the Jewish scholar Isidore Singer. When Hitler started his rise to power, Borglum was one of the very first public figures in America to condemn him absolutely and without hesitation, at a time when there were still mainstream voices, like Charles Lindbergh's, raised in his defense. He sometimes supported, sometimes attacked, the union movement but accepted a commission for a Sacco and Vanzetti memorial, explaining that whatever their politics, they had undergone an unjust and political trial. He was—at least in his own mind—an international diplomat, with plans for two major interna-tional reforms: a world court and an international authority to con-trol the world's vital waterways and canals.[20] Indeed, an International Criminal Court is now on the world's agenda.

In his dealings with elected officials, he demanded to be taken seriously, and he usually was. A 1941 telegram to South Dakota Congressman Karl Mundt captures something of his imperious sense of himself. "Phone White House. Propose that French fleet at Toulon be turned over immediately hoisting the American flag to our naval ambassador at Vichy as collateral for France's debt to America. Be quick about it. Wire me when you've done it. Gutzon."[21]

As one might expect of the author of such a telegram, he was famously pugnacious, fond of conflict with those he deemed less sincere, less creative, and less energetic than himself. This was pretty much everyone, and certainly anyone who saw things differently, including his colleagues during his very short-lived membership in the National Sculpture Society (he saw them as guardians of dead European convention), monopolists in the business wing of the Republican Party (enemies of the small farmer and artisan), and the executive committee in charge of the Rushmore work (petty-minded bureaucrats with no vision of a great national undertaking). In every case his criticism of his opponents involved not mere disagreement but withering moral attack. As his unlikely friend Supreme Court Justice Felix Frankfurter wrote of him, "It was all clear, black and white, passionate, uncompromising. . . . Gutzon was for war, for all sorts of war, six wars at a time. People weren't wrong; they were crooked. People didn't disagree with him; they cheated him."[22]

Borglum gained a reputation for being difficult that dogged him throughout his career, losing him commissions and interfering with his fund-raising for Rushmore, where from the first potential donors regarded him with suspicion because of his role in the collapse—because of bitter conflict with the organizing committee—of his earlier Stone Mountain project.

Given his contentiousness—the working title of his unpublished autobiography was "The One-Man War"—it is slightly surprising that he was never in an actual war. This was partly a matter of timing, although he did have opportunities. He was born in 1867, soon after the end of the bloodiest American war. The organized phase of the Indian wars was over before he had grown to manhood, with the exception of the Ghost Dance conflict, which was getting under way just as he was leaving Los Angeles for Europe in early 1890. In 1898, when the Spanish-American War broke out, he was living in London, depressed that he had not met his goal of greatness by age thirty, and painting murals for the Midland Railway Company's hotel in Leeds. He could have thrown up everything, gone back to the United States, and taken a commission with an auxiliary unit; after all, his soulmate, Theodore Roosevelt, who bore some responsibility for provoking the war, quit his job as assistant secretary of the navy to get in on the action. But it was Borglum's hope, and the hope of Jessie Benton Frémont, that he could build a reputation in the British and continental art world that would allow him to return home as a hero of the arts.

When he did come home, he was involved in several martial projects, although he never put on a uniform, something it's hard to imagine this superindividualist doing. He was greatly affected by the nation-building programs of Tomas Masaryk and Ignacy Paderewski, friends of his who were the unrecognized leaders of the unrecognized nations of Czechoslovakia and Poland. During World War I he made his Connecticut estate available as a training camp for volunteers for the army of a theoretical Czechoslovak Republic. These were young Czechs and Slovaks and Americans of Czech or Slovak descent who wanted to fight the Central Powers in the service of something that had never existed, an independent Czechoslovakia.

It is an odd historical fact that the sculptor of Mount Rushmore helped draft the Czechoslovak Declaration of Independence of 1919. His suggestions for that document included some lines that the Indians whose land includes Mount Rushmore might have appreciated:

> We . . . believe, that no people should be forced to live under a sovereignty they do not recognize. . . . We can not and will not continue to live under the direct or indirect rule of violators of alien or neighboring peoples. . . . We have been held in subjection by the force of arms, and the maintenance of our ideals has been secured only by stealth and against the tyranny of our oppressors."[23]

His World War I activities were not limited to the Czechs. Deeply involved in early aviation, Borglum became aware of a growing debacle in war procurement. Scrambling to develop an air force, the government had invested a billion dollars—a *billion* pre–World War I, pre-Depression dollars—in aircraft. For its investment not a single combat aircraft was ever delivered. The money was siphoned off by crooked contractors. The scandal was enormous, worthy of both the paranoia and the energy of a man like Borglum, and he seems to have recognized this. He persuaded

President Wilson to appoint him as a special investigator. He found evidence of the embezzlement that was bleeding the U.S. Treasury, as well as evidence of even more serious things: plots involving American manufacturers and British, French, and Japanese industrialists to prevent the creation of an American air force. He presented a detailed report to President Wilson, who did nothing. The scandal was too embarrassing, too embedded in the relationship between American commerce and politics. Eventually Wilson denied that he had ever authorized Borglum to undertake the investigation as a government representative. He had let him go ahead only as a private citizen. This infuriated Borglum, who published Wilson's original letter of appointment—in which Wilson says that the secretary of war will "clothe you with full authority"—to back him up, but he never did get an acknowledgment of his services. The government did not even reimburse him for the expenses of his investigation, a matter that clouded Borglum's opinion of Woodrow Wilson, the Democratic Party, and government in general for the rest of his life.

What Borglum thought of a particular American government, however, was quite different from what he thought of America's political mission. He poured tremendous energy into crafting Rushmore's philosophical statement. It was as important to him as the designs he sculpted in his studio.

Serious though he was, he was no stuffy theorist. On the contrary, he was a showman who understood that his message was in no way in conflict with some straightforward populist promotion, and he was the master impresario of Rushmore from the start of the project until his death in 1941. His tireless energy and inclination for the spectacular put together the marching bands, radio addresses, pageants, and fireworks that brought the world to the mountain. All had a high-minded theme: the great and glorious sweep of the history of the West—which Borglum thought of as cultural habits going back to Athens—into the geography of the American West.

The pageants, being transitory, could not continuously hold the public imagination. His writings and speeches are another story, and this very public man undoubtedly intended them to be read and consulted by concerned and patriotic Americans long after his death. This has not happened, and nowadays Borglum is known—if he is known at all—as the man who physically created Rushmore, not as its ideologue.

There are excellent reasons for this, even beyond the problem of Borglum's fulminations on the destiny of what he called the Anglo-Saxon races.

Like Custer, he was an extremely prolific writer. Unlike Custer, who was a surprisingly good writer—an astute observer of wit and charm who could mock his own vanity on occasion—Borglum wrote screeds full of romantic drivel and a striking historical naïveté: His writings are the thoughts of a man who is widely but not deeply read. Plowing through his papers, I often thought that this is what Ayn Rand's high school essays might have sounded like had they been written in English. The style may have been a hit in the America of his youth, a nineteenth-century America being remade by urbanization and technology that, struggling for sophistication, produced an era of florid writing. But nowadays his prose is tough going, and this, as much as anything else, may be why so very few people who see Rushmore read what Borglum wrote—in mind-numbing quantity—about its meaning. That's too bad, because Rushmore cannot be understood without knowing what Borglum thought he was doing.

It was Borglum's mission to make sure that American art was new enough, confident enough, daring enough, big enough, to be up to the task of honoring an energetic young nation. Its art had to leave behind the small and decaying art of Europe. Passages like this one are fairly typical. "We have built and are building, tearing down and rebuilding. . . . Monumental art must run as world work. It must see, form, and in no mistakable terms express the flood of power that surges in the race when it rises to great heights. American artists should be seers and should give, serve, and complete the spirit and concept of Columbus—of Washington—of Lincoln. . . . The spirit of the hour is world building."[24]

Typical, too, is the association of the artistic and the ideological, the new and the strong, the pure and the purifying. America was a fresh start for humanity, or at least for that part of it represented by the Anglo-Saxon races, with their creative genius: "If one wonders why a handful of freed souls in 1776, builders of a freed political peace in a removed virgin world, rise ever stronger in their service to civilization, ever firmer in the affections of a great people, he need but turn and study their silhouette against the blood-blackened skies of the hate-submerged Old World, wrecked and torn for two thousand years, or more, by the unslaked greed of despots."[25]

The idea of a worn, decadent, and bloodthirsty Europe and a virginal America ready to receive the best and most vital impulses of the Renaissance was a recurrent theme, one that Borglum returned to almost every time he wrote or spoke about Rushmore or about America. Perhaps this is not surprising, given his parents' flight from poverty and persecution in Denmark. He writes strikingly of a continent nearly empty of people before Europeans came: "Five hundred years ago these two great continents were quite silent; only the animals and birds and the seasons, bringing their life and sleep, gave action and color. Man, a red, fearful man, with his babes, roamed up and down our great national highways—the rivers and the plains. And the story is that in all our land there were less than a million."[26]

The story is incorrect, as it turns out, although the myth of a virgin land has served more pens than Borglum's.

Of all the mysteries of human history, the pre-Columbian population of North America is one of the most difficult to assess with any real certainty. It is also one of the most politicized; arguments for a high population can be taken as a defense of indigenous claims, whereas lower estimates can be used propagandistically, as a way of saying that Europeans displaced few natives and therefore cannot really be called colonials—which is obviously at least a part of Borglum's intention in this passage.

The best rough—very rough—guesses use information about epidemics to extrapolate back to pre-epidemic, pre-Columbian population levels. This is problematic, since it involves trusting contemporary diagnoses in order to estimate the course and mortality of disease. Where mortality statistics are available, sometimes they are factual and sometimes they are anecdotal; and there is always the problem of whether observers could accurately know whether they were dealing with "virgin" populations in the first place, or with populations already decimated and weakened by diseases that spread out through indigenous populations from beachheads of European settlement, preceding the path of any actual European into the continent. As early as 1910, anthropologist James Mooney, using very crude methods, estimated a pre-contact population north of Mexico at one million, and while this figure is almost certainly far too low it had a strong influence on later studies.

On the other hand, modern high estimates like that of anthropologist Henry Dobyns, who has suggested populations as high as 18 million in North America and from ninety to 112 million in the hemisphere, can get to this level only by assuming the very worst about the course of disease, recovery, and resistance—and then postulating a disease transmission that may have occurred but for which there is no particular evidence.

The general range of academic consensus nowadays is somewhere between two and seven million in North America, with much greater population density in Central America: perhaps 20 million in the dense city-states of Mexico and Guatemala. Anthropological geneticist Michael Crawford, after a thorough survey of various strands of evidence, suggests a total of 44 million in the New World[27]—2 million in North America, 25 million in Central America, 7 million in the Caribbean, and 10 million in South America. This an informed guess. Could it be higher, or lower? Certainly it could, but it is very unlikely that Borglum was close. To be fair, modern tools of demographic analysis were not available in his time.

Two of the most interesting plans that Borglum had for fully expressing the meaning of the monument never came to fruition. Had these plans been realized, Rushmore would today be less ambiguous, less in need of "interpretation."

He wanted to carve a brief, heroic history of the United States into the mountainside in letters three feet high, an inscription he called the Entablature. He asked President Coolidge, who had dedicated the mountain in 1927, to write the words. This was a stroke of political genius, for Coolidge's personal interest was a major factor in getting the project off the ground. In fact, the federal enabling legislation for Rushmore required that the words of the Entablature be written by Coolidge, but his efforts proved unsatisfactory as far as Borglum was concerned, and he created a minor scandal when he edited the former president's words and released them to the press without Coolidge's knowledge or consent.

After Coolidge died in 1933, Borglum—without consulting the Mount Rushmore National Memorial Commission, the organ set up by Congress to manage the executive tasks of building Rushmore—convinced the Hearst newspaper chain to sponsor a contest in which people all over the country would try to put the history of the nation in five hundred words, the winner to get a college scholarship and to see those words set in stone.

The contest stipulated that the following events, almost all of them having to do with the acquisition of territory, be included in the text: the Declaration of Independence, the Constitution, the Louisiana Purchase, the cession of the Floridas to the United States, the rise of the Republic of Texas and its entry into the United States, the Mexican War and the acquisition of California, the settlement of the Oregon boundary dispute, the Alaska Purchase, and the Panama Canal. Here's how Borglum described what he was looking for:

> In the fullest sense the great trek of the old world into the new, following that great child of the Renaissance, Columbus, meant more to the mind and soul freedom that resulted than all the discoveries of lands, or continents and their commercial value, to men and civilization.
>
> Too little has been thought—too little written, on the wide freedoms secured, the virgin worlds offered—unpeopled, untilled, ungoverned—the nomads incapable of resisting even this unorganized aggression of the invaders.
>
> No one HAS sung, painted or carved adequately the story of this irresistible God-man movement that fled its ancient moorings . . . following the sun into the unknown west—into the night![28]

Many of the submissions tell us about American popular views of history in the Depression era. Some speak of Leif Ericsson, some of "Israel's Children," nearly all invoke God. Some are hand-scrawled and hardly legible, some professionally printed and bound. There are many references to a "wild" and "virgin" land; most of the stories start with Columbus. There is no mention of Indians, at least in the submissions that have survived. There is a tendency toward a neoromantic style similar to Borglum's, lots of *e'ers* and *hereafters* and *thuses*. Some are dreary lists of presidents.

Dr. J. L. Edsall and George Reich concluded their submission with ringing phrases: "These heroes and the people with God's help have built up the most glorious Christian Republic of all times. A defender of christianity, morality and liberty in all future ages." Other applicants sent verse:

> Few dreams were ever more heroic, none were ever more sublime,
>
> In the march of human progress, since the inaugural of Time.
>
> In the Black Hills of Dakota, in the region of the pine,
> Mount Rushmore, far older than the Alps and Apennine,
>
> By the genius of the sculptor, has become a noble shrine.[29]

There was a fortuitous sympathy between Borglum's conception of empire and the attitude of the Hearst newspapers. The Homestake Gold Mine, a product of the Black Hills gold rush and an early acquisition of the mining magnate George Hearst, was the richest gold mine in the Western Hemisphere, the proceeds from which had financed his son William Randolph in building his newspaper empire.

The story that Borglum and Hearst wanted to tell never quite got told. The committee set up by the newspaper to select the inscription tentatively accepted five submissions, and Borglum, characteristically, rejected all of them.

Borglum never gave up the idea of formally explicating the symbolism of Rushmore. When he moved away from the Entablature, he began to focus on an even more grandiose scheme to convey the meaning of American political culture into the distant future: he decided to cut a Hall of Records into the mountain behind the figures, reached by a sweeping Grand Staircase. It would contain not only more statuary of important figures in American history but also details of the purpose of the memorial and the original paper copies of the Constitution and the Declaration of Independence. In his public speeches Borglum often said that the idea was inspired by a tablet that the French Canadian explorers, Francois and Louis-Joseph de La Verendrye buried near the present site of Fort Pierre in 1743, a sort of time capsule claiming the land for France. Citing this precedent showed a nice regard for South Dakota history, but the outlines of Borglum's plan had come up in his work before he had ever thought of Rushmore. He had designed something similar for the Confederate Memorial at Stone Mountain.

The Hall of Records is perhaps the most interesting and revealing part of Borglum's plan. Even more than the colossal figures, the plan for the hall shows the scope and the particular nature of his ambitions and of his conception of the American heritage. This is how Borglum described it in 1938:

On the wall . . . extending around the entire hall, will be a bas-relief showing the adventure of humanity discovering and occupying the West World; it will be bronze, gold-plated . . . [The entrance doors will interrupt] a panel 44 feet in height, surmounted by an eagle with the wings spread 38 feet. Pylons on each side of the panel, 49 feet in height, rise like two great protecting barriers; upon these are carved two colonial torches, the flames from which are more than 30 feet in length and in full relief [Borglum later in his plans substituted real flames high enough so the turning of the earth would cause them to flow continuously westward.] Cut into the panel on the edge are these words: "America's Onward March" and below, "The Hall of Records."[30]

There is certainly something magnificent about this, although he could also be ungenerous in his exclusive focus on the European heritage:

Neither will the records contain more than a brief résumé of the Indian occupancy here but will be specifically devoted to the progress that has changed the country since the first white man sighted America. . . . Inlaid in the granite floor will be a comet made up of minute stars and bearing the inscription "Westward The Star Of Empire Takes Its Way." There will also be set in that floor an Indian arrow of bronze with the words, "This arrow pointed to the North Star when this work was finished."[31]

The arrow is a quaint touch.

In an arrow pointing to an idealized point, in the inexorable push westward, Borglum was invoking a reverence for progress that goes back in European civilization to his beloved Greeks, progress that stagnated during the Dark Ages, revived in the Renaissance, and was elevated almost to a religion in the Enlightenment. It attained its full hold over the thought and action of Europe only during the industrial age, however, in the train of forces that were fencing off communal grazing lands and transforming the economy and culture of a region through the harnessed power of rivers and coal. All of Borglum's ideas about world history, about art, about the races of humanity, and about America make no sense outside the context of a relentless march toward the light, a struggle for Platonic perfection in which the world is constantly made and remade by individual effort and by the leadership of visionaries, in whose rank Borglum certainly counted himself.

Contrast this reverence for progress with the sense of permanence, stability, and repetitive cycles that dominates the traditions of most non-industrial societies. Consider that ubiquitous symbol of the Lakota, the medicine wheel, a circle divided into four quarters—black, white, yellow, and red. Quite a lot of meaning is packed into this simple design, which signifies the four seasons, the four directions, the four winds, and the four races of man (obviously a later philosophical addition; an older Lakota symbolism of the four races may refer to the four-leggeds, the two-leggeds, the wingeds, and the growing things[32]). The top two quarters represent the sky, the lower two the earth; together the four quarters and the two halves are the Six Grandfathers, a unity represented also on the mountain that came to be called Rushmore. It is a closed space and system that encompasses all the endless open spaces of the plains, of the world, and opens out into an eternity of cycles that, like the seasons, change and come back to the same place—not an engine of progress that obliterates the past and moves on.

Unlike the sacred circles of the medicine wheel, the round bowl of the sacred pipe, and the hoop of the Lakota nation, the symbols of European emotional sustenance were linear, directing their owners in straight lines through time and space and thought: the ships that brought Borglum's hero Columbus, the wagons and trains that brought settlers west, their books, their Bibles, their blueprints, the cultural knowledge unambiguously set down in writing that enabled them to master the world, to perfect it.

It was this cultural struggle that Borglum wanted to immortalize in Rushmore and in the Hall of Records, and in doing so he would, naturally, both use and display its most effective tools. Unfortunately for him, it took several acts of Congress to fund Rushmore, and by the time Borglum had run up a total bill for Rushmore of almost three-quarters of a million dollars, only about $150,000 of it raised privately, Congress balked and told him to stick to carving faces. The plans for a cultural archive were abandoned, and the hall is now represented only by a rough tunnel carved into the side of the mountain, a shelter for wild mountain goats. In a minor gesture that is almost an affront to the original plan, the NPS has recently interred a time capsule, a few engraved ceramic plates, in a shallow grave on the floor of this tunnel. The plates tell the story of the sculpture, how it was made and why.

This small time capsule may not add much to the knowledge of future generations. On a grander scale, the beliefs about time, history, and the endurance of cultural meaning held by Borglum and by many individuals and organizations associated with Rushmore can really only be called strange. In one of his most complete statements about the philosophical meaning of Rushmore, an article that appeared in the journal of the South Dakota School of Mines and Technology rather sententiously titled "The Political Import and the Art Character of the National Memorial at Mount Rushmore," he lists the great "national" projects of China, India, Cambodia, and Egypt, but says "None . . . have been so conceived, so located and so designed that they became a definite messenger to a posterity ten thousand, one hundred thousand, or, if the material survives the elements, a million years hence."[33] To put this in perspective, the high-water mark of Greek civilization came three thousand years ago, and although Greek thought is arguably the distant ancestor of modern American political structures, we turn to the Greeks as teachers only in an abstract and academic way; we study them as we study buried potsherds, invest them with the mystery and exoticism of objects not fully understood. A million years ago the human ancestor *Homo habilis* had just stepped off the evolutionary stage. *Homo erectus* was coming into his own, continuing and modifying *Homo habilis'* pebble tool industry and spreading out over Asia. The first productions that we believe had an artistic intent appeared about 960,000 years after that.

Borglum deliberately left Washington's nose one foot larger than scale to add another one hundred thousand years to the lifetime of his work; the recently completed renovations undertaken by the Mount Rushmore Preservation Society and the National Park Service are more realistically designed to ensure the full integrity of the work for twenty thousand years. This is not time on the scale of any human civilization to date.

Without an Entablature or Hall of Records, perhaps whoever or whatever is living on earth in the twilight of Rushmore's existence will see in these stone heads a work as inscrutable, as lacking in context as the stone heads that British sailors found on Easter Island. This was Borglum's worst fear and an example he often cited. If English words mean anything to the life forms of a million years from now and if some of the many words written about Rushmore survive in some form, what will these creatures learn?

5

THE PAGEANT OF PAHA SAPA

Borglum wanted to conquer time, to freeze a way of thinking about the nation and send it off into the distant future. George Orwell knew that if you want to control the future, you start with the past.

The town of Custer still holds a Gold Discovery Days pageant every summer, still puts on the show that Calvin Coolidge watched in 1927. I went to it to learn more about the conquest of the Black Hills in popular memory.

July 26 is the day before the anniversary of Horatio Ross's gold find, the single most important event in this town's history. Celebrating the date is more than a tradition: a substantial part of Custer's income comes from the gold legend and nostalgia for the Wild West. During the four-day celebration gunfights are reenacted in the streets for the benefit of tourists; the Hangin' of Flyspeck Billy is solemnly performed.

Justice is dispensed at the county courthouse, a modest and utilitarian building, one step up from a mobile home. But I knew there must have been a different one not too long ago. I found the building across the street, a solid stone construction with the detail and vaulted space that are the hallmarks of older civic buildings. The old courthouse has a story that goes back to 1973.

That was a time of awakening political consciousness for American Indians, on and off the reservations. While the larger society was grappling with the social stresses of the Vietnam War and the civil rights movement, Indians were learning how to be militants. By the early 1970s many younger Indians were no longer interested in working within the system established under white rule or even within the mainstream Indian solidarity groups, like the National Congress of American Indians, that worked with the government and American civil society. These new militants developed a style of fighting for treaty rights and human rights that would have been quite alien to many in the previous generation, who were trained in the mission schools to be ashamed of their Indianness and to aspire to the privileges of white normality; or else, if not ashamed, who were committed to seeking economic development and treaty rights by working through the tribal governments established under the Indian Reorganization Act of 1934.

This new militancy was partly a result of Government relocation and assimilation policies, administered by the Bureau of Indian Affairs, that offered incentives to young Indians to settle in the cities. The policy was developed by Commissioner of Indian Affairs Dillon S. Myer in the early 1950s. Myer was an advocate of the federal policy of "termination," under which the federal government tried to simply terminate all treaty obligations—and therefore all special relations with Indians that grew out of the pre-1871 practice of negotiating treaties with sovereign nations, such as land and hunting rights and tribal government—in exchange for a one-time fixed payment to each tribe that took the deal. Many tribes were pressured into accepting these arrangements in the interest, as it was explained to them, of "joining American society." For the tribes who were convinced or forced to accept termination, it was a disaster that caused great cultural and economic damage; virtually no Indian advocacy groups (nor the government) now defend it. Myer, like many of his time, felt that assimilation and absorption into the mainstream of American life was the only way for Indians to improve their standards of living. As a mechanism of assimilation, the relocation programs were supposed to provide transportation, job training, and help with employment and housing for Indians moving off the reservations. One effect of the program, of course, was that it made it much easier for reservation lands to be leased to whites or expropriated by the government.

Myer had had experience with relocating people when he worked with the War Relocation Authority, an agency that moved Japanese-Americans from the California coast to secure areas inland during the war. He modeled his Indian program on the WRA.

Many Indians led miserable lives in the cities, even those cities, like Cleveland and Minneapolis, that had sizable Indian ghettoes. The experience often helped to define their identities negatively: The culture of urban America was not theirs. Those who survived

alcoholism and drug addiction, petty crime, poverty, unemployment, racism, and imprisonment in the cities often came back to the
reservation with a new sense of Indian identity and a larger understanding of the damage they had suffered from colonialism.

The American Indian Movement was founded in 1968 in Minneapolis. AIM was modeled on the confrontational self-defense tactics of the militant black organizations of the late 1960s, focusing at
first on monitoring the Minneapolis police and preventing police
brutality against the Indian population. Originally an offshoot of an
anti-poverty organization called Citizen's Community Centers,
AIM ironically received a great deal of its early funding from program grants from the U.S. government and from organized religious groups, notably the American Lutheran Church.

The founders were Dennis Banks, Clyde Bellecourt, and George
Mitchell, three Chippewas from Minnesota reservations. These men
had extraordinary leadership skills, but their life stories were in many
ways typical of Indians with ties to reservations who were transplanted
to the urban environment. Banks was born in 1930 on the Leech Lake
Reservation, in northern Minnesota, and his early schooling was in the
Indian boarding school system, far away from his family and reservation. He joined the Air Force in 1953 and was stationed in Japan and
Korea. In the early 1960s he served time in Minnesota prisons for burglary, forgery, and parole violations. Banks has written that he found
the path of militant Indian identity while serving time in solitary confinement in the maximum security Stillwater prison. By the time he
became a founder of AIM, he was a recruiter for the Honeywell Corporation, who fired him when they found out what he was doing.

Clyde Bellecourt, born in 1936, grew up on the White Earth reservation, also in Minnesota. He—and his brother Vernon, another important AIM member—also did time in prison, where he earned a degree as a steam plant engineer and took correspondence courses in public speaking. He was also radicalized in Stillwater prison.

Although not a founding member, Russell Means would become perhaps the most outspoken and charismatic militant Indian leader of the 1970s. Means is a Lakota, born in 1939 on the Pine Ridge reservation, and he grew up spending time on the reservation with his extended family and also in California, where his father worked as a welder in the defense industry. Means as a teenager drifted into petty crime and drug addiction. In his twenties he studied accounting and computer science. He did many other things in California and throughout the Midwest and Southwest, including rodeo riding, teaching dance, working with an antipoverty program on the Rosebud reservation, and performing Indian dances for South Dakota tourists—a job he found most degrading. He never held a job very long though, and whenever his early life began to stabilize he would tend to take off on extended drinking binges.

Means' life and career demonstrate a rage fed both by the destruction of traditional Indian culture and by the family abuse that he suffered as a child, two things which, in Means' view, were directly related—his parents were formed to a great degree by the Indian boarding school system that warped so many of that generation. His memoir of his early life is a poignant and often tragic story. It gives a portrait of parents who tried hard to do their best by their children according to the conflicting values they had learned from their Indian families and at the Indian boarding schools; influences which were impossible to reconcile and which often left both parents and children desperately confused.

In 1969 Means was living in Cleveland, where he was a cofounder of the Cleveland Indian Center. Means first encountered AIM when he met members at a conference in San Francisco in 1969. Means was not at first impressed with AIM's tactics, but Banks later called him and asked him to help out with an AIM demonstration, a confrontation with the National Council of Churches at its convention in Detroit. Means joined, and went on to found the Cleveland AIM chapter.

As a Lakota he had a more prominent role in Sioux issues than the other AIM leaders, most of whom were Chippewa. His role at the Wounded Knee occupation that began in early 1973 was to make him a figure of national importance. Fiercely intelligent, fearless, and aggressive, Means has led a life punctuated by an astonishing amount of violence. He was involved in virtually every major confrontation of the Indian rights movement, as well as countless bar fights, prison fights, and—while monitoring human rights abuses against the Miskito Indians in Nicaragua in the 1980s—even a genuine aerial bombardment. He has been shot several times. He was stabbed in prison.

The AIM leaders of that period were smart and genuinely tough, street tough, prison tough. AIM members were known for their flamboyant reinvention of Indian garb, their style of confrontation, and their expressed reverence for traditional Indian ways. Still, the organization—especially in its early years—drew far more support from urban Indians than from reservation traditionalists, who may have sympathized with the anger of these alienated young people but who could not understand their methods of expressing it.

Although AIM is the most famous example of the new militancy, the awakening demands of Indians were also expressed by more mainstream Indian nationalists, as well as by other militant groups, such as Indians of All Tribes.

A pamphlet from the early 1970s suggests both the bitterness and the cutting humor that the militant Indian movements often used to great effect:

White Policy Proposal

It is hereby suggested that we create a Department of White Affairs for a trial period of 100 years. The department will be run strictly by Indians selected on the basis of their political affiliations and their incompetence in the business world.

White people will be looked on as white savages unless they adopt the Indian religion and Indian way of life. White religious holidays such as Easter and Christmas will be outlawed and all religious statues, medals, and musical instruments shall be confiscated by a newly created Indian mounted police force. It will be unlawful to wear a shamrock, eat haggis, fish and chips, pea soup or weiners and sauerkraut.

If a white wants to sell, lease or bequeath property, the

Department of White Affairs will make the final decision. At no time will a white be able to develop his land
without the consent of the Department of White Affairs.

From time to time advisors will be brought in from
the Congo, Indonesia and India to fill top civil service
jobs and teach the whites religion and culture.

It is quite conceivable that white lands will be expropriated for Indian interests in conserving the environment.

It is recommended that a series of treaties be undertaken
with the white nations for the ceding of their interests in
crown lands. They may keep the cities.[1]

Although a new organization, AIM saw a lot of action in South
Dakota. It had been at Mount Rushmore itself in 1970 and 1971,
about which more later; but its most famous interventions before
the occupation of Wounded Knee in 1973—or Wounded Knee II as
it is sometimes called—were in Gordon, Nebraska, and in Custer,
South Dakota.

This is the Gordon story. On the cold night of February 12,
1972, a middle-aged Lakota cowboy named Raymond Yellow
Thunder, just walking along the street, was kidnapped by some local
white hoods: Bernard Lutter, Richard Bayliss, and Melvin and Leslie
Hare. They beat him and then locked him in the trunk of their car,
drove him around town for a few hours, stripped him from the waist
down and pushed him out on the dance floor at an American Legion
post in front of hundreds of white people, most of whom didn't see
what was going on. They did this because, the Hares later told

investigators, they had a grudge against the legion hall manager, Bernard Sandage, who had expelled them from the hall a few weeks earlier. Yellow Thunder's tormentors put him back in the car trunk, drove him around once again, and then kicked him out in the freezing cold. He went to the local jail and asked to sleep there, something he had done before; the jail staff knew him. The officer on duty, noting his condition, offered medical attention, which Yellow Thunder refused. He walked out of the police station in the morning, and then crawled into a panel truck on a used-car lot.

He died there. The apparent cause of death was a brain hemorrhage brought on by blows to the head. These could have come from his attackers, or they could have come from rattling around in a locked car trunk while being driven over rough roads. The autopsy report said only that the injuries were not caused by a fist.

The attackers were arrested and charged with false imprisonment and manslaughter. AIM activists, invited to Gordon by Yellow Thunder's sisters and mother, came into town in a long convoy to protest this light treatment. American flags were suspended upside-down from their cars' aerials in the international naval distress signal, something that became an AIM trademark. Indian anger built an organized, determined, militant demonstration of power.

AIM took over the city hall, demanding that the town conduct a full investigation of the circumstances of Yellow Thunder's death and look into rumors that he had been tortured, perhaps even castrated. The demonstrators wanted the killers to be charged with first-degree murder, rather than the actual indictment that, in fact, more closely fit the law. They had no doubt that Indians suspected of committing such crimes against whites would have been charged with murder.

The demonstrators also wanted the town to set up a board of inquiry with equal representation of whites and Indians, dismiss the local chief of police and the prosecutor, name Indians to the police force and the Chamber of Commerce, make sure that Indian applicants were given equal treatment in employment, and listen to other long-standing Indian grievances. The city authorities of Gordon accepted many of these demands, including the dismissal of the police chief. Russell Means recounts that the chief, Robert Case, could only stutter helplessly as Means snatched off his cap and put it on his own head. Then Means went outside wearing the cap, and wrapped in an American flag, to address the gathering national press.

There was a new factor in politics in Indian country, and in the nation.

The AIM adherents believed they had won a major victory at Gordon, but Yellow Thunder's killers got off light. The Hares, sons of a wealthy white rancher, were convicted of second-degree manslaughter and false imprisonment, while Lutter and Bayliss were acquitted. They were fined $500 each on the imprisonment charge. For the crime of manslaughter, which carried a maximum penalty of ten years imprisonment, Leslie Hare ultimately served two years, Melvin ten months.

The Custer event unfolded against that background. On January 23, 1973, a white man from that town, Darld Schmitz, killed an Indian named Wesley Bad Heart Bull outside Bill's Bar in Buffalo

Gap, Custer County. Bad Heart Bull, who was refused entry because of an argument, fought with a man named James Geary, sometimes known by the nickname "Mad Dog," which he had acquired as a member of his high school wrestling team. Bad Heart Bull knocked Geary unconscious with a log chain. Some of the witnesses at Schmitz's trial said that Bad Heart Bull continued to beat Geary with the chain. Schmitz, who had been drinking, had a pocketknife with him, and he took it out and told Bad Heart Bull to drop the chain. They fought, knife against chain, and Schmitz stabbed Bad Heart Bull, who continued to fight briefly but then collapsed. Bad Heart Bull's friends put him in a car to take him to the hospital at Hot Springs, but the car ran out of oil and the engine burned out. They were overtaken by the ambulance carrying Geary to Hot Springs, which stopped and collected Bad Heart Bull.

Schmitz's pocketknife had nicked Bad Heart Bull's aorta. Perhaps he could have been saved if there had been no delay, but there was a delay and he died. Geary's injuries were so severe that he was kept in the hospital for a full month.

In later years the incident came to be highly exaggerated, embellished with claims that a hostile white crowd had surrounded Bad Heart Bull and that he had been stabbed twenty-seven times, tied to a car and dragged down the main street while the rednecks cheered. These things did not happen.

The killing has usually been remembered and described as symptomatic of two hundred years of racial history and conquest, rather than as typical of what happens when angry men get drunk and have weapons to hand. The second context is probably more accurate, but in the racially charged atmosphere of South Dakota in the early 1970s no violent encounter between a white man and an Indian was seen as racially neutral, and there were plenty of cases of genuinely racial murder and violent harassment.

The Yellow Thunder case was such an outrage, clearly racial, clearly a human rights violation, clearly unequal justice, which is no justice at all. Reasonable people could have called the Bad Heart Bull case self-defense. If this tragic, brutal and utterly stupid sequence of events had occurred between two white men, or between two Indians, it would have been a police matter but not a political one. If the history of whites and Indians in South Dakota had been different than it was, there would have been grieving and anger but there would probably not have been an explosion.

The state refused to indict Schmitz on charges more serious than second-degree manslaughter. Bad Heart Bull's mother, Sarah, many Lakota, and AIM thought the charge should have been murder. There were rumors that Bad Heart Bull had beaten Schmitz in a fight two days before Schmitz attacked him with a knife, that Schmitz had planned to kill Bad Heart Bull. This seemed to establish premeditation, the requirement for a charge of first-degree murder.

If Schmitz went out that night looking to kill Bad Heart Bull, or anyone else, it does seem odd that he would go armed only with a pocketknife.

Sarah Bad Heart Bull, Trina Bad Heart Bull, Eddy Clifford, Francis Means, and Robert High Eagle came to Custer on February 6 to testify at Schmitz's preliminary hearing. At the invitation of the Bad Heart Bull family, Dennis Banks and Russell Means brought an

AIM contingent to Custer for a demonstration that day. Many AIM people were already in nearby Rapid City for a three-day meeting on civil rights; announced in advance, the Custer gathering attracted the pre-emptive attention of the FBI, the South Dakota Highway Patrol, and the National Guard.

Robert High Eagle met with State's Attorney Hobart Gates. By this time the AIM contingent had arrived and was crowding the courthouse steps. After High Eagle left the meeting, AIM representatives Russell Means, Dennis Banks, David Hill and Leonard Crow Dog—great-grandson of the Crow Dog who shot Spotted tail and a spiritual advisor to AIM—went to talk to Gates. Neither High Eagle nor AIM could convince Gates to change the charge to first-degree murder.

After the meeting there was a confrontation in front of the courthouse. When deputies tried to push the crowd off the steps, Sarah Bad Heart Bull shouted obscenities at them. Mary Crow Dog, the wife of Leonard Crow Dog and the author of an important memoir of the period, says that Sarah Bad Heart Bull was then thrown to the ground and choked with a nightstick across her throat; she also says the cops were out of control, clubbing everyone indiscriminately and hurling racial threats.[2] An assembled crowd of Indians reacted by charging the building, attacking police, smashing the fixtures. High Eagle struck a Lieutenant Schmoll across the face with an iron pipe. The invaders, armed with clubs, knives, chain saw blades, and pipes, were pushed back by police with batons and then by highway patrolmen with tear gas. A Texaco station across the street provided a convenient source for firebombs.

Russell Means remembers the police ripping Sarah Bad Heart Bull's clothes off and clubbing her on the head, as well as stripping and fondling Indian women. Means fought furiously, and after he was eventually handcuffed he was then clubbed on his elbows. When the police realized who he was he was thrown into a bully circle of armed vigilantes who kicked him around a bit. One of these thugs, addressing a policeman by his first name, begged to be allowed to take Means home for a day to work him over.

Some of the Indians tossed gasoline and flaming torches into the courthouse and into the nearby Chamber of Commerce, which, being wood, quickly burned to the ground. By the end of the day several patrol cars had been torched, along with the sign at the edge of town that said "Welcome to Custer, The Town With The Gunsmoke Flavor!"[3]

Two days later, at an open meeting in Rapid City with Mayor Don Barnett, Dennis Banks said, "We've carried signs to protest illegitimate acts against our people, but they have never listened to us; but they did listen to us February 6 in Custer. They're going to continue to listen to us from this day forward. We're going to burn down those racist towns. These people want us to live within their system and obey their laws, but they are not ready to lay down the law against their own kind. . . . We are trying to teach non-Indian people that Indians are people too."[4]

Legal proceedings against AIM and its leaders for their part in the riot stretched on for years.

So there I was, in Custer for the pageant and in front of this historic courthouse, which is now a museum. Inside is a room full of minerals, some with beautiful crystal structures. Lakota weapons, ritual objects, and crafts are in another room. The sacred Lakota pipe is displayed with the bowl separated from the shaft; part of its power comes from its symbolic joining of male and female, and to join the parts in a profane setting is disrespectful. I've noticed that museum authorities throughout Indian country are aware of this, although many Indians do wonder what their sacred objects are doing in white museums in the first place.

There is a mockup of the inside of a frontier mine. There are the original newspaper clippings—the *New York Tribune*, the *Chicago Inter-Ocean*—announcing the discovery of gold in the Black Hills. There is the old courtroom itself and, on the second floor, a pioneer school, protected by rope barriers. There is a local man's extensive knife collection.

I was curious about when this building stopped being used as a courthouse and whether the disuse stemmed from the riot, although I was shy about making a point of it. I asked the elderly woman in charge of the museum. "Oh, since 1973," she said, and the date answered my question. "Since the uprising. They never used it after that." I was struck by her choice of word, which seemed to acknowledge something, but defensively. She was friendly, with just the hint of a challenge in those old gray eyes.

A fairly detailed history of the building makes no mention of AIM or the events of 1973, unless you count this tidbit typed on a small piece of paper pasted onto a time line as an afterthought: "1972. American Indian Movement Leaders make presence known in the southern Black Hills and take on federal law-enforcement officials at

Wounded Knee II." The typist got the year wrong: Wounded Knee
II began in February 1973.

The pageant I came to see is called the Pageant of Paha Sapa.
Paha Sapa is what white people believe the Sioux call the Black
Hills, although those who speak Lakota as a first language are more
likely to say Khe Sapa, which means "black mountains" rather than
"black hills." Trees make the Hills look black from a distance. The
Hills have been around for millennia, the pageant since 1924, when
the Custer Women's Civic Club decided to raise money for a new
building, assembled the townspeople to plan a production, and
charged admission to see it. They got their building, which was
eventually dedicated by Grace Coolidge on August 11, 1927, the day
after her husband dedicated Rushmore.

The pageant takes place on Pageant Hill, a wide field in a park on
the edge of the Hills, which enclose the town. Just a few miles down
the road is the spot where the Gordon party, the first organized
white civilian expedition into the Hills, built a stockade for protection. When this stockade was dedicated as a local monument in
1925, it was compared to one of the touchstones of the nation itself:
"As the rock of Plymouth was the first outpost of civilization in the
reclamation of a new continent, so the original Stockade which is
here reproduced today was the first outpost of white men in the conquest of this wonderful little inland empire of the Black Hills." The
rest of the speech lauds the gold fever of the pioneers and appraises
each aspect of the beautiful Black Hills in terms of how much cash
it has generated for the local economy, then ends with a benediction:
"May these beautiful mountains and valleys which we love with an

undying affection become the permanent abode of all that is highest and best in Christian civilization!"[5]

Not so far from the site of the original stockade is a monument to Annie Tallent, "The first white woman in the Black Hills. . . . The world is a better place because she lived in it." Oddly, Tallent's title was first claimed by a black woman, Sarah "Aunt Sally" Campbell, a cook with the Custer party, who announced herself "the only white woman that ever saw the black hills"[5]—at least as reported by William Eleroy Curtis of the Chicago Inter-Ocean, who might have been inviting his readers to snicker. Or perhaps not, which may only prove the relativity of race.

The sky was terribly blue. A dirt road ran through the park that is the unofficial edge of the stage. Vehicles and campers were all lined up on one side of the open field, with spectators sitting on truck gates and lawn chairs. There were no Indian spectators.

The pageant began. The text that is used each year is essentially unchanged from the original production of 1924, and it is a lengthy production because the announcer on the tinny microphone goes back to the beginning of time to tell the story of the Black Hills. It is a complete origin story, with various spirits calling forth all the flora and fauna of the Hills, the minerals, the people. There is a cast of hundreds—birds, flowers, animals, trees, "God's Messenger," the "Gold Trolls"—because this is truly a community event, and everyone's kids take part. Parents and relatives strain to glimpse their children or their neighbors' children across the large field.

The cosmology is biblical, of course, and although the Bible is a new import in these parts, in this pageant the Black Hills began with

Genesis: "Let there be light!" There's an hour of dancing children, then white men come to the Hills. God's Messenger tries to push them away, but they ignore her. After quite a long while there is an intermission.

The origin tale has a parallel with traditional Lakota stories, although the white folks' version is obviously adapted to these lands rather than inspired by them. The Lakota version is more specific to the place, although it is disputed by those Lakota elders who do not adhere to the recent myth of origin in the Black Hills. It tells of seven spirits who made the land sacred to the Lakota. The first brought them the Hills for eternity. The second brought the sacred fire, deep in the earth, the life-giving heat that the whites know as volcanic activity, a source of destruction and renewal. The third spirit brought the waters of the Hills, the healing waters of the Hot Springs area. The fourth brought the air in Wind Cave, where this Lakota legend says that humans first emerged from the underground Buffalo Realm. The fourth spirit brought the rocks and the minerals, including all that Homestake gold. The fifth spirit brought medicine, the herbs of the Hills. The sixth brought the buffalo, the deer, the elk, the eagle, all those creatures around whom the physical and conceptual world of the traditional Lakota was built. The seventh spirit brought the Hills as a whole, a totality, a heritage, a continuity for the people.

In the second part of the pageant the prospectors come, Custer rides through and calls out to the spectators, "You guys seen any Indians?" Horatio Ross finds gold. Annie Tallent helps to build the stockade, but the army tells her she has to leave because of the treaty.

The real Annie Tallent, a very tough woman who was far more eloquent than these actors, made an ignominious departure from the Gordon Stockade on a government mule. She had some primly practical words to say about the treaty in her memoirs. "Ignoring the ethical side of the question, should such treaties as tend to arrest the advance of civilization, and retard the development of the rich resources of our country, ever have been entered into?" A few pages later she is even more sure of herself and of her role as an agent of fate: "The gold-ribbed Black Hills were to be snatched from the grasp of savages, to whom they were no longer profitable even as a hunting ground, and given over to the thrift and enterprise of the hardy pioneer, who would develop their wonderful resources and thereby advance the interests and add to the wealth of our whole country."[7]

Indians raided the wagon trains, massacred some settlers. For this pageant, unlike the 1927 production described in the *Rapid City Journal*, it was apparently impossible to find Indians who were willing to take part, so it was white men in paint and feathers, with saddle blankets over their saddles to make it look as if they were riding bareback, who attacked. I noticed them sitting on their horses in the "off-stage" meadow between scenes, talking with the stage manager, who carried a walkie-talkie. "Are we done yet? No, we still have to raid the fort. That's right, honey, have to go raid the fort. All in a day's work." When it came time to gallop off, they had almost comical difficulty handling their horses, although they never quite fell off.

Flyspeck Billy was hanged and the pageant concluded with a reaffirmation of community. "Custer City, Mother City, oldest and highest town in the Black Hills, slowly have you grown, but within your borders there has been built up a spirit of great loyalty and fellowship. . . . To you, Custer City, first born of the Black Hills towns, and to our great Nation and State, we pledge our loyalty and devotion."[8] "The Living Flag" was solemnly presented to the audience.

There is a certain fit between the lines spoken from Genesis, the parents anxiously scanning for their offspring in the play, and the content of the play, which is about struggle and triumph, very much in the Western (both kinds of Western) tradition. Although this version of history leaves out a lot, it is a comfortable reaffirmation of the world the spectators live in. They will come back to see it every year, encouraging their kids, taking time to reflect on the perseverance of their ancestors and the wisdom of God, who told the Gold Trolls to place the gold in the ground "so that man could eventually find it." Eventually the children of the children here today will take part. The production values may be amateurish, but the pageant itself is a discourse on origins, on destiny, on identity. It is tribal history, evolving and taking on meaning with each year.

Millie Heidepriem, who wrote the pageant script that is still followed today, said of it:

the American Indian, like the ancient Greeks and Norse, made up in his childlike imaginative mind fanciful tales and legends which explained, satisfactorily to him, the workings of the universe . . . The second part of the pageant has for its theme the lure of gold. . . . The real history of the Black Hills begins with the coming of

145

Custer's expedition in 1874. . . . The third part is patriotic and symbolical, personifying those characteristics
which build a strong cooperating community and which
honor the memory of the pioneers."[9]

The pageant tells this "real history of the Black Hills," while
Rushmore proclaims the national version, arrogating history to
itself in the same way that the Custer pageant does. It makes perfect
sense that Borglum's memorial should be here in the Black Hills, in
this part of America that embraces so much of our national drama of
restless exploration, entrepreneurial risk, cultural evangelism, and
relentless expansion.

6

THE HEARSTS

The Pageant of Paha Sapa was all about gold. Gold was the undoing of the 1868 treaty, and gold, from the Homestake mine, made George Hearst rich. The Hearst papers were built on this gold, and William Randolph Hearst made Theodore Roosevelt president. Theodore Roosevelt ended up on Rushmore. Homestake was an original sponsor of Rushmore.

A little less than a year after the Custer party found gold, in August of 1875, John Pearson and six others prospected Deadwood Gulch in the northern Hills. The group found gold, and a picturesque gold-rush city sprang up, complete with gunfighters, prostitutes, and pigtailed Chinese laundrymen providing services for gold dust. Wild Bill Hickok, Calamity Jane, and many other characters who would have had a hard time in the more urbane environments of the settled cities walked the streets, building their own legends and also, unknowingly, a future base for tourism revenue in these Black

Hills towns. Deadwood, like Custer before it and Lead after, was briefly the largest town in the Hills.

Alerted by Pearson's strike, Fred and Moses Manuel, French Canadian brothers, struck the "lead" ore outcropping that gives the town its name in April 1876. It took its name from what the Manuel brothers very much wanted to find: a homestake strike rich enough to set them up in a home and business.

The Homestake turned out to be the mother lode that everyone had been looking for. The Manuels, knowing that they didn't have the capital or the technology to develop their strike, sold it to L. D. Kellogg, a purchasing agent acting on behalf of a syndicate headed by George Hearst of San Francisco. Hearst was so enthused by Kellogg's description of his new property that he came out for a look. Hearst's mining fortunes had gone up and down; shortly before the Homestake purchase he had had to sell many household effects, including his wife's carriage horses. The Homestake mine was incorporated in California in 1877. Less than three years later it had produced more than $1.3 million in gold. Hearst would never be anything but rich again.

By this time the Manypenny commission had come and gone, and the Hills were about to boom, the picks and shovels delving, the saloon keepers and the gunfighters moving in.

Hearst was a savvy operator with experience in the geology and technology of mining in Missouri and California. He stayed for more than a year, examining the potential of neighboring claims and buying them up if they were worthwhile, conducting assays and surveys, and protecting the legal position of his new investment. Hearst was well aware of the effects of the Manypenny commission and the Senate's ratification of the act of 1877 and considered that matter closed, his interests in the Black Hills secure as far as Indians were concerned. Although the law had been ignored where it benefited Indians, men like Hearst could turn to it unabashedly as a protector. As he wrote to his partners, James Haggin and Lloyd Tevis, regarding a competing claim of the neighboring Giant mine: "You can bet your life I have made up my mind to fight the thing out on the old line at all hazards as it shows the most damnable frauds ever perpetuated in any country. I will hurt a good many people. As I wrote you, if we succeeded in finding out the fraud and maintain our rights there would be more squealing than was ever heard of before."[1]

The Giant suit was just one of his legal activities; at various times during his sojourn in the Black Hills he had thirty or forty suits pending against other claims.

The Homestake operation used the latest technology. It introduced railroads and the most modern, powerful stamp mills to the Black Hills, those crushers that broke up the ore by dropping big weights on the mined rock. It eventually brought in telephones and electric light, and it continued to buy out the other mines that had sprung up around the mother lode.

It also became an enormous magnet for skilled and unskilled labor, importing many expert miners from Europe—the "Cousin Jacks" of the Cornish mining region who had worked the tin mines for generations, so that already by the eighteenth century they were working far out underneath the ocean. The Cornishmen were joined by Irish, Italians, Scandinavians, Finns, and Slavs, all eager to have the security of working in a mine that was not likely to play out anytime soon. Although Chinese were seldom employed in the mines, they were a vivid presence in the development of the Hills, with a small Chinatown in Lead, where they ran restaurants and laundries. The Mining Museum in Lead today displays some tiny, beautiful objects that were discovered in an expansion of Homestake's open cut: a delicate crystal medicine bottle, holed coins dating from the Qian Long period of (1736–95), an enameled ink box.

Homestake jobs were good jobs by the standards of the day, the region, and the industry. In the 1890s three-quarters of the Homestake miners did not speak English, and their polyglot settlements in Lead were the beginnings of a truly American process of assimilation into a New World identity. These settlements were also the seal of the industrial transformation of the Hills.

By the early years of the twentieth century the Homestake had become an enormous venture, a regional behemoth. As a 1952 guidebook says, "Lead is the Homestake and the Homestake is Lead; the two are inseparable."[2] Owing to an early conflict between the mine's claim to the ore under the town of Lead and the original survey of the town, the mine ended up owning virtually all the real estate of Lead. Residents did not buy the lots on which their houses stood; rather, they leased them from the company and could be evicted on ninety days' notice.

In the 1880s the Homestake expanded into what is nowadays called the news media. The immediate spur for this was water, in Lead as elsewhere throughout the West a major factor in politics, business, and public relations. Mining requires a lot of water. When Homestake manager Samuel McMaster acquired a water source near the competing Father DeSmet mine—water that for practical reasons the Homestake could not use but that it wanted to make unavailable to the Father DeSmet—the Father DeSmet manager, Gus Bowie, retaliated in kind, acquiring water rights near the Homestake. McMaster pressed the case that under U.S. mining law, water rights had to be exercised in order to be retained. The Father DeSmet then attempted to give free water to the city of Deadwood. In response, McMaster helped the city's signed water contractor, the City Creek Water Company, to pursue legal action against the city for breach of contract. The city put the issue to a referendum, and to win the populace over, both mines acquired local newspapers— the Homestake bought the *Deadwood Pioneer,* and the Father DeSmet founded the *Evening Press.*

Homestake had an unusual management style that could best be described as an authoritarian but for the most part benevolent paternalism. Good labor relations were fostered by a great deal of company involvement in the welfare of the town and the workers. As early as 1879 the mine provided free medical care for employees and their families and eventually built the town's hospital. When that hospital became obsolete it built after that the Black Hills Regional Medical Center, in nearby Deadwood.

The mine became the center of not only the town's economy but its social organization. It sponsored the town's schools, its recreational clubs, its country club, its ethnic marching societies, the American citizenship training classes—and controlled its politics.

Homestake pamphlets from the 1980s proudly describe the town's recreation center—it burned down in a fire in 1989—with its opera house, library, swimming pool, and bowling alleys.

What the pamphlets don't say is that most of these amenities were first housed in the Union Hall of the Lead City Miners' Association, a rather passive union that looked after the welfare of its members without confronting the interests of the company. When the mine became an affiliate of the more radical Western Miners' Federation in the early 1890s, and workers began to agitate for union membership for all employees, the Homestake's manager at that time, Thomas Grier, instituted a new policy: the Homestake would no longer employ union members. In support of this policy he shut down the mine in 1909 and kept it closed for more than a year.

With the resources of the local and of the Western Miners' Federation stretched, a small group of workers formed a "loyal legion" in 1910 and begged Grier for work. Grier reopened the mine, importing other scabs from mining regions all over the country. The unions were broken and bankrupted. The *Lead Daily Call*, a reactionary paper associated with the mine, for several years thereafter published the names of merchants who had supported the strike, suggesting that Homestake employees should not patronize them— and given the power of the Homestake in this single-employer town, the suggestion was more than polite. Many merchants were driven out of business by these means, although they could be removed from the blacklist by humbly begging the Homestake's pardon.

Grier got his union-free mine, and union-free it remained even after the Wagner Labor Relations Act of 1935 guaranteed the right of collective bargaining—such was the trauma of the lockout in the memory of this town and such was the company's control of the mine. The Homestake did not again have a union workforce until 1965, when the workers became affiliated with the United Steelworkers of America.

In the aftermath of Grier's action, the Homestake went to great lengths to ensure worker docility, increasing its paternalistic benefits and building the recreation hall. The Homestake could afford to be generous; it had won complete control of Lead. In an article comparing Butte, Montana (an entirely unionized mining town with famously terrible management-labor relations), and Lead, the *Engineering and Mining Journal* remarked that Lead had better working conditions. "The only condition is that the miner shall have nothing to say about it himself."[3]

Today the Homestake mine dominates the town of Lead, in rugged territory high up in the Black Hills. So much of the ground underneath the town has been dug away by the insatiable requirements of mining—the Homestake, using the most modern methods, has to crush five tons of low-grade ore to get an ounce of gold—that large areas of land on the surface cannot be built on for fear of collapse. Although Homestake had legal problems in the 1970s and 1980s over its habit of releasing toxins directly into Gold Run Creek,[4] in more recent times it has been careful to pay attention to environmental protection. Modern gold mining requires a great many toxic substances, including cyanide, which is used in the amalgamation process. Tourists visiting the Homestake works can view a complicated series of pools through which runoff water passes before it is released into the environment, and in these pools trout swim peacefully. If any of them go belly-up, the valves are closed.

The introduction to a Homestake centennial pamphlet pays homage to the romance of its pioneer beginnings without mentioning the conquest that it required: "WILD! RUGGED! A PATHLESS WILDERNESS! That was the Black Hills of Dakota Territory in the early 1870s. It was an untrodden and mountainous region far from the paths of civilization—where fortune beckoned with a glittering smile. . . . Truly, the Homestake was a contemporary of the roving Sioux, the grizzled prospector . . . and the hardy pioneer."[5] The pamphlet then turns to the Bible for a vindication of the universal appeal of gold, in Genesis 2:11–12: "The whole land of Hav'ilah, where there is gold; and the gold of that land is good."

In 1927 the company was one of the first major sponsors of the Rushmore project, contributing five thousand dollars, an amount matched by each of the three major railroads serving the Black Hills region, the Chicago and Northwestern, Burlington, and Milwaukee. Five thousand dollars may not seem like much nowadays, but these were the largest original private donations. Homestake also contributed much of the blasting powder and other tools used in creating Rushmore; and many of the men employed in drilling, carving, and blasting on the mountain's face were laid-off miners from the Homestake, Etta, Columbia, and Keystone mines—Depression-era employment casualties. Homestake contributed a million dollars in value to the renovations at Rushmore in the 1990s through a complicated real-estate swap, and Harry Conger, chair of Homestake, was also the chairman of the national Rushmore campaign that raised money for the renovations.

Homestake contributed to the drama of American history in ways more practical than Rushmore's symbolism. Homestake gold financed George Hearst's newspaper, the *San Francisco Examiner*, which was the organ of his political career. William Randolph Hearst took over the *Examiner* when his father was elected by the California legislature to the U.S. Senate in 1887. In 1895 William Randolph moved to New York. The elder Hearst, on his death in 1891, left his estate entirely to his wife, Phoebe Apperson Hearst, but the widow was very generous toward her son.

When he came East, Hearst bought the *New York Journal*, where he further developed the populist, sensational style that had had an enormous effect on the *Examiner's* circulation. One of Hearst's biggest projects in New York was his support of nationalist rebels in Spanish Cuba, beginning in the mid-1890s. Rebel guerrilla actions led to a brutal clampdown by the Spanish authorities, eventually including the mass internment of suspected rebel sympathizers in *reconcentrado* camps where Spanish forces could keep an eye on them.

As Ronald Reagan saw the Nicaraguan Contras as freedom fighters, Hearst seems to have sincerely seen the Cuban struggle against the Spanish as an analogue of the American Revolution. Like Reagan, he was not about to let the facts get in the way of his truth; he knew the sort of stories he wanted about Cuba. His newspapers were to play a role in completing the work of Simón Bólivar and José San Martín, driving Spain out of the hemisphere once and for all.

Hearst beat the drums for war with Spain for several years before he got results, and he cooked up some great reading in the process. Hearst reporters consistently filed melodramatic reports of Spanish atrocities and especially of the alleged tortures carried out by the "beast" Valeriano Weyler, the Spanish general sent to put down the rebellion. These stories usually sprang from the imaginations of his reporters in Havana, since their attitude about the conflict had led the Spanish authorities to ban them from the war zone. Rebel atrocities went unreported.

The Hearst newspapers created international incidents. He made a Cuban heroine out of Evangelina Cosio y Cisneros, a beautiful girl who had been imprisoned by Spain for violent independence activities. To Hearst, she was "the Cuban Joan of Arc," and to spice things up, a near-victim of the beastly lust of a General Berríz (whose attempt on her virtue had of course been foiled—a non-virginal Joan of Arc would never do).

By the time all this made it into the Hearst papers young Evangelina—whom the *Journal*, oblivious to the technicalities of Hispanic surnames, consistently called "Miss Cisneros"—was in prison not as a combatant but for defending her honor from the attacks of Berríz. Hearst mobilized a massive national campaign among the women of America to save Evangelina from the Spanish rapists, arranging for thousands of cables to be sent to the Queen Regent of Spain and keeping the outrage before the public for weeks. Finally he brought the affair to a dramatic climax: his reporter Karl Decker went to Havana, rented a house next to the prison and, on the night of October 8, 1897, using a ladder as a bridge, crept across to the young lady's barred window. The *Journal* reported that Evangelina's cellmates slept the sleep of Morpheus—she had been secretly supplied with opiates to put in their coffee so that they would not awake—as Decker sawed through her bars and spirited her away. In fact all of this drama was quite unnecessary because all the prison guards had been bribed with the *Journal's* money. Decker and the young lady could have walked out the front door of Recojidas prison. But how exciting would that be?

Decker, writing as Charles Duval (supposedly to confuse the Spanish authorities) summed up the *Journal's* perception of its role like this:

> Evangelina Cosio y Cisneros is at liberty, and the journal can place to its credit the greatest journalistic coup of this age. It is an illustration of the methods of the new journalism and it will find an indorsement in the heart of every woman who has read of the horrible sufferings of the poor girl who has been confined for fifteen long months in Recojidas prison. . . . [6]

To which the *Journal's* editorial comment added:

> The *Journal* is quite aware of the rank illegality of its actions. It knows very well that the whole proceeding is lawlessly out of tune with the prosaic and commercial

nineteenth century. We shall not be surprised at international complications, nor at solemn and rebuking assurances that the age of knight errantry is past. To that it can be answered that if innocent maidens are still imprisoned by tyrants, the knight errant is yet needed. The *Journal* is boundlessly glad that it has rescued Evangelina Cisneros from the unspeakable Weyler's hands, Spanish law or no Spanish law, and the comity of nations to the contrary notwithstanding. The *Journal* is ready to stand all the consequences of what it has done.[7]

Especially since the consequences were a massive circulation boost. What the *Journal* did was to spend an entire week in self-congratulations and congratulatory telegrams from all over the world, from journalists and journals, politicians, Princess Kaiulani of Hawaii, ordinary people and the Pope himself, lauding the act, comparing it to the escapes and attempted escapes of Mary Queen of Scots from the Tower of London and the Marquis de Lafayette from an Austrian dungeon.

When Decker and Hearst smuggled Evangelina into New York, Hearst sent his reporters out to meet her ship in the harbor, put her up at the Waldorf-Astoria, and bought her an entire couture wardrobe. She was then accompanied downtown by an enormous parade featuring naval cadets and regular army soldiers of the unrecognized Cuban Republic to a glittering reception at Delmonico's Restaurant, where representatives of the Daughters of the American

Revolution made the anti-colonial theme explicit. The celebrations continued in Times Square with fireworks, searchlights, and the military bands of the 69th and 7th Regiments, provided by the Journal.[8] Hearst was a man who knew how to do an international incident up right.

But Hearst's most important story—the one that finally got the United States into war with Spain—was, of course, the fate of the *Maine*.

On February 15th, 1898, the U.S. battleship *Maine*, sent to Havana harbor as a military presence during a time of rising tensions, was rocked by two enormous explosions. More than 250 sailors were killed. The nation went wild. When the Star Spangled Banner was played in theaters, the enthusiasm of the theater-goers almost caused riots.

At the navy department, a small audience gathered as the tiny ensign flying on a model of the *Maine* was solemnly set at half mast. President William McKinley was hung in effigy in some parts of the country for his reluctance to fight, although he soon appropriated $50 million for a presidential discretionary defense fund.

Given the state of late nineteenth century naval forensics, no one can ever know for sure whether the *Maine* was sunk by accident or sabotage. Hearst was sure, though. Two days after the event the *Journal* was flatly declaring that the explosion was caused by a torpedo: "Torpedo hole discovered by government divers," although on the next page there is a small article reporting that the first thing the divers will do when they reach Havana will be to make a thorough inspection of the hull. Over the ensuing weeks the Hearst papers served up a constant froth of war hysteria, such as a fictionalized account of an attack on New York City by the visiting Spanish cruiser *Vizcaya*, made to look like a news article.[9] Meanwhile, President McKinley and his cabinet struggled to negotiate with Spain, and the Spanish government tried to find a way out of the situation that would not lead to the fall of the Spanish monarchy, which would have been the inevitable result of leaving Cuba without a fight. Hearst, who hated McKinley, poured scorn on his efforts and wrote of the diabolical influence of a pacifist Wall Street and an American public gone soft. He published diagrams showing exactly how the Spaniards had detonated a mine under the *Maine*—a mine now, not a torpedo—using wires strung from the water up to Morro Castle in Havana harbor.[10] Soon after the explosion he began running "American People's Views," printing hundreds of citizen appeals to the most warlike national impulses.

Spain couldn't do anything right. When, immediately after the explosion, Spanish army officers in Havana sponsored formal rites for the victims led by the Bishop of Havana and donated land for their burial, the *Journal* was infuriated:

> American citizens in Havana are highly incensed that these things should be. They ask, 'Why should American seamen who have been blown to atoms aboard their own ship in a Spanish harbor during a time of peace be the objects of such apparent display of sympathy? . . . it is generally believed that the acts of the Spanish officers in paying for the funerals and giving aid for burials are

directed by advices from Madrid. The indignation of the
American residents of Havana knows no bounds.[11]

Hearst ran completely fabricated stories of Spanish desecration of
the bodies of the American martyrs on the docks of Havana. Eventually, and partially due to Hearst's constant badgering, McKinley
agreed to a congressional ultimatum that he knew Spain could not
accept. War was officially declared on April 25, 1898. The young
assistant secretary of the navy, Theodore Roosevelt, who had also
been doing his able best to provoke war, resigned his position to
organize a volunteer regiment of cowboys and Indians, miners and
(in a proud acknowledgment of the war-fever solidarity of the American public) Ivy League boys in tailored khakis—the Rough
Riders—and get in on the action.

Roosevelt was fascinated by war, intensely anxious to prove himself not a coward. The example of his father, who performed valuable but non-combat service during the Civil War, seems to have
haunted him. In the days before the First World War gave whole-
sale slaughter a bad name, his romantic notion of war was not
blunted in the least by seeing actual men killed in combat, or by
killing: Roosevelt's memoir of the Rough Riders is full of admiring
descriptions of strong, healthy young men giving their lives for the
cause, refusing to take cover under fire, refusing to go back behind
the lines when wounded. He wrote of disciplined fire and stoic resignation to death and dismemberment, of a desire only for glory (in
contrast to the Spaniards, whom he describes as shooting in panic
and running at the first opportunity). A vague sense of unreality

hovers over all his descriptions: can war really be this much fun? Roosevelt lovingly describes the officers' toast to themselves en route to Cuba: "The officers: may the war last until each is killed, wounded or promoted."[12]

And indeed the experience of war seems to have done very well for Roosevelt's peculiar vitality. In the aftermath of the surrender of Santiago de Cuba, the most important battle of the war, when his troops were sickening and dying in squalid, dysentery and malaria infested camps, Roosevelt remarks that he was one of only two officers who were not sick a single day. After his troops came home to camp at Montauk, Long Island, he wrote, "Many of the men were very sick indeed . . . I was myself in first-class health, all the better for having lost twenty pounds."[13]

As the American Century dawned, the United States found itself in control of the destinies of the former Spanish colonies of Cuba, Puerto Rico, and the Phillipines, and became for the first time a colonial power beyond its own lands.

The war had one result that was of less immediate importance than empire-building, but it was a result that mattered in the long run. Were it not for Hearst, an eager young colonel of irregulars might never have led his troops up San Juan Hill on the road to Santiago, at least as the newspapers and later memory would have it. In fact it was Kettle Hill, a less important Spanish emplacement, that Roosevelt charged, with spare eyeglasses sewn into his uniform and hat. But Hearst created the legend of Roosevelt at San Juan Hill, and without Hearst there might not have been President Theodore Roosevelt. There would have been different faces on the mountain.

Roosevelt became a contender for the New York governorship, then a compromise candidate for Vice President in 1900. When McKinley was assassinated in 1901 at the Pan-American Exposition in Buffalo by the anarchist Leon Czolgosz, Roosevelt stepped into the presidency. His career path had been marked by his love of adventure, his enthusiasm for war, the support of the Hearst media. He was launched toward the presidency fighting Spanish colonialism, and ended up on a monument to American colonialism, a monument in the Black Hills, which brings us back to the present.

Homestake runs a small boutique and gift shop that sells gold jewelry, much of it Indian-made, directly to the public, as part of its public-relations and tour operations. The store also sells a medallion, one ounce of pure gold, with a buffalo design, that eternal symbol of the West. The wild buffalo are almost gone now, their disappearance part of the whole complex of events that made Homestake possible.

The mine has done more than extract gold. In 1965, in association with the Brookhaven National Laboratory, the cosmologist Raymond Davis built a solar neutrino detector deep in a Homestake shaft. The device was designed to track the course of neutrinos—those mysterious particles that are tremendously important to the edifice of modern physics theory—in an enormous vat of cleaning fluid. The idea was that solar neutrinos, which can pass through solid matter, would not be detected anywhere but deep in the earth.

This scientific sideline is very important nowadays, because a crisis looms over Lead. The price of gold has been falling consistently—in September 2001 it is $270 an ounce, as compared to around $335 an ounce for much of the past decade—and the quality of the ore coming out of the mine is dropping. The cost of producing Homestake gold has exceeded the market price. Homestake has been divesting itself of real estate since 1984, selling houses to their owners and getting out of the business of running the town's infrastructure. It has turned the water distribution system over to the city government. Homestake will close up its operations in Lead permanently by the end of 2001.

This town has never had any other base of support than gold mining, any other major employer than Homestake. Lead hopes to use the deep hollow spaces underneath it for a world-class national neutrino laboratory. Will this work? It is hard to believe that science can inject as much money into the town as an industry that once employed twenty-five hundred people did. It is true that there will be lots of work for construction contractors and for miners while the laboratory is being built, and people are hopeful. Bumper stickers in Lead in the summer of 2001 read, "I ♥ Neutrinos"; a flyer on the door of the city hall advertised Neutrino Day.

Mayor Dennis York is optimistic. He told me that there are many other things that can be done underground besides gold mining and the study of neutrinos and that Lead could become the center of a South Dakota high tech efflorescence. The shielding from cosmic rays make the former Homestake mine a good place to produce computer chips. The navy does underground research, and it also needs an underground listening station to monitor worldwide nuclear weapons testing.

Two things I learned from Dennis York are that tobacco can be used in bone marrow replacement technology, and that tobacco grown underground is best for this purpose.

It was a little more than a hundred years ago that miners were scooping riverbed sand into wooden rockers to shake out tiny bits of gold. Indians were attacking the intruders on their sacred lands, the place where they held their sun dances and vision quests. Frontier merchants were setting up their shops. Now the town waits with some anxiety to see if the government will deliver funding adequate to the task of setting up a neutrino lab for experiments that will perhaps alter scientific theories about what matter is, what time and space are. A different kind of vision quest, perhaps, with different requirements than the sincerity, willingness to suffer, and spiritual purity that were required of candidates for the original. The "sealed book" has been opened indeed.

7

LITTLE BIGHORN

Funny how the Custer legend lives on. The defeat on the Little Bighorn—the victory of the Greasy Grass, from another point of view—didn't change the unfolding drama of Western settlement. It was soon followed by the death of Crazy Horse, the exile of Sitting Bull. The Indian victory, ironically, brought the crackdown that opened the gates to mining and settlement and stripped the mystery from the Black Hills. Eventually, Rushmore put its stamp and seal on the opening of the land.

Driving the empty stretch of Montana highway between Broadus and the town of Crow Agency on my way to the anniversary ceremonies, I stopped to pick up an Indian hitchhiker.

He was a big man, but friendly and so soft-spoken that I had to lean over to hear him in the small car. He was Cheyenne and Hidatsa from North Dakota, and when I told him where I was going, he smiled a big beautiful smile.

"Custer, yeah, we sure kicked his ass."

He told me he'd been in the marines and asked where I was from. I mentioned all the places I grew up. He stared at me intently. "No. I mean, where's your *blood*."

My ancestors were Jews from Poland, Ukraine, and Russia, I said. They came here about a hundred years ago. I wondered what he'd make of this. It seemed pretty far away from the plains, from anything Indian. But as usual, things were less orderly than I'd assumed.

"My mother, she was Polish. Mixed-blood. Her dad came from there. He couldn't speak any English, nor any Indian. He could play the fiddle, though. Man, he could play the fiddle. My mama told me about how he had a barbershop in Poland. And they came and took it away from him. Just because he was Jewish, he didn't belong. So they thought they could just take it away. Like he didn't matter, like they used to treat the black people here."

I glanced at him. He looked as full-blood as full-blood can be, which means nothing.

It was something to think about as we headed toward the site of a battle determined by conflicting notions of racial destiny. I felt a little chagrin for wondering whether a Cheyenne Hidatsa from North Dakota would have a hard time understanding the reasons Jews might want to leave Poland.

I thought about all the white people in Indian country who claim a great-grandmother who was half Cherokee and, with her, some tiny mental corner of Indian identity. I've always found such claims silly, and I've noticed that Indian people are more at ease with me when I make it clear that I am not going to announce myself their kin. So it was sort of a kick to think that my Cheyenne Hidatsa Polish Jewish passenger and I might in fact be related.

Just before the turnoff to the battlefield a group of Lakota on horseback were wheeling and charging against the backdrop of the rolling hills, green that year after bountiful rains. The group is called the Big Foot Riders, who first rode a pilgrimage to Wounded Knee in the freezing weather of December 1990, the massacre centennial, restoring their spirits by reaffirming their connections with horses. They make it a point to appear at events important to the Lakota journey. Painted and bonneted, they rode in a fast circle, calling out with their high-pitched, yipping war cries while Lakota singing and drumming boomed from the fringes of a crowd of Indians in the distance. This music will transport an unwary *wasichu* to another place, make his hair stand on end, and if you have never heard it, no description will suffice.

The riders carried feather-trimmed ceremonial staffs and blew on eagle-bone whistles. Some of them used saddles.

I stopped the car to watch. One car pulled out of the line and paused next to me. A cheerful Indian woman called through the window. "Ain't'cha proud? Them's South Dakota Sioux!"

Maybe she noticed the South Dakota plates on my rental car. There was something teasingly ironic in her tone, addressed to my *wasichu* face, but nothing unfriendly.

A few hundred yards off in the grass to the north of the memorial cenotaph for Custer and his men there was an honoring dance for Indian veterans of all wars, Indian wars, U.S. wars. It was run by Cheyennes and included a victory dance with some of Custer's captured guidons. A veteran in U.S. army dress uniform put war paint on the cheeks of those who requested it, teenagers in buckskin and feathers, in Michael Jordan T-shirts, grandmothers carrying their grandchildren. I did not know just how to approach this ceremony. I was not exactly unwelcome to watch, not exactly welcome. At the 120th anniversary events in 1996 a group of tourists apparently believed a Cheyenne group was putting on a costume pageant for their benefit, and were surprised when told to stay well clear.

Recent years have seen a lot of new thinking about the battlefield. It is one of the few places in the country where large groups of Indians and non-Indians encounter each other *as* Indians and non-Indians when they're not selling anything to each other. Events on the anniversary day, June 25, are carefully calibrated to honor and respect the political and actual descendants on all sides in the battle.

It wasn't always like this. At a conference on the political history of the site following the 125th anniversary of the battle, in 2001, I heard the renowned historian of the West Robert M. Utley—who served as a guide at the battlefield when he was a teenager—talk about the interpretation of the site through most of its history as a national monument. Utley described superintendents quite taken with the idea of the heroic, dashing general and disinclined to present any other point of view. "Indians participated in all the anniversary events. But they never said what they themselves might think about these events. And we never asked them."

When Utley was a teenager, the train station in nearby Hardin, Montana, had segregated waiting rooms for Indians and whites.

Indeed, several of the former site historians and superintendents who spoke at this gathering mentioned that their first interest in the battle had grown from seeing the Custer-glorifying Errol Flynn film *They Died with Their Boots On* (all of them later came to have a more sophisticated view of Custer). Up until the 1960s the militarist tradition was very strong, fed by a victory in World War II and by the sterling record of the Seventh Cavalry in that war and in Korea. The Seventh fought hard at Manila. It was the first unit to enter Seoul. Brice C. W. Custer, the general's grandnephew, was the lieutenant colonel of the Seventh during the breakout from Pusan during the Korean War. This Custer told Utley that the men of the Seventh were far more inspired by the legacy of George Armstrong Custer than they were by the fight against world communism.

The battlefield is no longer about the glory of Custer. It focuses on the historical context of the battle and on the stories of all the participants. The new approach mostly works. The first time I came for the anniversary, in 1997, I was a little taken aback by an introductory message from Superintendent Gerard Baker, which began with the words: "VICTORY DAY CELEBRATION." His list of the day's events included, among other Indian-hosted events too numerous to mention, a victory march and dance by the Northern Cheyenne Warrior Societies; an appearance by the Oglala Sioux Tribe Veterans' Posts 269 and 281; a prayer at the location of the proposed Indian Memorial; a noon meal sponsored by the Northern Cheyenne Warrior

Societies; traditional songs offered by singers of the Northern Cheyenne and Lakota Nations; and prayers offered by Indian elders.

Baker is of Mandan and Hidatsa descent. The first Indian superintendent, Barbara Booher, of Cherokee and Ute descent, served from 1992 to 1994. She invited all the tribes who took part in the battle, as well as the Seventh Cavalry, to participate in commemoration ceremonies. Baker continued this approach, and his successor, Neil Mangum, who is not Indian, has done the same. It is a tradition now. On later visits I knew what to expect, although unlike Baker, Mangum has not gone out of his way to emphasize the battle as a victory, and the event has mellowed into a festival of cultural exchanges and expressions of mutual respect.

What would Sitting Bull or Custer have made of all this? I doubt that either would have been inclined to honor the other as a brave and worthy foe doing his duty as he saw it, the position that is the order of the day. I doubt that either would have agreed with Mangum when he describes the battle, as he is fond of doing, as "Americans fighting Americans." But we are living now, and they are not.

With my Polish Jewish Cheyenne Hidatsa friend I walked down the path into Medicine Tail Coulee below the visitors' center, looking at the white stone markers showing where soldiers had been cut down by the Sioux and Cheyenne, who swarmed across the Little Bighorn to the southeast. They drove Custer's soldiers before them along the ridge and back to the north, away from Major Marcus Reno and his men, taking refuge in the cottonwoods below.

Custer's commanding officer, General Alfred Terry, had suggested that Custer not divide his forces, but Custer sent Reno to attack the southeastern tip of the village and sent Colonel Frederick Benteen—he and Custer despised each other—off to guard the ammunition train, calling for his assistance just before he went into battle. Reno rode out from about where the Garryowen post office stands today and burned a few lodges, only to be driven back into the cottonwoods and then across the Little Bighorn.

By the time he crossed the river Reno had the brains of Bloody Knife, Custer's favorite Arikara scout, splattered across his face.

Reno fled to high ground and spent several days besieged on what is now called Reno Hill, his men and Benteen's forming a dismal defensive ring. The soldiers were picked off when they came down to get water, until the approach of General Terry's infantry a few days later convinced the Lakota-Cheyenne-Arapaho confederacy that they had done enough.

Custer and the men under his direct command attacked a little after Reno did, from the north. The killing fields of the men of the Seventh stretch all along the ridge he rode down from, and then down into the valley toward the coulee. Their original graves were marked with tipi poles taken from the abandoned village three days after the soldiers died. Now they have tidy white markers: "U.S. Cavalryman Fell Here."

Many of the Indians besieging Reno and Benteen wore clothes and carried weapons taken from the dead cavalrymen who fell with Custer. They must have been a disturbing sight for the soldiers crouched behind their earthworks, parched with thirst.

Looking back up toward the presentation dais and canopy above the trail, where an Indian group was performing a dance, my Cheyenne-Hidatsa companion reacted to the show with irritation. "Ha! Them Crows—they were on Custer's side, his scouts. They were traitors, really."

I asked him how he could be sure, from this distance, that those were Crows under the canopy.

"It's a Indian thing. You just know."

I asked whether there were continuing tensions between the Cheyenne and the Crow. After all, they live just down Montana 212 from each other, about twenty miles apart. "Well, yes, we sure do live close together. But, well, you might say, some of that old—friction—is still there. Crows."

These rolling hills surrounded by what is now the Crow Indian reservation in southeastern Montana must have seemed very far from home to Custer and his men, many of whom were themselves immigrants who found a trade in the army of their adopted land— English, Scots, Swiss, Germans, Irish, Danes, a few Italians, a Russian, a Hungarian.

As I walked the grounds I imagined how exposed they must have felt in this landscape—alien motes. The land is bright, hot, alive with the sounds of insects. A half mile or so to the northwest, near where the NPS access road joins Montana 212, is the Crow Agency Casino, definitely not here in 1876. No one will see its gaudy lights until dark.

A military cemetery located on the battlefield grounds is for soldiers who did not fight with Custer that day but who ended up sharing the ground where he fell. "In Memory of our Comerade,

John H. Cruis, Sargent of C company, 25th Infantry. Died July 30, 1893, aged 45 years." "James N. Davis, Saddler Troop D, First U.S. Cavalry. Died December 9, 1885, aged 40 years." These matter-of-fact details still have some power to evoke the lives of men whom no one living now remembers.

The cemetery was open for military burials into the 1970s. Bill Henry, chief historian at the site from 1967 to 1969, recalled at the battlefield conference in 2001 that soldiers killed in Vietnam were buried there almost every day of his tenure, many of them Indian, many of them local. He remembered ceremonies jointly led by Catholic priests and traditional medicine men, with Indian women up on the rise behind the cemetery, wailing and ululating.

A small museum houses photographs of battle participants, weapons recovered from the battlefield, cultural and historical notes. Before a period painting of the slaughter in full-blown romantic style, a very blond young boy, five or six years old, wailed: "Mommy, what's happening with those cowboys? Did the Indians kill them all?"

On the hillside past the museum and the gift shop stands the cenotaph on the mass grave of the men who fell with Custer. The gravestones of other men, many of them marked "Unknown Soldier" but some with names glaring whitely in the sun—the civilians Arthur "Autie" Reed, Boston Custer—lie scattered along the hillside, and more lie at the bottom of the slope, although visitors cannot go there.

Although there has been a focus on Indian memorial services in recent years, the Custer monument is far from friendless. James

Welch, a member of the Montana Blackfeet tribe who wrote a book and a film script about the Custer myth and the Little Bighorn battlefield, describes a 1992 event in which white Custer buffs solemnly poured out water on the ground for the thirsty souls of the cavalrymen. I find it interesting that white interpretations of ceremonies that touch on Indian life—even ceremonies for whites—are seldom confined to the ecclesiastical impulses of white culture but spill over into a sort of animistic paganism. It is as if the ritualizers recognize how ethereal is their abstract god, how far from the grime and blood and terror that was seen on these dusty ridges, and have unconsciously decided that faux Indian ways will better serve. It's a puzzling sort of tribute.

On an early visit, I watched as a group of white men in period costumes held a service for Custer's men. They were sponsored by the *Battlefield Advocate*, a private magazine and organization that has tenaciously clung to the image of the heroic general in the name of resisting "political correctness." The organization and its leader, Wayne Michael Sarf, used to have a semiofficial advisory role at the monument, but as the more Indian-oriented interpretation took hold, this relationship ended. Indeed, relations with Superintendent Gerard Baker became so bad that the *Battlefield Advocate* people eventually took the extraordinary step of petitioning the president of the United States for his removal.

When Gerard Baker stepped down as superintendent in 1998— for reasons unconnected to the *Battlefield Advocate* campaign, after a tenure that earned the praise and support of his NPS supervisors— he left with death threats against him. Baker told me that he considers this a measure of his success in opening the door to the Indian side of the story at the Little Bighorn.[1]

So Gerard Baker was not invited to the *Advocate*-sponsored ceremony, where a white man with a Pawnee haircut, in hilariously inaccurate plains Indian garb—including shiny black leather trousers with the seat cut out—spoke of "healing." He read a poem that invoked the Four Directions and the Great Spirit. The men in costume had made a special "flag of healing" that has been displayed around the country. "Come on and hold this flag, this flag that the General is unfolding," he asked of us. The General indeed bears a striking resemblance to the original. "This is important, this is our medicine. People from all over the country have touched this flag. Help us to put aside both our differences and our similarities."

On later anniversary visits I saw none of this kind of thing. It was replaced by solemn roll calls of the dead of both sides and wreath-laying ceremonies at the cenotaph and at the site of the future Indian Memorial. And if some of Custer's modern supporters may veer on silliness, it is too easy to dismiss the man as the vain fool that his opponents would have him be.

He was not, perhaps, the world's greatest military strategist. But he was no cartoon, no one-dimensional glory hunter. He was brave, beyond any question. He could write, and he wrote prolifically for many sporting and general-interest magazines of the day. His nineteenth-century prose, while ornate, is not cloying or overly sentimental, although he does portray his own actions in the best possible light (a habit that caused some of his brother officers to drop the *f* in the title when referring to his book *My Life on the*

Plains). He was interested in the world around him. He did not tol-
erate the mockery of others, but he could laugh at himself and his
reputation for foppery:

> When the alarm of "Indians" was given, and in such a
> startling manner as to show that they were almost in our
> midst, the question was not "What shall I wear?" but
> "What shall I do?" . . . A modern Jenkins, if desiring to
> tell the truth, would probably express himself as follows:
> "General Custer on this occasion appeared in a beautiful
> crimson robe (red flannel *robe de nuit*), very becoming to
> his complexion. His hair was worn *au naturel*, and per-
> mitted to fall carelessly over his shoulders. In his hand he
> carried gracefully a handsome Spencer rifle. It is unnec-
> essary to add that he became the observed of all
> observers."[2]

Custer was capable of an empathy that many of his contemporaries—and my contemporaries—lack:

> If I were an Indian, I often think I would greatly prefer
> to cast my lot among those of my people adhered to the
> free open plains rather than submit to the confined limits
> of a reservation, there to be the recipients of the blessed
> benefits of civilization, with its vices thrown in without
> stint or measure. The Indian can never be permitted to
> view the question in this deliberate way. He is neither a

177

luxury nor necessary of life. . . . When the soil which he has claimed and hunted over for so long a time is demanded by this to him insatiable monster, there is no appeal. . . . Destiny seems to have so willed it, and the world looks on and nods its approval. . . . Where and why have they gone? . . . Ask the Saxon race.[3]

He was no sentimentalist, however. Reflective he could be on occasion, but he did not forget his mission, and he did not forget his race. When rumors flew that General Sherman—a man who did not shrink from devastation—might run for president in 1876, Custer speculated on how his fellow Ohian[4] might run Indian policy. "There would be one grand Indian war, and then there would be no more Indians. It would settle the Indian question beyond the tom-foolery of Quakers and sentimentalists who don't seem to know that every Indian everywhere is simply a brute. You can't civilize an Indian any more than you can teach a rooster to lay goose eggs."[5]

An Indian monument will soon stand not far from the Custer cenotaph. The idea of erecting one has a long political history. As early as 1925, a Cheyenne woman named Nellie Beaverheart petitioned the government for a monument to her father, Lame White Man, who had died in the battle; this petition was ignored.

The next time anyone lobbied for an Indian monument was in 1972, when AIM organized caravans of cars from around the country to converge on Washington, D.C., an action designed to draw attention to Indian treaties and to persuade American political leaders to honor them. This effort was called the Trail of Broken

Treaties, and it culminated—although this was not planned in advance—in the dramatic capture of the BIA building in Washington just before the election that saw Nixon win a second term as president. One of the caravans started in Seattle, where important tribal fishing rights battles were being waged. It was led by Russell Means of AIM and Hank Adams and Sid Mills of the Survival of American Indians Association. The caravans stopped off at reservations all across the country to pick up cars full of supporters, and, among other places, this caravan visited the Crow reservation near the Custer battlefield.

While the demonstrators spent the night with the Crow, a sculptor with the group made a plaque honoring the defenders at Little Bighorn. This might have been an uncomfortable moment, for after all the Sioux and the Crow were hereditary enemies, and the Crow had given aid and comfort to Custer throughout his career on the plains, including providing six of the scouts—Curley, Goes Ahead, Hairy Moccasin, Half Yellow Face, White Man Runs Him, and White Swan—who had accompanied him to the battle. The scouts knew of the massive gathering of Sioux and Cheyenne and tried to tell their commander. Why didn't he listen? Custer might have been thinking of a last-minute presidential nomination at the Democratic convention in Saint Louis that summer, and needed the glory of a quick victory. At any rate, Custer dismissed their fears and released them from service before the event. Having failed to convince him of what they knew was to follow, they cleared off, seeing no necessity for suicide.

In the pan-Indian spirit of the caravan action, however, the names of these scouts were added to the plaque. This pleased the Crow.

The group brought the plaque to the battlefield site the next morning, equipped with cement and tools to install it. In his memoirs, Russell Means recounts that the superintendent begged them not to go through with it. He promised to see to it that an Indian memorial was authorized through the proper channels. The Indians took him at his word and dispersed.

In 1976, the centennial year of the battle, there was still no monument. Means and AIM came back. This was not a good time for Indian-white relations in the Western states. The shootout at Oglala had occurred the year before; on the Pine Ridge reservation the tribal chairman, Dick Wilson, was engaged in a reign of terror directed against Indian civil rights activists and anyone who opposed his rule. In the wake of the AIM-inspired occupation of Wounded Knee in 1973, many whites saw any Indians who stood up for themselves as dangerous, violent militants who had to be confronted—and many Indians involved in civil rights or traditionalist activities expected all whites to react to them in this way. Grievances and mutual misunderstandings had the potential to explode into violence, and often did.

In this atmosphere, the NPS tried to forestall any unpleasantness by scheduling the main commemorations a day earlier than the anniversary, on June 24. Crow Indians who worked at the battlefield tipped off the AIM people about the change in plans. When a caravan of about seventy-five cars, led by Means, John Thomas, and Oscar Bear Runner, appeared at the battlefield, it was met by a huge contingent of law enforcement agents, including county sheriffs, Bureau of Indian Affairs police, FBI agents, Parks Service rangers, and highway patrolmen.

What followed was a very curious scene. Some of the police had attack dogs on leashes. The AIM activists had anticipated this tactic and had come prepared with two bitches in heat. The attack dogs responded to a higher duty and went AWOL, chasing after the bitches and taking their handlers out of the action. The demonstrators walked on into the parking lot, where the ceremonies were going on. Brice Custer—son of Brice G. W. Custer of Korea, great-grandnephew of the Custer of the plains—had donned period costume for the event.

Means mounted the podium and made a speech demanding that those assembled show respect for the sacred pipe carried by Oscar Bear Runner. Means pointed out that whereas Americans were celebrating their nation's centennial, Indians were celebrating the centennial of the battle as "a year that gives us pride and dignity. We bear no ill will."[6] The assembled crowd, who thought the Indians wars safely in the past, must have felt somewhat confused, but they applauded him. The Lakota traditionalist Frank Fools Crow performed a ceremony at the battlefield.

At the ranger station Means again demanded an Indian monument. Again the superintendent promised to arrange one.

In 1988 Means and a group of AIM members built a makeshift concrete memorial near the cenotaph. It read: "In honor of our Indian Patriots who fought and defeated the U.S. calvary [sic]. In order to save our women and children from mass-murder. In doing so, preserving rights to our Homelands, Treaties and Sovereignty." The plaque stayed in place for more than two months, from the anniversary date of June 25 until September 8, when the NPS had it removed. It has since been moved into the museum, as part of the history of the site.

In 1991 a bill sponsored by Ben Nighthorse Campbell, at that time a Democratic congressman from Colorado and the only American Indian in the Senate, authorized the Indian monument and changed the name of the site from the Custer National Battlefield Memorial to the Little Bighorn Battlefield Memorial. The only conditions for the new monument were that it was not to overshadow or detract from the Custer monument and, in an interesting attempt to assert quantitative nonpartisanship, that its base be the same size as that of the cenotaph.

The monument will be a reality. It is perhaps unfortunate that the design was eventually awarded to a white artist in a blind competition. Of course, the choice was controversial. When I asked Russell Means about it, I was surprised by his view of what the monument should represent, though not by some of his other objections.

> We end up with a white man's monument to our people that is as far removed from the theme of peace through unity as you can possibly get. In fact, what's been done, to my mind, is to lionize the three different Indian groups that were there fighting and winning . . . it hasn't anything to do with the theme that was put forth . . . how

do you gain peace through unity by lionizing fighters, in our case warriors? My elders said 'Peace Through Unity . . . Austin Two Moons, Enos Poor Bear, one a Cheyenne, one a Lakota. I know they meant for Indian people to build that monument.

The monument, like most modern monuments, is allowed no public funding.[7] That is where the story stands now, although Superintendent Mangum is setting aside part of the ten-dollar entrance fee toward the monument, and private donations are coming in. At the anniversary in 2001 a donation of more than seven thousand dollars was announced—from the Seventh Cavalry Association. Bill Richardson, the veteran of the Seventh who announced the donation, emphasized that "we strongly support this memorial and we will continue to do so." So far have we come.

In 1999, Nellie Beaverheart's request was realized when the Park Service dedicated markers to two Cheyenne, her father, Lame White Man, and Noisy Walking. The Park Service will place markers wherever an Indian casualty can be verified. Verification is, of course, much harder for Indians than for the soldiers, whose final resting places were set down in notebooks. Maintaining an unliteral racial shorthand—what colors are we, really?—the Indian markers will be of red granite, as distinct from the white granite markers of the soldiers.

As I left the battlefield area on my first visit, heading down the hill toward the evening celebration on the rodeo grounds, I passed the general himself, or a good facsimile thereof, strolling alone down the hill and into the sunset, plucking on a Jew's harp. He looked like a man who has the blessing of knowing exactly who he is.

Down by the campground, which is next to the Crow rodeo and powwow grounds, I followed a small path that quickly took me out of sight of any human-made object. Soon I heard hoofbeats behind me. An Indian kid, maybe sixteen, came galloping up on a small black pony, coming very, very fast. He wore jeans and no shirt or shoes, his long black hair streaming out behind him in the wind. The pony had no saddle, and was guided only by a rope halter. As the boy approached, he called out to me, "Did you see a brown and white pony come this way?" I hadn't, and told him so, but I'd been walking only a few minutes. He slapped the pony's rump, accelerated, and was gone.

All stereotypes about Indians and horses aside, this kid looked as though he'd been born on a horse. Horse and rider were magnificent. The Indians at the Little Bighorn could ride like that, no doubt.

Later that night, at the powwow that closed the Indian celebration of the anniversary, Superintendent Baker started the dancing around the circle of the fire. He had doffed his ranger uniform and hat and wore beaded buckskins and a wolf pelt. He shook a ceremonial staff as he moved to the drumming and singing, in that shuffling gait that is meant to imitate the movement of the buffalo. Unlike the pageant participants at the cenotaph earlier that day, he did not appear to be in costume.

There was a buffalo meat feast, much dancing and singing by

firelight, and games of chance by kerosene lamps in the tents, tourists with cameras mixing with the Sioux and Cheyenne and Crow in their braids.

Later, sleeping in my rented car around two in the morning, I heard voices.

"Someone in there."

"Sleeping, already?"

A big rock slammed into my car door, making it known that sleeping before the last dance has been danced, the last bowl of buffalo stew eaten, was a rejection of Indian hospitality. The rock throwing shook me up. I drove back to Broadus, Montana, to find a motel to sleep in.

One more Custer site to visit. I wanted to track the general to his final resting place.

Many tourists expect to find his tombstone at the battlefield, but he is not there. The burial party that returned to the site a month after the battle gave him an elaborate stone cairn, but his remains were returned to West Point in the following year, where, despite his 1861 thirty-fourth place graduation—in a class of thirty-four—it was hoped that he would inspire later generations of cadets. His wife, Elizabeth Bacon Custer, dedicated the remainder of her very long life to preserving his memory. She insisted on an appropriate memorial next to the administration building. She got her monument, not one but two—she hated the first offering and got another more to her liking: her husband on a high pedestal, redundantly brandishing both pistol and saber. This monument was erected in

1879, but by 1884 it was already perhaps a little embarrassing. After all, the man had led his entire command to destruction. The statue was sent to a New York foundry for repairs.

There we lose track of it. In 1965 the pedestal reappeared in the Cadet Cemetery, shorn of its hubristic occupier, replaced by an Egyptian obelisk. The viewer can see in this cipher whatever meaning he finds most appropriate.

The inscription notes that Custer was killed at the Battle of the Little Bighorn, along with his entire command. A bronze buffalo head protrudes from the side of the pedestal, lending an air of incongruous exoticism that would be more startling were it not for Custer's Elysian neighbor, Brigadier General Egbert L. Viele, Class of 1847. Viele was the chief engineer of an early New York Central Park plan in 1856, and the engineer of Prospect Park in Brooklyn. His crypt, perhaps fifty feet from Custer's, is a complete Egyptian fantasy, a huge pyramid with columns, scrollwork, Egyptian lions guarding the entrance.

Despite such opulence, Custer seems to be more fondly remembered than Viele. When I visited the site more than a century and a quarter after his death, there were fresh blue roses on the grave, a small but very crisp American flag.

8

BORGLUM AND THE

KU KLUX KLAN

N ational Park Service rangers give a short orientation talk at the Sculptor's Studio, part of the Rushmore Complex, where Borglum's models, an explanation of his plans, and various artifacts from the drilling and blasting are on display. When I saw this presentation, a clean-cut young ranger from Nebraska told the story of Doane Robinson's original idea and praised the political skills of Senator Peter Norbeck and Congressman William Williamson in getting Rushmore legislation passed. He spent some time on Borglum's vision, genius, and persistence. He called a cute little girl out from the crowd to assist him in demonstrating the pointing technique that transferred the measurements from the models to the mountain; she held a stick of dynamite while he talked about blasting.

He mentioned Stone Mountain, Borglum's previous mountain-carving project, in passing. I wanted to know what this young ranger thought of Borglum's ideas about white supremacy. How compatible could these ideas be with a modern evaluation of patriotism? After the ranger had finished his presentation, I asked him whether a discussion of Borglum and Rushmore was complete without mentioning Borglum's ties to the Ku Klux Klan. He looked uncomfortable. "Well, I had heard that he had some Klan connections."

"He had a leadership role in the Klan. That's one of the reasons the Stone Mountain project fell apart, you know. Two Klan factions were feuding over its administration, and Borglum played his cards wrong." The Klan angle on the story is discussed in only one of the many books about Rushmore and Borglum—Howard and Audrey Shaff's biography, *Six Wars at a Time*, which is sold at the Rushmore gift shop.

"Well, there were a lot of problems at Stone Mountain. He wasn't totally in control of the work. Anyway, we don't really go into Stone Mountain very much in our Rushmore presentations."

I asked him, more directly, whether Borglum's white supremacism should influence how we think about the meaning of Rushmore today; after all, so much else about the monument is associated with his personality. He gave a crisp and clear response. "I don't think that anything that Borglum may have thought or done personally has any relevance to Mount Rushmore as a national memorial. The meaning of Mount Rushmore is to honor these four presidents, our leaders. "

That's not the official meaning of the monument. Still, my question stands. Should it matter for those viewing Rushmore today that

Borglum worked with the Klan? The answer is not simple. What exactly were Borglum's Klan connections? Was he merely a fellow-traveler, or did his soul resonate to the vibrations of what would today be called racism? Most people of his time believed that a hierarchy of races was not a delusion but the clear consensus of science.

Six major books have been written about Borglum and Rushmore, and enormous numbers of smaller books, pamphlets, and articles. They have all contributed to the public image of Rushmore through their discussions of its creator. Most of the authors, to the extent that they talk about the personality of the sculptor, present him as a classic American original, perhaps with certain faults, but faults that were understandable by-products of his genius and his romanticism—he was irascible, slightly paranoid, perfectionist, intolerant of criticism and small-minded people, generous beyond his means.

The story that presents Borglum as a gruff but fine man has some serious lacunae. He did stand firm in his conviction of the superiority of the Nordic European "race" and in defense of its destiny as the great civilizing influence in the world. He was consistent about this when he was on the subject of European supremacy, although he could recognize injustice against other peoples when this organizing concept was not threatened. The idea pervaded all the realms of his opinions, and especially that of art. As he wrote in his "Ten Commandments for Sculptors," in a passage that perfectly displays his puritan and romantic sensibilities:

In ideas, don't copy the primitives, the barbarians—

189

and don't spend your youth tracing the archaic products of mentally limited, cramped, Asiatic and African
"Sculpture."

If your tastes are below your chin, do as Gauguin and
all his illy trained followers do; go and live with the
animal world; wallow in their physical impulses and be
one of them; deceive yourself.

Don't think you can produce anything that will find
its way into the record of culture of our people that was
not conceived in your own soul and reflects the best,
purest of our civilization.[1]

Of Borglum's biographers—who include his wife, his son, and a
good friend of his son, none except Howard Shaff and Audrey Karl
Shaff say anything at all about his membership in the Ku Klux
Klan or his lifelong anti-Semitism and white supremacism. The
Shaffs, to their credit, go into these matters in some detail, but
seem a little defensive about it: "We . . . felt a strong obligation to
make sure our readers understand that the socially acceptable
Klansmen of the 1920s were not the same radical, racial fanatics
who exist today in the splintered organizations that carry the
banner of the KKK."[2]

It is hard to tell, from this distance, just what Borglum thought
he was doing with the Klan. The Shaffs suggest that he was
looking for an organization that he could direct as a force in
national politics, which is certainly true as far as it goes. Indeed
there was something about the populism of the Klan that attracted

him, something that he came to associate with the struggles of farmers and working men.

Borglum had become involved in the long fight against railroad and banking interests that were ruining farmers; his belief that agriculture was at the spiritual heart of a strong and honest nation was typical of his romantic temperament. He had taken a passionate interest in farm politics in the Dakotas in 1916 and later lobbied energetically for the Non Partisan League, a group intended to transcend politics in the national interest. He had some admiration for Robert La Follette of Wisconsin, the leader of the anticorruption, anti–big business progressive movement of the early twentieth century, although he later concluded in disgust that La Follette had allowed himself to become a cat's-paw of socialists, anarchists, and Bolsheviks.

Perhaps it was an almost desperate delusion, but he saw the Klan, which was an enormous and truly national organization in the early twenties, as the vehicle that might finally give him some influence on national policy, and he fought furiously to direct and control the Klan's largely self-defeating efforts in the conventions and elections of 1924. He would have been attracted to the Klan's paranoid style, too; Borglum was always ready to see a conspiracy against him, especially if it involved Jews.

Just a few years before getting involved in Klan politics, in 1920, Borglum had served on the board of the Inter-Racial Council, an organization whose name meant something slightly different than what it might now; the "races" it concerned itself with were the Irish, the Poles, the Lithuanians, the Germans. It lobbied for more or less unrestricted immigration. The Inter-Racial Council was sponsored by major corporations and industrial organizations that were concerned with a ready supply of cheap labor. Even so, it supported a fair bargain, and spoke out aggressively against nativist attempts to exclude immigrants from citizenship and from unions, and against "English-only" laws in journalism and public gatherings.

In the years of Borglum's association with the Klan he abandoned this accommodationist agenda. An extended, if disorganized, statement about his national program came in an undated draft of a telegram on Klan goals addressed to his good friend the Klan leader D. C. Stephenson. In this undisciplined, misspelled outpouring we can see the standard elements of Borglum's political thought: the romance of the farmer; the concern with the heroic individualist myths of America coupled with a paradoxical, almost socialistic sense of the government's responsibilities; the faith in capitalism juxtaposed with a contempt for capitalists; reverence for what he conceived to be strict constitutionalism; and convictions of xenophobia and white supremacy.

> Four matters of paramount importance are before the Nation at this hour. . . . We join with the Farmer Northwest and South in common demands for the relief promised, and the same aid and protection given that is enjoyed by Alien manned city industries be given to the home Farm Industries.
>
> Second we demand laws and immediate regulation resisting the mongrel hoard that is fleeing from its own

responsibilities in Europe and pouring over our National Border bringing disease, ignorance, immorality and contempt for our laws our language and our customs in search only for our wealth. Immigration from the slums from the decay of Europe must cease if America is to continue a free peaceful protestant people . . .

Third we propose while America should remain steadfast in her principal of evading entangling alliances that is remain forever free from offensive partnership with foreign nations, and as a fundamental principal in Nordic blood is order under law, we the greatest aggregate of this race under a single constitution can no longer hold aloof from the establishment and participation in the direction of a worlds law and a worlds court.

Fourth we demand that henceforth and specifically in the present determining of delegates for the Presidential Convention of nineteen twenty-four that these conventions shall be free, representative, uncontrolled by Alien or group interest tyrannizing over free expression of the conventions vote we demand that the South shall have their white mans representation in our Presidential Convention and that partisan use of Negotiable negro delegates shall cease to be used to determine clique nomination of a convention, or form the basis of Federal patronage of the South.[3]

The story of Borglum and the Klan is important to understanding

Rushmore and to understanding a continuity of meaning with the earlier Stone Mountain project, which is where Borglum became involved with the Klan.

In 1915, Helen Plane, an elderly Confederate war widow who was president of the Atlanta chapter of the United Daughters of the Confederacy, convinced that organization to sponsor a memorial to the Confederacy. She wanted a portrait carved on the broad cliff face of nearby Stone Mountain: a head of Robert E. Lee, perhaps twenty feet high. The group formed an executive Stone Mountain Memorial Association, and Mrs. Plane got in touch with Borglum, already one of the most famous American sculptors, who was excited by the project. Sam Venable, the owner of the mountain and the quarry behind the cliff, agreed to donate the carvable area if a sculpture could be completed in twelve years. Borglum, characteristically, convinced Mrs. Plane, the United Daughters, and Venable that he had to carve a much larger memorial than they had originally planned. Borglum envisioned the columns of a huge army marching across the cliff face, led by Lee, Stonewall Jackson, and Jefferson Davis. He set about developing methods for projecting an image onto the rock face and for carving that image once he could trace it.

What he wanted to put under the mountain was as ambitious as his plans for the carvings. It clearly prefigured his plans for the Rushmore Hall of Records. He wanted three main underground halls, named for the state of Georgia, the Daughters of the Confederacy, and the Venable family. The halls would be lined with vaults, with thirteen communicating windows for the thirteen confederate states. There would be thirteen bronze stars sunk in the floor. The walls were to be covered with Founders' Rolls honoring Confederate soldiers, the names to be chosen by those who donated one thousand dollars or more to the project.

In a rock bay near the vaults Borglum wanted to build an amphitheater with the largest pipe organ in the world. In a cavernous chamber there would be cases for "relics" donated by survivors. There would be an enormous granite stairway to a broad central avenue connecting the halls, and a central bronze incense urn on the avenue.

What did all this have to do with the Klan?

The original Ku Klux Klan was founded in Pulaski, Tennessee, soon after the Civil War, by six friends who had theatrical pranks, not terror, in mind. What they came up with was a sort of fraternity, with initiation rituals and an odd, hooded costume. Galloping around the countryside at night, they found that people took them seriously and were frightened, especially superstitious blacks. Soon the young and growing organization developed an agenda, one that sought to use the power of their mysterious appearances to put the social order back the way it had been before the humiliating recent defeat and the arrival of the hated carpetbaggers.

The flair for the dramatic that the founders showed became a hallmark of the Klan, adding to both its appeal to potential members and its ability to frighten its targets—blacks, Catholics, Jews, the foreign-born, "immoral elements."

What had been a loose and undisciplined organization was remade along more formal lines in 1867, when the Confederate general Nathan Bedford Forrest called a meeting in Nashville and gave it a plan and a purpose: to defend the Constitution, Southern honor, the weak and the oppressed. He also gave it a ranking system, using the exotic titles that are both chilling and ridiculous today: a Grand Wizard was at the head of an Invisible Empire made up of Realms, which corresponded to the states and were headed by Grand Dragons. Lesser dominions were headed by Titans and Cyclopes. The ordinary Klansman was a Goblin.

The growing influence of the Klan was directly related to the end of the relatively mild, "presidential" phase of Reconstruction and the beginning of the more punitive "radical" phase, in which Congress sought to truly remake the South, destroy the traditional centers of Southern political life, and see to it that blacks could vote and participate in Southern society. The Southern governments that had been approved by Lincoln and Johnson were overturned by Congress, and what looked like a long-term military occupation settled in. The Klan saw a new battle for the soul and traditions of the South. The races had to be kept separated and in their accustomed roles, and blacks kept out of the militias and the polling places.

This early Klan opposed not only full civil rights for blacks, Jews, and Catholics but also lawlessness (if not instigated by the Klan) and immorality. On night rides throughout the South, Klansmen attacked bootleggers, divorced or separated men and women, loafers, and gamblers almost as often as they attacked black militiamen and Northern schoolteachers, although the consequences for the latter groups were usually more severe. For those who wanted to fight back, the Klan was hard to combat because so many of its members by night were respected judges, sheriffs, councilmen, and jurymen during the day.

A few years later, however, the Klan was having a harder time presenting itself as a force for traditional conservative values. Anonymous men often do things they would not do in the light of public recognition, and the Klan's growing propensity for violence, as well as the difficulty of enforcing limits set by a central council or leader, had given it a bad reputation and was causing it to lose much of the popular support it had once claimed among rural whites in the states of the Confederacy.

Perhaps more important, most of its fundamental goals were secure. Northern military rule had provoked the white Southern power structure into finding new ways to manipulate the black vote and stay in power. Social reforms had stalled; the races were not in danger of mixing.

In 1869, saying that the goals and membership had become perverted, and responding to increasing federal pressure, Nathan Bedford Forrest disbanded the Klan as an official organization and had its records and rolls burned. Not every chapter paid attention to this, and official extinction of the Klan was hardly the end of vigilante action throughout the South, but the Klan as a formally administered organization was dead and remained dead until it was revived in 1915—at Stone Mountain.

The rebirth of the Klan had a lot to do with a novel, *The Clansman*, and the movie that was made from it, D. W. Griffith's *Birth of a Nation*. Both had an enormous impact on American popular culture. The 1905 novel was written by a North Carolinian, Thomas Dixon

Jr. Dixon was a politician who had become a fiery Baptist minister with a large following. He then moved on to reach a larger audience on the lecture circuit. He was famous for his oratory.

The Clansman is part sentimental love story (it is subtitled *An Historical Romance of the Ku Klux Klan*) and part hate screed. It tells the stories of two sets of lovers after the Civil War, a brother and a sister from the North who fall in love with a brother and sister from the South. It features an insanely evil caricature of Thaddeus Stevens, the radical Republican who pushed for direct congressional rule of the South and wanted to use that rule to create socioeconomic justice, redistributing land to former slaves. Dixon's Stevens character ("Austin Stoneman") was intent on wrecking and humiliating the South by the imposition of "negro domination"; what this meant to Dixon was the rape of white women by subhuman blacks, the constant trope of white southern racial hysteria that may well have its roots in a subconscious guilty knowledge of the impunity with which white men raped black women in the Old South.

The Clansman was a very popular novel, and Dixon adapted it for the stage. When D. W. Griffith was looking for a suitable subject for what he conceived as the first epic of the moving-pictures age, he came to Dixon. Together they created a tremendously powerful work in the new language of film, featuring Sherman's devastation of the South, Northerners malevolently encouraging the unbridled lust of depraved freedmen, and heroic Klansmen riding to the rescue of besieged white feminine virtue, all set to a dramatic score taken from Wagner and from black spirituals, to be played live in the orchestra pits of thousands of cinemas.

The movie opened in 1915 to ecstatic reviews in the South and riots in the North. There was talk of censorship, but Dixon arranged a private showing for President Woodrow Wilson, who was a Virginian and who also happened to be a college friend of Dixon. Wilson, a racist through and through, was much moved by the piece. "It is like writing history with lightning," he exclaimed, and added, "My only regret is that it is so terribly true."[4] Dixon also showed it to Chief Justice Edward White, who confided to Dixon that he had himself been a member of the original Klan, in Louisiana.[5] With the approval of the president and the chief justice of the Supreme Court lending an air of legitimacy, the film went on to break all box office records, taking in eighteen million dollars gross, even though the entrance price was an unheard-of two dollars for a good seat—a value of perhaps forty dollars nowadays.

Birth of a Nation, which helped the revived Klan recruit, opened in Atlanta just after the first modern Klan ceremony was held at Stone Mountain. America in the early years of the twentieth century was a more sociable and socially organized country than it is now, and fraternal organizations were much more common. The *Atlanta Journal* and the *Atlanta Constitution* frequently listed events sponsored by fraternal orders, including the Woodmen of the World, the Masons, and the Knights of Malta. Fraternal orders had their own contest for the best float in Atlanta's Harvest Festival Parade, an annual event that in 1915 took place a month before *Birth of a Nation* opened in December. Top prize winners were the Pilgrim Knights of Oriental Splendor, the Junior Order of American Mechanics, the Daughters of America, and the Woodmen of the World.[6]

The times may have been ripe for a xenophobic, nativist revival. Europe was tearing itself apart. Paranoia about war and foreign agents was rife. Just before D. W. Griffith's show came to town the *Atlanta Journal* had published a ferocious editorial on the threat of foreign domination—an editorial that sounds just a bit familiar in our own time of protests against the World Trade Organization and political opposition to an international criminal court:

> If the agents or powers of foreign Governments are to determine how our industries are to operate, with whom our commerce shall be conducted and what our national policies are to be, the United States will cease to be a sovereign Power and become a mere vassal of European monarchies. . . . It is the urgent duty of Congress to deal with this matter at its approaching session . . . it should . . . amend the present laws to reach spies and plotters, whatever their nationality may be and in whatever way their crimes may be undertaken and accomplished."[7]

On December 6, President Wilson gave an address to Congress on war preparedness that focused heavily on the disloyalty of the foreign-born and the need for "Americanism." "There are citizens of the United States, I blush to admit, born under foreign flags but welcomed under our generous naturalization laws to the full freedom and opportunity of America, who have poured the poison of disloyalty into the very arteries of our national life."[8]

In the midst of war fears a movie that opened just prior to *Birth of a Nation*, titled *Battle Cry of Peace*, was packing houses in Atlanta. In it hostilities develop between the United States and the nation of "Ruritania." Propagandists cry for peace, and their efforts ensure that when actual war breaks out, the United States is unprepared. The Ruritanians bomb New York, with much bloodshed and carnage. In the *Atlanta Journal's* reviews, the movie is reported to be a powerful military recruitment tool.[9]

And then *Birth of a Nation* came to town. It was not just a film; it was a much-advertised and much anticipated cultural event. It had already been playing in New York and in many Southern cities for months, buoyed by Wilson's endorsement. The film toured with a fifty-piece orchestra providing the soundtrack. Reviews in the *Atlanta Journal* and the *Atlanta Constitution* eloquently convey the mass sentimental hysteria about the work and the raw racial fears of the time and place.

> [Birth of a Nation] swept the audience at the Atlanta theater Monday night like a tidal wave . . . Race prejudice? Injustice? Supression? You would not think of those things had you seen "The Birth of a Nation." For none but a man with a spirit too picayunish and warped for words would pick such flaws in a spectacle so great and whole-hearted as this. In the first place, the picture does every credit to the negro race, lauds those faithful old black people whose fealty to their masters led them to dare the anger of mistaken fanatics, shows the true

progress they have made since in industry and education. This picture is too big a thing to be bothered by such a gnat's sting of criticism . . . you smile sympathetically, too, at the darky buck-dancing on the corner and the little pickaninnies rolling funnily in the dust . . .

. . . then the Klu Klux Klan gathers. The scenes which follow defy description. In the little town of Piedmont the blacks are celebrating, far away across the hills the Klan assembles. Back and forth the scene changes— one moment a street in Piedmont swirling with mad negroes, the next a bugle blast from the orchestra and out of the distance the riders of the Klan sweeping on and on. Back to the street and house where a white girl trembles in fear before the black horde without back with the bugle blast to the onrush of the Klan. They are coming, they are coming!

. . . And after it's all over, you are not raging nor shot with hatred, but mellowed into a deeper and purer understanding of the fires through which your forefathers battled to make this south of yours a nation reborn . . . [10]

The *Constitution* describes Austin Stoneman, the Thaddeus Stevens character, in this way:

. . . You are ushered into an ante-chamber in Washington where a misguided man is plotting a black regime among white people—where a mulatto woman dreams of empire. You live through a period of ruin and destruction in the country where you were born. You see the plot executed and that same country humiliated and crushed under a black heel. Former happiness is shattered by the arrogance of ignorance. You sicken at the sight of an attempt to enforce marital racial equality. Again and again the unbearable hideousness of the days of reconstruction is borne in upon you . . . You could shriek for a depiction of relief—and, yes, retribution.

. . . a troop of white figures upon spirited horses dashes at breakneck speed into the picture and wheels into position . . . Men grimly determined upon a last desperate chance to rescue women and homes and civilization from an unspeakable curse are gathering for the work at hand . . . .Freedom is here! Justice is at hand! Retribution has arrived![11]

One who paid to see the movie was an ambitious dreamer named William J. Simmons, from Talladega County, Alabama. A failed clergyman, he had been preaching in the Methodist church from the age of fourteen, and had preached in rough mill towns like Opp, Alabama, where—as he told it—he had to fight men to get them to come to church. Simmons left the organization in 1911 when he was refused an urban assignment and became a professional fraternal organizer, an occupation in which an energetic man could make a good living on commission in the 1920s.

Simmons was a "joiner," and had joined just about every fraternal order he came across. He decided to form his own organization. Although Griffith's movie is often credited as the catalyst of his action, he himself would say that he had been dreaming since childhood of forming a new incarnation of the Klan. Perhaps his early fascination was based on the tales of Klan terror he would tell of hearing from the "darkies" as a child on a small farm in Alabama, tales he later related with great enjoyment. His father, a doctor, had been a leader of the original Klan.

He may also have been influenced by the power of an early, delirious incident brought on by illness. Such episodes can subtly affect a man's life. Simmons was talkative and wanted desperately to be a leader.

Simmons wrote and copyrighted the oath and rituals of his reformed Klan, and on the night before Thanksgiving Day 1915 he took fifteen robed initiates—including John Bale, the Speaker of the Georgia legislature, a member of the original Klan—up to the top of Stone Mountain, where he had arranged a canteen of fresh water, a flag, a Bible, and a sword on a stone altar propping up a sixteen foot cross soaked in kerosene. He explained the significance of each item, and noted that the sword had wounded a Confederate and killed two Yankees in the Civil War. Then the cross was set on fire.

The Klan oath was administered by Nathan Bedford Forrest's grandson, Nathan Bedford Forrest III, by the light of the burning cross. Stone Mountain—the site of Gutzon Borglum's first attempt at mountain carving, which shared in concept so many of his romantic ideas about the meaning of honor, sacrifice, and patriotism—was ground zero of the twentieth-century Ku Klux Klan, its very altar. Sam Venable, the owner of the mountain, who had been persuaded to donate the cliff face for the monument, was one of the new initiates of the reborn Klan on that night.

When *Birth of a Nation* opened in Atlanta on December 7, 1915, Simmons was ready. On December 19 a small ad appeared in the *Atlanta Constitution*. It featured a crudely hand-drawn figure of a hooded rider on a rearing horse, burning cross in hand. It is the only handwritten advertisement I came across in the Atlanta papers of the time.

KNIGHTS OF THE KU KLUX *KLAN*.

For Home, Country and Each Other. A High-Class Order for Men of Intelligence and Character. The World's Greatest *Secret*, Social, *Patriotic*, *Fraternal*, Beneficiary Order. Chartered by the State of Georgia December 6th, 1915.

Col. W. J. Simmons, Founder and Imperial Wizard, 85 W. Peachtree Place, Atlanta, Ga.[12]

Helen Plane, the original force behind the monument, was cheered by the revival of the Klan. She specifically requested that Borglum add some Klan figures to the design to honor those who had headed off black and carpetbagger "domination" of the South. Later, as we shall see, the officers of the Stone Mountain Association came to be predominantly Klan members.

Men joined Simmons's revived Klan for all kinds of reasons, only one of which was a hatred of minorities and those found wanting in morals. The childish rituals and strange language of the Klan—Simmons's copyrighted opening ceremony for a meeting ran to eight pages, the closing ceremony to five—gave members a sense of hidden knowledge and self-importance. Indeed, many of Simmons's early recruits were important men in their communities—bankers, businessmen, merchants.

The law of "Klannishness," which in practice meant steering business to fellow Klansmen, was attractive to potential members, and white Protestant tradesmen benefited from the Klan, because it led aggressive boycotts against Catholic-, Jewish-, and black-owned businesses, often publishing lists of businessmen who were Jewish or Catholic. It also led campaigns against politicians known to be Jewish or Catholic, which, at certain times and places in the 1920s, was a decisive factor in local politics.

After the United States entered World War I in 1917 the Klan's advocacy of "100 percent Americanism" was congenial to wartime patriotism, and newly minted Klansmen busied themselves with breaking up industrial strikes and persecuting leftists, "aliens," and loose women who struck at the moral foundations of the country, harming the war effort. After the armistice, the Klan was a sponge that soaked up the fervor not spent in wartime. The social changes that followed the war also helped Klan recruiting, and such things as the growing emancipation of women and the access to high-paying industrial jobs that blacks gained during the war were played up by the Klan as signs of the apocalypse to come if right-thinking Christians didn't take action.

Although Simmons did expand his Klan, he was not a talented organizer, not a very practical man. He knew he needed to bring in professionals. In 1920 he formed an alliance with Edward Young Clarke and Elizabeth Tyler of the Southern Publicity Association. Their usual line of business had been organizing things like the Harvest Home Festival, the Better Babies Parade, and Red Cross blood drives in Atlanta. In fact, the Better Babies contests and parades may not have been all that far from Clarke's Klan work: they were public searches for little Übermenschen. The *Atlanta Journal* reported from one such event:

> At least 10 perfect babies have been found among the hundreds of youngsters entered this week in the Better Babies show at the auditorium. . . . Mrs. James M. Savitz, a member of the committee in charge and herself the mother of four eugenic sons, declared . . . "most of the babies are very close to the standard . . . except for some slight imperfections that in any other context would go unnoticed. The hundred physicians conducting the examinations are drawing the line close, however, and even discolored skin or nails disqualify a child and count against the average."[13]

A week later the *Journal* showed pictures of "Georgia's Finest

Baby," Claude Lewis Trussell Jr., seven and a half months old, who won the gold medal by scoring 99 percent on some fanciful scale of baby perfection.[14]

When Clarke and Tyler took up with Simmons, the Klan grew exponentially, and the new chief recruiters collected eight dollars of every ten that came to the central headquarters through initiation fees and the sale of regalia. This was a high price for Simmons to pay for skilled help, but Clarke justified his large commission by the lost dollar value of the Jewish and Catholic clients and business connections he was giving up in going to work for the Klan.

Still, Simmons came out ahead. Clarke and Tyler turned Klan recruiting into a money-making machine. They very efficiently reformed the membership process, creating an army of "Kleagles"—recruiters—organized hierarchically, with Clarke as Imperial Kleagle. Like Clarke, the Kleagles were paid on a commission basis. The Kleagle who brought in a new member got a cut of the initiation fee, passing on the remainder to regional and national officers all the way up to the Imperial Wizard—and to Clarke and Tyler—in Atlanta. Simmons built himself an enormous Klan mansion and headquarters in Atlanta, which he named Klankrest.

This was another motive for joining the Klan: it could provide a very good living. Only a year or so after Clarke took over recruiting, Simmons's organization of a few thousand had grown to one hundred thousand members. Clarke, the former friend of Jews and Catholics, had entered into the spirit of his work and taken to making speeches about defending the white race against "mongrel civilizations." He proposed that blacks be sterilized.

He also undertook fund-raising work for the Stone Mountain project, not officially as part of his Klan duties but through the Southern Publicity Association. Still, he had found the work through the Klan, after the committee chairman, Forrest Adair, and Borglum himself had carefully considered whether Clarke's known Klan connections would help or hurt their cause.

By 1924, the high-water mark of the 1920s Klan, it had millions of members, and it had penetrated several Northern and Western states, notably Indiana and Ohio. Soon after that there was a national backlash against the Klan, and its rolls began to decline, never again to include such a large number of American households. The public perception of the modern Klan began to shift. From a somewhat eccentric fraternal organization it came to seem a thuggish group out of the mainstream. This was instigated in part by public revulsion at continuing Klan violence. One of the most famous incidents was the exceptionally gruesome slaying of two white Klan opponents in Mer Rouge, Louisiana, on August 24, 1922. The victims, Watt Daniel and Tom Richards, were flogged, tortured with a a blowtorch, and run over by a tractor before being drowned, and many of the law-enforcement officials of the town participated. Mer Rouge got the nation's attention. Several states and municipalities responded with laws to ban hooded processions and organizations with secret memberships. Newspapers, the *New York World* in particular, took up anti-Klan crusades.

Stone Mountain continued to hold a special place in Klan culture. Klan initiations were regularly held there through the 1920s, while

Borglum was still involved with the sculpture project. It was again an altar of rebirth when the third distinct phase in the history of the Klan began, the post–World War II resurgence that quickly produced splinter groups and feuding factions. It was here, in May 1946, that the Klan held its first post-World War II mass induction. Two hundred initiates, in front of a crowd of more than two thousand, took the oath before Grand Dragon Samuel J. Green of the Association of Georgia Klans (the parent organization had been disbanded in an attempt to avoid paying back taxes). Klan rallies were held regularly at Stone Mountain right up until the 1970s.

Borglum's project at Stone Mountain ended in a dramatic pair of conflicts. Both of them involved the Klan.

One of these conflicts was with the Stone Mountain executive committee and especially with the man who became the chief officer of that committee in 1923, Hollins Randolph, a devoted Klansman and an important player in Klan politics. The other conflict was with the leadership of the Klan itself. Each situation involved a coup, one in the Stone Mountain executive committee and one in the leadership of the Klan. To understand the connection between the conflicts we must make a detour into the quarrels of the Klan in the 1920s. This is where the story of Stone Mountain politics and the story of Klan politics became the same story.

Borglum was introduced to the Klan by his friend Sam Venable, the owner of Stone Mountain. His period of working directly with the Klan began when his fund-raising efforts led him to David Curtis Stephenson, known to associates as Steve, the "Old Man" (although he was in his early thirties at the time of his Klan career), the Chief, or, in the style of a military intelligence officer, G1. Stephenson was a phenomenon, a born political genius, immensely ambitious and charming. By the time that Stone Mountain was really getting under way in the early 1920s, he was a major figure in both the Indiana Klan and in mainstream Indiana politics.

In a time when identity was less a matter of pieces of paper and more one of imagination, Stephenson was truly a self-made man, inventing and reinventing himself in roles that advanced the yearning for power that was always a central aspect of his fantastic and highly emotional life. When Borglum met him he had already had a colorful career as a showman but was turning to his true calling, politics. A drifter, an itinerant reporter and typesetter, before the war a professional organizer for the Socialist Party in Oklahoma, he came to Evansville, Indiana, in 1920. With a respectable job as a stock salesman for a coal company and a new wife, he seemed to be settling down a little, leaving behind a past that included the abandonment of his first wife and child and a history of drinking and seduction that had forced him to leave many a small town in a hurry. His charm, organizing ability, and a fictive war record that involved active service in France and the rank of major (he had actually spent the war as a recruiter and an officer candidate in Minnesota and Massachusetts) made him a popular and efficient leader of a veterans' group in Evansville.

It was just at this time that Clarke and Tyler were starting to remodel Simmons's moribund Ku Klux Klan as an aggressive business organization with a broad national base, and Evansville—with a small but visible nonwhite, non-Protestant, non-native-born population—was an attractive site to launch their first recruiting drive outside the states of the Confederacy. Stephenson's skills earned the notice of the recruiter Clarke and Tyler sent to Evansville; and Stephenson, the veterans' organizer whose own real record as a veteran perhaps left him feeling he had something to prove, was attracted to their program of patriotism and 100 percent Americanism. Beyond that, he saw the potential of the Klan to be a truly national vehicle for his political ambitions, much as Borglum did—especially since there seemed to be a policy vacuum at the top level. Stephenson met with the Atlanta leadership and found them primarily concerned with marketing and rituals. He had bigger plans for the organization, and when, soon after his Atlanta meeting, the Klan moved him to Indianapolis and gave him the title of King Kleagle, or chief regional officer, he got started in earnest.

He was tremendously successful. In the early 1920s Stephenson was able to recruit seventy percent of the white, native-born, Protestant men of Indiana to the Klan. On the commission system, this made him a very wealthy man and also gave him great influence in the state.

Stephenson liked money, but it was not his main motivation. He had a talent for consolidation of power, and he went about it in imaginative ways. In Indiana in the 1920s, there was a state-chartered group called the Horse Thief Detective Association, part-time civilian law enforcement officers who, with an authority left over from the days of universal horse transportation, could pursue, arrest, and hold without warrant suspected horse thieves. The organization had persisted into a time when horse thievery was virtually nonexistent, using its charter to pursue car thieves and take vigilante action against boot-leggers and perpetrators of vice.

Most interestingly from Stephenson's point of view, new chapters could be started on the initiative of an existing chapter or member and the payment of a $6.50 filing fee. Stephenson became a Horse Thief Detective and began to set up new chapters all over the state, adding about three thousand members to the existing eleven thousand, an increase that was almost entirely made up of men whom he had recruited to the Klan and the Detectives simultaneously. This meant that he had, in effect, a private police force, highly loyal to him personally, with the legal powers of pursuit and arrest.

Stephenson inspired tremendous loyalty and even adoration, and his Klan power overflowed into legitimate politics. By using strikingly modern methods of polling, advertising, and getting out the vote, he helped to elect Ed Jackson as Indiana secretary of state in 1922 and—even after Stephenson split bitterly with the central Klan organization in Atlanta—governor in 1924. Stephenson's disciplined organization also helped to elect a state treasurer, a state supreme court judge, several mayors, members of the state assembly, and many lesser officials. Once in office, many of these officials worked to pass legislation that favored Stephenson's multifaceted business interests. Another favorite tactic was for Stephenson's legislators to propose laws that would hurt powerful interests—and then withdraw the proposals after Stephenson collected a fee from the interests affected.

The first meeting between Stephenson and Borglum has not been documented, but they both attended a national "Klonvocation" in

November 1922, an event that was a major turning point for the Klan. Imperial Wizard Simmons—who had been on an extended vacation from his Klan duties, leaving Clarke in charge, which had led to some resentment in the ranks—called the meeting more for entertainment and ceremonial purposes than for serious business. Stephenson, a rising star in the Klan, went to Atlanta in a private train car, his expenses paid by his loyal Indiana organization.

Simmons thought the assembled Klan was there to parade, to hear some speeches, have a good time; and incidentally, approve a constitution and formally vote to enthrone him, Simmons, as Imperial Wizard and Emperor. "Emperor" was a ceremonial title used for what the Klan fancied to be affairs of state, and Simmons had held both titles simply as the founder of the organization.

Simmons seems to have been something of an innocent. He was unaware until the last moment that there were far more complicated things than his own agenda going on at the Klonvocation.

Klansmen were plotting. Some of the most powerful men in the organization, including J. C. Comer, the Grand Dragon of Arkansas, H. C. McCall, Grand Dragon of Texas, and Kyle Ramsay, Louisiana Klan secretary, joined by Simmons' own bodyguard Fred Savage, were tired of his rather aimless leadership and had decided to replace him.

While Simmons was obsessed with Klan rituals and publicly disavowed the violence associated with the organization—and while he had left most of the real organizational work to Clarke and Tyler—there was a more activist wing of the leadership that wanted to do more than recruit, recite oaths, and wear odd costumes. The man that Comer, McCall, and their allies chose was a Texas dentist, Hiram Wesley Evans, former Grand Titan of the Texas Klan Province #2 and the Klan National Secretary. He was a true believer who joined the Klan out of allegiance to the idea of white supremacism, not to fool around with rituals. Evans was not concerned with romantic nostalgia for the original Klan. He was a leader of Klan terror in Texas, and was proud of it. Under his leadership the Klan maintained a special "whipping meadow" along the Trinity River in Dallas.

Stephenson was recruited to the coup the night that he arrived in Atlanta for the Klonvocation. That night, Stephenson, Savage, and Evans circulated among the assembled Klan members in their hotel rooms and told them that Simmons wanted to split the Klan powers, with Simmons remaining as Emperor and Evans taking on the administrative role as the new Imperial Wizard.

Then Stephenson and Savage paid a late-night call on Simmons, whom they found sleeping, and told him of an evil plot. The next day, they said, during Simmons' nomination ceremony, a group of the assembled Klansmen were going to attempt to defame him with tales of scandalous immorality. "There is a certain crowd of men here who say that if you are nominated for the office of Imperial Wizard tomorrow, they will get up on the floor and attack your character. And we've just come to tell you that the first man who insults your name will be killed by a sharpshooter right on the spot as he speaks. There'll be enough of us with firearms to take care of the whole convention, if necessary,"[15] Savage assured Simmons.

Simmons was distraught. He had thought he was giving a party and a pageant. Imagining the convention hall soaked in blood during his triumphal moment, he asked if anything could be done to prevent it?

Maybe this, suggested Savage helpfully. Refuse to let your name be put into nomination. Get the group to nominate Evans, the dentist from Texas, instead. You've wanted to drop the day-to-day anxieties of running the organization anyway; you can be Emperor and keep all the honor of the position, while Evans takes on the work of being Imperial Wizard. But you'll be the real leader of the Klan.

Amazingly, Simmons fell for it. Evans was nominated and acclaimed, and immediately he began remaking the Klan in his own image. During the next few years the struggle between the Emperor and the Imperial Wizard would become increasingly public, to the delight of the anti-Klan newspapers such as the *New York World* and Georgia's own *Enquirer-Sun*. Simmons was pushed aside. Although Evans had promised to set up the new Emperor in an ornate "throne room" to receive visitors, no throne was forthcoming, and Simmons spent his days hanging around other people's offices at Klan headquarters. He soon found out that Evans had rewritten the new constitution to arrogate all powers of the Emperor to the Imperial Wizard.

Simmons grew bitter and isolated and eventually left the Klan. He sued his old organization over the use of its rituals and oath, which belonged to him by U.S. copyright, and won a settlement of almost $100,000. That sounds like a lot, except that Simmons had been taking in almost $35,000 a day from the national Klan before the coup, even after Clarke and the local Kleagles had taken their cuts.

Simmons used the money to set up the Knights of the Flaming Sword, and proclaimed himself Monarch.

Borglum attended a prayer breakfast with Simmons, Evans, Stephenson, and the other coup leaders on the morning of the convention coup, and his presence there—noted by William Shepherd in *Collier's* magazine—is one of the very few times his Klan affiliation ever came to public light; he was usually very, very discreet about it. Immediately after the coup, Borglum was named to the Imperial Kloncilium. This was the Klan executive board. He was no outsider, no foot soldier. For the brief time that he was on this committee, Gutzon Borglum, the sculptor of Mount Rushmore, was a high officer of the Klan.

For a while Stephenson's power grew, and he and Borglum tried to guide Evans towards an application of power on a national scale, towards a more respectable public face. Borglum was willing—or Evans believed he was willing—to try to set up a private meeting between Evans and President Harding. In June 1923, Borglum and Stephenson attended the new Imperial Wizard's secret strategy meeting in Washington.

Although Borglum and Stephenson left the meeting feeling that Evans was not a man of vision, Evans was at first reluctant to cross Stephenson. Mindful of the role that the Indiana organizer had played in his coronation, he formally appointed Stephenson Grand Dragon of the Northern Realm at an enormous July 4th Klan rally in Kokomo, Indiana, in 1923. Stephenson made a dramatic entrance, arriving in a private plane flown by his personal pilot, something that was a tremendous novelty at the time. At his investiture Stephenson, who in his Klan associations seems, like Borglum, to have been attracted to the Klan more from ambition than from race hatred, gave an ornate speech about the Constitution—the speech of a bombastic amateur historian, very similar in style to Borglum's writing. Stephenson sent Borglum a copy. He did not wear a Klan robe, although Evans presented him with one, and in fact Stephenson insisted to the end of his life that he had never owned nor worn one.

Simmons later complained to journalist William Shepherd that a pathetic old drunk was seated with the ceremonial party on the dais, and that Stephenson's people whispered among the crowd that this figure was Simmons. Such deceit would not have been unusual for Stephenson, who had a genius for the arranged detail. It is impossible to say whether it was Stephenson who invented Simmons' presence or Simmons who invented Stephenson's invention of Simmons' presence. Each had reason to discredit the other.

It was during the period immediately after Stephenson's investiture that Borglum reached the true depths of his racial nastiness. He showed Stephenson articles not intended for publication outside of Klan circles. Writing to Stephenson on the question of immigration, he displays a faith in biology as destiny that, in this form, goes back to the nineteenth century writings of the French racial theorist Joseph Arthur, le Comte de Gobineau, whose writings were to influence the Nazis. Such ideas were not rare in Borglum's time, and sometimes leaned on a misunderstanding of Darwinian science, which to modern eyes only makes the thesis more drearily predictable. But Borglum's writing is mixed with flashes of real venom.

He seems to have been trying hard to get into the spirit of the Klan, and to have succeeded all too well.

[The Nordic races] have been and continue today the pioneers of the world. They are the builders of world empire . . . it may safely be said that all invention, analytical science, deductive philosophy have been pushed forward . . . by these venturesome peoples, who have subdued savages, beautified and peopled what was in the Roman day the wilderness and is now the richest, most comfortable, best established, most sought portion of the earth . . . America has been peopled by these free, independent thinking races . . . the dark races have never moved in block or with any group conviction but always from the urge of individual misery . . . the oriental has no constructive initiative. The dark races were also moved by the desire to attach or associate with the more prosperous of strange peoples. Here we have in the filtering of Asiatic and North African blood [into Europe] the complete vitiating of the vigor and intellect of the civilization existing in these once pure European peoples.

The Nordic has ever been a camp maker; the Mediterranean . . . a camp follower. The one establishes, creates, builds, the other attaches, feeds upon, corrupts . . . it is not overstating the case that while Anglo-Saxons have themselves sinned grievously against the principle of pure nationalism by illicit slave and alien servant traffic, it has been the character of the cargo that has eaten into the very moral fiber of our race character, rather than the moral depravity of Anglo-Saxon traders . . . [in southern Europe] no student of ethnology, or history or government or political economy need look for other cause of three thousand years of rape and rapine . . . than the mongrel blood that has destroyed original race purity . . .

And so on, and so on, for nine pages. At one point the man who would later glorify the conquest of the "West World" and who was himself the son of an immigrant, a Mormon religious dissident from Denmark, writes with completely unconscious irony:

We are the enemies of no people, of no creed, of no political isms, when *applied in other countries*. As the sons of our fathers we claim the same indigenous right to protect ourselves from invasion of "isms" alien to our own . . .

He appends a Notes section that includes the following observations.

Every step in the course of west world civilization has been opened up by Anglo-Saxon Americans. Mexico is one hundred years behind Turkey.

If you cross a thoroughbred with a jackass you get a

mule. If you cross a pure bred with a mongrel dog you get a mongrel.

So in races, as Madison Grant states: "Cross an Englishman with a Hindu, the offspring is Hindu; Englishman with Chinese, offspring Chinese; Englishman with Negro, offspring Negro; Englishman with Jew, offspring Jew."

If you cross any of the others with each other it is curious that the lowest race in civilization is the strongest physically and breeding (crossed) is always down. A Negro and Jew will produce Negro, but Hindu and Jew—Jew. Chinese and Jew, offspring Jew; Italian and Jew, offspring Jew; any European race and Jew, offspring Jew.[16]

Elsewhere in his correspondence with Stephenson Borglum suggests that something very like slavery should be re-established in the United States, in regard to "alien" workers:

There is only one colony in the United States and the federal government must assume guidance of colonies of Poles, Hungarians, Italians, and break them up in a proper humane manner by American schools and complete American control. A certain portion of all aliens should have their labor designated for them until such time as the government could control its trained and untrained labor market and move the surplus as needed.[17]

When Evans, paranoid and jealous, turned against Stephenson later in 1923, Borglum interceded on his behalf. The Evans-Stephenson split was to become a major issue in the Klan, echoing through the elections of 1924.

Borglum corresponded with Stephenson for many years and tried hard to work with him against what they both saw as the coarsening influence of Evans in the Klan.

Borglum had begun to grow disillusioned with Evans soon after the coup. As one of his Klan responsibilities, the sculptor sat on a policy committee that was to form a new national program for the Klan. He took to this work with his usual energy. Forming national programs was the kind of thing Borglum lived for, and he still believed that he could turn the Klan into something like the populist self-help organizations in defense of farmers that he had seen in North Dakota. Typically, however, he was disappointed in the failings of lesser men, and disgusted to find, once again, that his political ideas were not honored and recognized. Speaking of the report produced by the committee and its chairman, Clarke, he wrote petulantly to Stephenson:

> . . . you can well imagine my astonishment . . . to find a totally different committee had been created without reference to what I had done . . . I am now thoroughly convinced that the South will continue in its bondage;

that the nigger will continue to nominate the President of the United States; and that the Klan, as such, will not raise an intelligent, helpful, constructive finger to free the South and to free the nation from that damnable situation. And that is true because you have not five men on the Kloncilium that you can trust with the task, or three with any part of it . . . [18]

Six months later, after meeting with Evans on a mission of reconciliation for Stephenson, with the upcoming 1924 Republican presidential convention in mind, he was even more fed up with the Klan and its leadership's inability to forcefully proclaim a national program.

. . . a Jew, a negro or a Romanist could not crawl into a more cowardly position nor seek neutral ground more quickly than did every Klan leader I appealed to, the Dr. included, except Andy, since you and I talked. Then I brought up the Negro question, who the President has insisted shall not only be awarded their usual representation in this Republican convention, but some southern states shall have an increase of negro delegates. The Dr. has completely backed down on that matter too . . . My Northwesterners are standing shoulder to shoulder, I glory in the little part I've been able to play and the confidence I hold there, we are going on, and we are going to succeed, the entire power of organized Judism cannot stop us.[19]

Whatever his disgust with the fading political potential of the Klan, Borglum's disappointment suggests the emotional investment he had made in it.

When Stephenson, hounded by Evans and accused (probably falsely) of embezzling Klan funds, was forced to yield his Grand Dragon title only a few months after receiving it, Borglum was about ready to give up on the Klan. He turned his back on Evans and sided with Stephenson, suggesting a partnership outside of the Klan in terms tinged with his usual sense of his own messianic destiny:

> . . . I wish you could somehow abandon all these other organizations and devote yourself in a large way to National affairs, preparing yourself to take a part in National work. You have demonstrated so abundantly your ability and leadership, why not use that for National purposes entirely rather than for so called "fraternity" purposes. . . . The last two Conventions have demonstrated to me that there is but one way of affecting our National life, and that is through large economic movements, such as the farm movement, cotton movement which is the detail of the movement to force National production and National marketing. . . .
>
> . . . Steve, I want you to be in on this, but I want you to come into it *on your own account*, wholly and solely committed to the economic salvation of the great producing body of American citizenry.[20]

Borglum's friendship with Stephenson and the rift with Evans were enormously important at Stone Mountain. There, Hollins Randolph was a loyal Evans partisan, which meant that he and Borglum saw each other with growing hostility and suspicion. Evans wanted to consolidate control over the monument, the more so since the idea of a Confederate memorial was popular in the South and the Klan needed to burnish its civic image. Borglum was not going to put his monument at the service of Evans's organization.

National politics entered the picture, too. The Evans faction was preparing to come out as a force at the Democratic convention of 1924 by supporting William Gibbs McAdoo, a candidate who was rumored to be sympathetic to the Klan. Borglum, who considered himself an independent-minded Republican, could on occasion support a Democrat for president—he campaigned enthusiastically for FDR in 1932—but McAdoo was closely associated with Wilson, and Borglum despised Wilson as weak and dishonest; he had never forgotten how Wilson had distanced himself from Borglum's World War I aircraft investigation, refusing even to pay his expenses. Borglum eventually came out very strongly for the Republican nominee, Calvin Coolidge, the incumbent who had ascended to the presidency after Warren Harding's death in San Francisco the previous year. Coolidge was the man who would, of course, eventually be indispensable to the success of the Rushmore project.

Hollins Randolph took Borglum's refusal to back McAdoo as a sign of his Northerner's perfidy. Co-operation between the sculptor and the Stone Mountain committee was becoming increasingly difficult.

This would have been a bad time for Borglum to be publicly identified as a Klansman. Joseph Pulitzer's *New York World* had been doing spectacular exposés of Klan terror for more than a year. At the Democratic convention the *World* kept the spotlight on Klan leaders and Klan candidates, doing features on Evans' presence at a hotel near the convention. Almost every day of the Democratic and Republican conventions the *World* pressed them to adopt an anti-Klan plank. Mindful of Southern votes, neither party would denounce the Klan by name. At the Democratic convention the pro- and anti-Klan forces came to blows on the floor. Although there were other important matters on the agenda—United States membership in the League of Nations, the International Court of Justice, farm relief, women's rights, prohibition—the question of whether or not to denounce the Klan by name became the overwhelming issue.

McAdoo was not a Klansman but he was counting on Southern support. Evans and the Klan had let it be known that if they could not be sure of McAdoo, they would throw their support to Indiana Senator Samuel Ralston, a good friend to the Klan.

McAdoo's refusal to denounce the Klan was to be his downfall. His candidacy was over when he was greeted at the convention and in newspaper editorials with jeers of "Ku Ku McAdoo!" In a test of endurance that seemed to go on forever in the New York summer heat, the deadlocked convention swung back and forth between McAdoo and his strongest challenger, New York governor Al Smith, before finally nominating the compromise candidate John Davis on the 103rd ballot on July 9, after meeting for almost two weeks. It was the longest American political convention on record.

Borglum's split with Randolph over the 1924 election was a serious blow to their co-operation at Stone Mountain. Stephenson, still close with Borglum, had been more of an embarrassment than a rival to the Evans Klan throughout the election. For all his canniness, he had a reckless and violent quality that destroyed him soon after he reached his point of greatest power.

In 1925 Stephenson was a defendant in the most spectacular trial in Indiana history. He was accused of kidnapping a twenty-eight-year-old clerk, Madge Oberholtzer, and repeatedly raping her on an overnight train from Indianapolis to Chicago. When they reached the city Oberholtzer was checked into a hotel with him and then, accompanied by a Stephenson bodyguard, she slipped out to buy a hat. She bought the hat and, surreptitiously, some mercury bichloride powder, which she swallowed; a month later, when she was dying, she said that she did this as a way of forcing Stephenson to take her back to Indiana. There was some doubt at the trial as to whether Oberholtzer's death had been caused by the poison or by infection from the deep bites that Stephenson had inflicted all over her body.

Stephenson went to prison on a conviction of murder in the second degree, a conviction on which he would serve thirty-three years of his thirty-years-to-life sentence, although he was constantly appealing and garnered a great deal of media attention.

When the state Republican establishment, many of whose members were adherents of his Klan faction and beholden to him for their positions, failed to protect him, and when his protégé and political creation Governor Ed Jackson, mindful of how it would look, refused to pardon him, information about Stephenson's connections with powerful politicians began to leak out of Stephenson's prison cell in Michigan City, Indiana. Soon the state was embroiled in an enormous bribery scandal, fed by information from Stephenson's "black boxes," the repositories of his political IOUs. The scandal eventually enveloped Indianapolis City Controller W. C. Buser, Marion County Republican Party chair George Coffin, and Governor Jackson himself. At the federal level, it led to investigations of Klan-orchestrated corruption in Indiana and in the campaign of U.S. Senator Arthur Robinson.

All of these men were close to Stephenson and to the Indiana Klan. The investigations and Stephenson's continuing incarceration—he served the longest sentence ever served for second-degree murder in Indiana—led to generations of speculation that he was being kept locked up because of the political establishment's fear of what he might reveal if he were freed or because of what he had already revealed. The scandal was a major factor in public distrust of the Klan after 1924.

Stephenson remained close to Borglum until Borglum's death in 1941, and close to his widow Mary after that, corresponding with them from prison. The Borglums always insisted that he had been framed for political reasons. There is some evidence that this may have been the case.

Borglum's friendship with Stephenson, on top of his now open dislike for Evans and his refusal to help the McAdoo campaign, made Borglum's position increasingly difficult with the Stone Mountain Committee. However, the proximate cause of their final conflict was the success of a fund-raising scheme that Borglum had arranged with the federal government, in which a Stone Mountain half dollar, designed by Borglum, was sold for a dollar, the profits being given to the project.

The scheme was wildly successful. It eventually raised almost three million dollars. This made the fund a tempting source of income to Randolph, whose accounting practices, according to audits made soon after Borglum had his final falling out with the committee, were found to be less than orthodox. After many years of being underfunded, the Stone Mountain project had enormous potential income in 1924. To keep control of this windfall and to use it to increase the influence of the Evans branch of the Klan, Randolph called a surprise meeting of the Stone Mountain executive committee, packed it with his allies, and changed the nominating rules, taking it out of the control of original officers affiliated with the United Daughters of the Confederacy. This action meant to Borglum that Randolph was his enemy and the enemy of the project. Although the coins had already been minted, he prevailed upon the Treasury Department and President Coolidge not to release them to the association for distribution to advance buyers.

Infuriated, Randolph and his new committee fired Borglum and attempted to hire his assistant, Jesse Tucker, to finish the job using Borglum's models and designs. Tucker reported the plan to Borglum, who destroyed his studio models and pushed the working model at the site over the cliff, smashing it to pieces. Randolph, believing that under Borglum's contract the models belonged to the Stone Mountain Association, called out the police.

This led to one of the most dramatic scenes of Borglum's career, as he and Tucker, fugitives from the law, fled in a wild car chase to North Carolina, where Borglum's friend Angus McLean was governor and refused to extradite him to Georgia. This turned into an affair that lasted for years and almost ruined Borglum's chance at Rushmore; the Stone Mountain Association and much of the Southern press did their best to brand him as a saboteur, a vandal, and a thief and flooded the South Dakota civic organizations enlisted as Rushmore fund-raisers and sponsors with pamphlets to that effect.

Many influential people in the South and Southwest were willing to listen to Randolph, one of their own. In 1928—three years after Borglum's flight from Georgia—Henry Johnston, the governor of Oklahoma, when asked by Randolph if legal action against Borglum was justified, replied in the ringing tones of a lost style of public discourse:

> The murderer has taken that which he cannot restore. The incendiary by firebrand may destroy the homes of the poor and the rich alike. The despoiler of childhood leaves wreckage in his pathway. . . . The act of Herr Borglum is an act of murder, of destruction, of arson, of desecration, of vandalism. . . . Borglum has the heart of a criminal . . . . He has wounded the heart of the South . . . he is beyond the pale of decent manhood . . . Prosecute every case that you have against him. . . . Let the case become another monument erected to the memory and virility of the men who followed Jackson and of the

devotees of Robert E. Lee. Though I knew I would lose, I would prosecute this case through the last court with definite intensity, even as a warrior wounded unto death and at the point of being hurled from a precipice would yet defy his destroyer.[21]

Well! This sort of thing followed Borglum through the rest of his career and finally made it impossible for him ever again to work at Stone Mountain, although to the end of his life he was certain that he would be invited back to finish the task after others had tried and failed to accomplish it.

The association gave the contract to the sculptor Augustus Lukeman, a far lesser talent than Borglum, who blasted all of Borglum's work off the mountain—Lukeman sometimes justified this act by saying that Borglum had sculpted Lee wearing a hat, that there might be ladies among the observers, and that the real Lee would never have kept his hat on in the presence of a lady. Lukeman spent a tremendous amount of money, and accomplished very little. Sam Venable spent the rest of his life locked in conflict with the association, regretting deeply that any committee led by the likes of Hollins Randolph had got its hands on his mountain, but he was unable to regain control. At one point, after Lukeman took over, Venable was reduced to writing rather pathetically to Borglum: "Dear Gutzon—could you in any way get some paper to publish that Lukeman is a Jew . . . it would create a pause among many people in our Country."[22]

Furious with the organization for its actions at Stone Mountain, its rejection of his plans and its treatment of Stephenson, Borglum ended his Klan affiliation absolutely in 1925. But whatever his modern apologists may say of this embarrassing episode in his life, there is more to it than his crackpot hope to redirect the Klan's political energies. Before the Stone Mountain debacle, before the disintegration of the Klan as a powerful nationwide entity, during the time that Borglum and Stephenson were trying to influence the leaders and capture the direction of the Klan, Borglum seems to have enthusiastically embraced the Klan's white supremacism. His writings from this period give the impression of a man trying on a set of ideas, being tempted by their radicalism. They express a much more extreme form of racism than he practiced in any other period of his life, before and after.

Much of this may be, as his biographers Howard and Audrey Karl Shaff would have it, the temporary focus of a man dazzled by purely political possibilities, one who might take positions contrary to his better nature and later feel ashamed of them. What is interesting about Borglum's racism and xenophobia from this period, however, is that while it may be a cruder version, it is perfectly consistent with his long-standing conviction of western cultural superiority. This, indeed—no matter how embarrassing to the monument administration and to his biographers—is part of the legacy of Mount Rushmore. It is not an accident or a by-product, but something intended by the sculptor to signify a fact of life: the triumph of right, of good, of enlightenment, of the Nordic races, in the conquest of the "West world."

A postscript.

Downtown Atlanta still has some remnants of decaying Southern charm, but it is mostly plastic strip malls punctuated by slums and traversed by broad avenues with strangely bucolic names, along which commuters careen with reckless ferocity: Peachtree Boulevard, Piedmont Way.

Apparently Atlanta is famous for its bad drivers. In three days there I saw four fatal accidents.

When I asked the desk clerk at my hotel where to go to see some of the town, he directed me to the suburb of Buckhead, which is full of yuppie bars in strip malls. The malls have the greatest number of "adult clubs" I've ever seen in suburbia. This is ultra-"Family Values" Cobb County. Newt Gingrich used to represent this district.

In the Fulton County library, two ladies earnestly discussed the Book of Revelation across their study carrels. "No, you see Jesus knew that would happen *before* the sea turned to blood. . . . This was the meaning of the prophecy in . . . Wasn't that what Paul referred to in his Letter to the Corinthians?"

Walking in downtown Atlanta, I saw a plaque commemorating a famous event. The word *reconciliation* is prominent in the inscription, and at first I took it for a New South, post–civil rights marker. But no. It commemorates the reconciliation of Jefferson Davis and James Longstreet, one of Davis's estranged generals with whom he had not spoken since the dark days of Reconstruction. At the dedication of a statue to U.S. Senator Benjamin Hill in 1886, Longstreet, seeing Davis giving a speech on this spot, impulsively strode up to the platform and embraced him. All the bad blood was washed away.

At least all that particular bad blood. What joy a black person might take in this historic event is hard to imagine.

Most of the white people I saw in the town and in the suburbs were pressed and clean, in polo shirts and sneakers and perfectly brushed hair. The black people in the suburbs were more or less in the same style. Black people in downtown Atlanta were sullen and, when circumstances required them to engage with me, almost inarticulate. In America class masquerades as race—but we react to it as race.

At the entrance to the metro station a group of hate-crazed Black Israelites were holding forth in their bizarre garb (I thought they were a New York thing?) showing how the Bible proves that they are the real Jews, the chosen people, and that the "so-called white Jews" and other "so-called white people" are devils and usurpers who have never contributed a single thing to civilization. It occurred to me that this is Borglum, reversed. They'd attracted a medium-sized crowd of black people of all ages and, so far as I could tell, classes. It was impossible to say whether the onlookers were attracted by the entertainment value of insanity or whether they took the rants seriously.

I wandered over to a park where some sort of rock event was going on. Virtually all the spectators were white, well-groomed professionals, many of them carrying babies. Virtually all the guards and support staff were black.

A band was playing a medley of classic rock songs, each song segueing into the next with an identical beat, every now and then cycling back to Queen's "We Will Rock You." The band played all the traditional numbers: "Jack and Diane," "Sweet Home Alabama," "Walk This Way," "After Midnight" (the Eric Clapton version, of course, not the superior J. J. Cale original), "Born to Run." The musicians were competent but utterly without creative spark.

They headed into a Rolling Stones tribute set. Suddenly some-thing occurred to me. Would they–? Surely not here, not nowadays.

By the time they'd run through "Honky Tonk Women," "Sym-pathy for the Devil," "Gimme Shelter," and "Satisfaction"—what other song rightfully ends a Rolling Stones tribute set?—I figured we were safe. But then those signature open-A-tuned, five-string-guitar, Keith Richards–special seven chords rang out, those four sin-gular notes following right behind them, as insinuating as death, one of the most instantly recognizable and powerful openings in the whole rock canon.

Unfortunately I cannot quote the lyrics to *Brown Sugar* here, but no doubt they would be familiar to many readers: the slave ships, the cotton fields, the slaver having the time of his life as he whips the women, with rape—and the enslaved women's enjoyment of rape—strongly implied.

No reaction at all from the white crowd as the servants' faces went blank. It was just another song to them. The middle-aged rock-star wannabes onstage, the balding guys with their ponytails, the female backup singer imitating Stevie Nicks imitating a Gypsy, all seemed to be having a great time, stomping and yelling it out. I pretty much ran out of the park.

The song was not intended as a provocation. The performance was completely unconscious. I was thinking, Is this part of why the Black Israelites can get a crowd together—so blacks can hear them call whites devils?

From this, on to Stone Mountain, cradle of the reborn Klan.

Rushmore may be a national monument, but Stone Mountain

Village—as distinct from the town of Stone Mountain, Georgia, which is a real community—is a theme park. The village sits on huge, carefully manicured grounds that offer paddleboat rides, golf courses, a standard-gauge railroad, an antique car and treasure museum, and a Confederate museum with dusty, out-of-date exhibits—which don't get as much traffic as the amusement park. There is a 330-room hotel. There is a nightly laser light show on the bas-relief sculpture, reduced from Borglum's original plan to three figures, Jefferson Davis, Stonewall Jackson, and Robert E. Lee. There is an aerial tramway to the top of the mountain. You can see all the attractions for seventeen dollars plus seven for parking.

The stone carving was eventually finished, but not by Lukeman. The state of Georgia took over the project in 1958 and hired a Yankee, Walker Hancock from Massachusetts, to finish it. It was dedicated in 1970, a bas-relief carving on the side of the mountain comprising the figures of Jefferson Davis, Robert E. Lee, and "Stonewall" Jackson. President Nixon was supposed to give an address, but he was busy, so Vice President Spiro Agnew stood in.

The museum has a silly exhibit on the making of *Gone With the Wind*—silly until you realize what Sherman and the burning of Atlanta still mean around here. A historical section, actually very informative, tells of the development of settlements around Stone Mountain. The story here echoes that of the Great Sioux Reservation. The Creek and Cherokee lost slices of their land as the government kept promising to leave them in peace if they would only move farther west. When the Stone Mountain area was opened to white settlement by the Treaty of Indian Springs in 1821, the government surveyed the land and distributed it by lottery. Stone Mountain itself, after several transfers of ownership, was quarried for its granite, which is now found in the steps of the U.S. Capitol, the locks of the Panama Canal, and the capitol building in Havana, among other places. The Cherokee were eventually removed a lot farther west—to Oklahoma—in 1838.

There is a brief mention of Klan activity at Stone Mountain, although nothing is said of the active support of Venable, Borglum, Randolph, and Plane, the key figures in the early history of the monument.

Despite all the amusement park attractions, the mountain itself is the star, a stunning mass of igneous rock rising straight and sheer into the sky. The carved area on its side looks a little ludicrous, a huge blasted field in which the three bas-relief horsemen march across the mountain, the horses' legs fading away into the granite.

From on top of Stone Mountain all Atlanta and a great deal of the surrounding region is laid out for the visitor. On the windswept bald dome it is very hot, far up above the wispy clouds.

Ironically, Stone Mountain has accomplished what Rushmore has not. The crowds who come here are what is now called "diverse." While it was conceived as a monument to white supremacy, the world has changed around it and the multicultural Atlantan sprawl is now lapping at its edges. At a suburban shopping-mall cinema just like every other suburban shopping-mall cinema I've ever seen, a billboard advertised a "Bollywood Film Festival," catering to the many Indians—the other kind of Indians—who have moved into the neighborhood. When I rode the tramway to the top of the mountain, I shared the car with Hindu and Iranian women and their children, the Indians in saris, the Iranians in long dresses and headscarves. The Iranian women spoke to each other in the beautiful Persian language, then broke off to speak to their children in broadly accented English. The accent was backwoods Georgia, not Tabriz.

Yes, quite a few black Americans too, pressed and polo-shirted in good suburban style. Before coming here I assumed that black people would shun a monument to Davis, Jackson, and Lee. I was wrong. They shell out for the tramway and the railroad ride—complete with a comedy team that stages an incompetent holdup—just like everyone else.

And I realized something. The American Way has won here, but not as Borglum and the Klan assumed it would. Stone Mountain is business, it's entertainment, with all meaning and historical significance leached out of it. The park is owned by the state of Georgia, but its day-to-day operations are handled by Silver Dollar City, a conglomerate that runs several other amusement parks, including Dollywood, Dolly Parton's commercial fantasyland. The company's mission statement reads: "Silver Dollar City, Inc., is a company dedicated to creating memories worth repeating! We immerse our guests in unique, highly themed environments that bring to life the adventure, entertainment and wonder of another century."[23]

At Stone Mountain and later at Rushmore, Borglum never doubted the eternal and universal meaning of his message. It just goes to show.

9

INDIANS PERFORM AT RUSHMORE

I ndians appear on the margins of the official Rushmore story from its beginning, never quite as agents of action, but as colorful extras in the unfolding narrative. Rushmore and Indians are the chief attractions in a part of the land where the opening of the frontier is only a few generations back. There is a certain rugged sentimentality in that; and asserting a vision of American destiny, the blessing of the American natives—whether sincere, contrived, extorted, or imagined hardly matters—is a sort of shortcut to affirming the authenticity of the settler heritage. Indians participated in all of the official dedications and ceremonies at Rushmore until the 1970s, when their blessing became more problematical.

Let there be no doubt: the Indians who participated in the early ceremonies at Rushmore did so because they wanted to, many without pay. At a time when Indians had been taught in boarding schools and by government agents and missionaries for several generations that their culture was inferior, that their best hope lay in embracing white values, white economics, and white religion, white colonials were not the only ones lacking a sense of irony at the Rushmore pageants. Indeed, Indians from the various reservations clamored for representation if they felt they had been slighted in the program. Some paid positions existed, and a need to earn a living, coupled with a desire to show whites that Lakota culture had its own glories, won other Indian participants. If education, display, and making some money could be combined, why not? Henry Standing Bear, a friend of Borglum's, who was old enough to remember Red Cloud's War and the Little Bighorn, once wrote to Borglum:

> I wish to know if you will be able to use a 100% Native American in any of your exhibits this summer.
>
> I am one of the few remaining real Siouxs. I was a young man when "Long Hair" [Custer] made his fatal mistake; I knew the land when Buffalo were plentiful and the Sioux really had meat to eat; I was a Scout in the service of the United States Army when our Cheyenne cousins were misled; I am glad to say I was not present at the Wounded Knee massacre, but was on duty after that tragedy.
>
> My services are frequently in demand by those who want the typical American; I have been exhibited in all large eastern cities; I was one of three representatives of the tribe taken to Chicago to represent the city of Deadwood a few years ago; the other two were ill and it

remained for me to carry on alone. I have testimonials to show I did my part well. . . . I was in Washington, D.C., this spring; I expect an engagement in Colorado later in the year, but if you have any place where a genuine American can be used, please let me hear from you.[1]

When Borglum came to the Black Hills for the initial dedication in 1925, he wired ahead to Doane Robinson in Pierre, "SHALL BRING SOME COSTUMES FOR CEREMONIES. CAN YOU GET A FEW REAL INDIANS FOR SPECTATORS."[2] The Associated Black Hills Commercial Clubs found some. The non-Indians who made it up the mountain from Keystone were treated to an overture from a thirty-piece band, speeches from congressmen, and elk sandwiches. Charly Black Horse and a party of six gave a "war dance" and an Omaha walking dance.[3]

Borglum gave a speech in which he promised that a part of the ancient stone behind him would be a statue of George Washington "within a twelvemonth!"[4]

Then Borglum and some assistants climbed to the top of Rushmore and summoned an Indian on a horse to preside silently over the rest of the proceedings. It is not known whether the indian wore his own clothes or one of Borglum's costumes.

Then, in complete solemnity, enormous British, Spanish, and French flags—representing former European claimants of the Black Hills—were raised and then lowered by men in frontier costume. The flag raisings were accompanied by salutatory volleys from the Fort Meade cavalry and the lowerings by the national anthem of the country in question, in accordance with the habit of treating flags as totemic objects, homes national to spirits that demand respect. This ceremony sealed the passing of the land from aboriginals whose own totemism was considered by whites to be a proof of their primitivism.

Finally, the American flag flew over the gathering, the band played the "Star-Spangled Banner," and a minister gave a benediction. The American flag remained aloft as the ceremony closed and the crowd headed back to Keystone.

The next dedication of the mountain came when President Coolidge vacationed in the Black Hills in the summer of 1927. His blessing was vital to the Rushmore project. Private funds in adequate amounts had not been forthcoming, and government support—and presidential enthusiasm—was going to be necessary for the completion of the project. It was during this presidential vacation that Borglum captured Coolidge's interest and invited him to write the text of the Entablature.

Throughout his visit Coolidge was the subject of much adoring press coverage, and Indians extended honors to him, too. In an event widely covered by the press, on August 4, at the Days of '76 gold rush celebration in Deadwood, Coolidge was ceremoniously inducted into the Sioux Nation, and named Chief Wanbli Tokaha—Leading Eagle. Coolidge agreed to visit the Pine Ridge reservation on August 17. The Indians would have preferred to perform the ritual on the reservation, but the convenience of the tourists and local businesses took precedence.

The ceremony was performed by Chauncy Yellow Robe, who, in

magazine photographs, is shown first in a business suit, then in buckskin, with a feather bonnet over his close-cropped hair. It is hard to imagine what the reticent, buttoned-down president made of the procedure, which involved being fitted with his own traditional eagle-feather bonnet. The ceremonial address, given in the Lakota language by Henry Standing Bear, is a masterpiece of diplomacy, with much more hinted at then stated, and with an implicit agenda.

> Mr. President, it is a great honor to us that you have come among us and into our camp. We have nothing to give but our national respect, receive you into our people as one of us, and confer on you the honor place in our tribe left vacant by Sitting Bull, Spotted Tail and Red Cloud.
>
> It is fitting that we are here standing side by side as brothers on this historical ground which was the very part of these Black Hills for which our people have long struggled against the whites and made our people and your people enemies.
>
> We are here today as your people. In our relationships with your people our forefathers handed down to us the tale of certain lamented events like the Custer battle, but marked as memorials to high and worthy examples for a future relationship more enlightened.
>
> Today we are here together again, in an event which shall mark in our history and in which one of the greatest

of American peoples shall pay their highest national respect to you, by adopting you into the tribe, making you their High Chief, giving you a name to uphold.

Our fathers and chiefs, Sitting Bull, Spotted Tail and Red Cloud, may have made mistakes; but their hearts were brave and strong, their purposes honest and noble. They have long gone to their Happy Hunting Ground, and we call upon you, as our new High Chief, to take up their leadership and fulfill the same duty call from which they never did shrink, a duty to protect and help the weak.[5]

The President spent a day at the Pine Ridge reservation two weeks later. In a message as diplomatic as the speech of Henry Standing Bear, Indian leaders of the Niobrara Convention of the Episcopal Church greeted Coolidge and remarked on the contrast between conditions of the present day and fifty years past, when

those who killed Custer hated the white man. Now in the same place are gathered hundreds of Christian Indians, engaged in religious meetings. . . . We seek not the lives of our white brothers; it is rather some of them who seek what little we possess.

. . . You hold our fortune in your hands; you and your successors control our destiny. With the passing of the old free life, the old world of the Indian disappeared forever. If we live at all, we and our children must live the new world of the white man, and we must have your help to do this.[6]

Coolidge, in his reply, seems to have missed the point. He referred to the "Battle of Wounded Knee," which he called "the last event of enough importance to be listed by the War Department as an Indian campaign."[7] This was tactless at best. Coolidge was speaking in Pine Ridge Village, a few miles from the mass grave. He did not visit the site.

Speaking to an Indian audience, he brought them the news that there were "over 200 tribes and bands in the United States, each with its own name, tongue, history, traditions, code of ethics and customs, which have the effect of law with Indian tribes."[8] He then said,

> Many Indians are still in a primitive state, although strongly influenced by white contacts, and thousands are as civilized as their neighbors. . . .
>
> Within recent years, agriculture and stock raising have been gaining ground in the economic progress of the Indian people; but many of them are still unable at this time to take their places in the world as self-supporting farmers, mechanics, manufacturers and skilled laborers.
>
> Since the enactment of the General Allotment Law and the establishment of schools for Indian education, there has been remarkable progress made in their

advancement and development, and they are being trained and encouraged to become self-supporting.[9]

It is not fair to judge a president of the 1920s by the standards of political discourse prevailing eight decades later. Still, leaving aside the condescension of this speech, one would have expected him to be careful about the truth and to have his people do decent advance work.

In fact, the Pine Ridge Oglala Sioux and other Sioux tribes in the region were in bad shape. Starting near the turn of the century, many of the Sioux were indeed becoming self-sufficient, living lives less close to the edge of destitution, as cattle ranchers—an occupation that had some distant cultural resonance with the old hunting way of life that had disappeared with the buffalo. But at the time Coolidge spoke, this economic upturn was ending. The economic problem on Pine Ridge went back not only to the taking of the Black Hills but to the land grabs and the further evolution of the reservation system— indeed, to the General Allotment Law that Coolidge praised.

Settlers—now mostly farmers and ranchers rather than prospectors—poured into western Dakota Territory in the 1880s. Congress responded by passing the Dawes Act in 1887, a measure that involved tradeoffs between local, state, and federal powers and that had a complicated set of interests behind it. The Dawes Act was at least partially an attempt to straighten out land relationships and make land available for settlers and railroad building in advance of eventual statehood for North and South Dakota. The act apportioned land to Indian heads of families on application for a land patent, thus destroying the cultural claim to common tribal use of the land. This was, of course, part of a longstanding American ideological prejudice against any sort of communalism; as early as 1838 the Commissioner of Indian Affairs, Hartley Crawford, wrote with assurance, "Common property and civilization cannot co-exist."[10]

Under the Dawes Act Indians would receive from eighty to six hundred and forty acres of land, depending on the quality of the land, the size of the family, and the version of the legislation in force at the time. It provided for a twenty-five-year "patent in trust," during which the government would serve as trustee over the land granted while the patent holder learned white ways and took up farming, after which he would receive a "patent in fee" and would be able to sell his land. When allotments had been finalized, the government would have the right to distribute "surplus" land—that not allotted to Indians—to settlers at a fixed rate, the price to be paid to the Indians but the money held by the government and invested on their behalf.

The 1877 agreement with the Sioux being in effect, the Dawes Act did not apply on the reservation right away, but Congress unilaterally drafted an "agreement" in 1888 that would effectively extend it to the Sioux with their consent—except that homesteading was allowed on Indian land before the process of allotment had even been completed. Under the formula for allotment in the agreement, the Great Sioux Reservation had more than twice as much land as the Indians "needed," so large chunks could be excised right away.

The reservation was to be broken up into six smaller reservations centered on the old Standing Rock, Cheyenne River, Crow Creek,

Lower Brulé, Red Cloud, and Spotted Tail agencies, the places where the old chiefs had settled down with their bands. The Sioux, pressed to accept this plan by a commission led by Richard Pratt, would have none of it. Although Pratt produced some Indian signatures, Congress found evidence of manipulation and bad faith and did not allow the plan to go into effect without the Indians' consent.

In pursuit of a similar plan, General George Crook reappeared among the Sioux in 1889, again as a member of a commission, offering essentially the same plan on slightly better terms. Under this plan, the government would buy up nine million acres left over after allotment for resale to settlers at low cost. Indians who accepted patents in trust would become U.S. citizens. There was a certain urgency on the government's part this time, for in February the legislation was passed that would create North and South Dakota out of the Dakota Territory and admit them to the Union in November of that year. Unless the plan was implemented, most of the new state of South Dakota west of the Missouri, except for the Black Hills area, would be off-limits to white homesteading. A Republican Congress and president, Benjamin Harrison, had been inaugurated in 1888, and the Dakota Territory settlers were known to be heavily Republican. Once statehood gave them the right to vote, the more of them there were, the better.

Crook was a better negotiator than Pratt. He feasted the Indians, allowed them to dance a little—the Indian Department had classed dancing as an "Indian Offense" since 1883—and worked on individual "progressive" leaders in isolation from the traditional councils and assemblies, which had resolved in advance that they were not even going to talk to Crook and his commission. Armed with promises that the old ration agreements would not be broken, threats that the alternatives would be worse, and copious presents, Crook won over many influential moderates at the agencies, who had learned the lesson that the government could take their lands with or without their consent, with or without compensation.

The Lakota as a group struggled to understand the agreement, debated it, talked about it, listened to their leaders. They sought ironclad assurances that their rations would not be cut, that the other subsidies put in place by the treaty of 1868 would remain in force. They demanded and received assurances of compensation on unrelated issues, as for ponies seized from the Red Cloud and Red Leaf bands by the government in 1876. They also asked Crook to present further bills for damages and land to the government on their behalf, which Crook said he would do but that he insisted could not be considered part of the negotiations in hand, although the Indians may have considered that acceptance of these bills was conditional upon acceptance of the agreement.

In the end many signed, led by "progressives" like John Grass at Standing Rock, Chasing Crow at Cheyenne River, and American Horse at Pine Ridge. They did this not because they were happy with the agreement but because they believed it was the best deal they could get.

Crook did not win over Red Cloud, and he did not win over Sitting Bull, the very last important Sioux leader to surrender to the reservation system—although Sitting Bull had spoken in favor of the plan a year earlier in Washington, if the Sioux could get a better price than was offered at the time—but Crook could plausibly claim[11] to have secured the signatures of three-quarters of the adult male population that the treaty of 1868 required; the guardians of Indian policy had insisted on at least this much. The agreement was enshrined in the Great Sioux Act of 1889.

Two weeks after Crook left, Congress reduced the Sioux appropriation for the coming fiscal year by 10 percent, and the Indian bureau cut rations accordingly. The meat ration on the newly defined Pine Ridge reservation went down 40 percent—which resulted in a tremendous loss of prestige for all those "progressive" chiefs who had spoken for the agreement.

The extent to which private ownership of land was a severe cultural imposition may be judged by the lengths to which Indians went to avoid being assigned allotments.

> They would run away when the Allotting Agent with his crew of assistants came into their neighborhoods and conceal themselves in the thicket, or ride back over the hills, leaving only a cloud of dust to mark their pathless course. . . . But a patent was recognized by law as having effect as soon as it was duly signed (by the agent, not the Indian) and recorded, no matter whether or not the allottee accepted it.[12]

By 1891—the year after Wounded Knee—"trust" Indians, those with patents in trust, were allowed to lease their land to settlers for up to three years, later changed to five years, subject to the approval of the Indian agent. "Competent" Indians could lease their land without any restrictions, and by 1910 any Indian could lease land. The whole question of leasing of Indian land posed a dilemma from the white point of view, for efforts to impose white values were frequently incompatible with efforts to relieve Indians of their land. The sight of Indians living in idleness, sustained by lease income from white ranchers, disturbed many white agents and other government observers.

This terrible twenty-year period in Lakota history gave rise, starting in early 1890, to the syncretic religious revival—part Christian, part traditional expressions of despair—that eventually ended with the slaughter at Wounded Knee. The Hills and the buffalo were gone. The remaining lands of the Lakota had been split up into a patchwork of private holdings unsuited for agriculture. Their annuities, on which they were greatly dependent and which they viewed not as handouts but as the fulfillment of treaty obligations, had been reduced by Congress after the agreement of 1889, and the official reduction of the beef ration was further diminished by the elimination of the "fifth quarter," the organs that whites did not consider edible but which had formed an important part of the Indian diet. Witholding them was another attempt to remake Indian habits in the image of white civilization.

Whites attempted to dictate the political course of the Lakota as much as their religious and economic course. This meant breaking the power of the chiefs. In 1877-78 Red Cloud lived briefly on the Missouri, and then finally got an agency for the Oglala on White Clay Creek, near the Nebraska border, about seventy miles south of the Black Hills country. Spotted Tail's Sicangu settled at Rosebud Creek to the east. But the new agency villages no longer took the names of the chiefs. They were called instead Pine Ridge and Rosebud, a significant change and a calculated reminder that the government considered the old chiefs irrelevant—and that Indians who cared about the future should, too.[13]

In 1882, Red Cloud was officially deposed as Chief by Valentine McGillycuddy, the agent at Pine Ridge between 1879 and 1886. McGillycuddy was at least an honest and competent agent. These traits didn't mean that his relations with the people whose destinies he oversaw were all that good. Ever since it had become clear that the whites interpreted the 1868 treaty far more narrowly than Red Cloud did, the aging chief had made a post-treaty career of objecting to the agents assigned to his people, and he particularly disliked McGillycuddy. In the summer of 1879, during a rare visit to the agency by Interior Secretary Carl Schurz, the ultimate federal arbiter of Indian Affairs, Red Cloud made annoying demands for the fulfillment of treaty obligations and for the removal of McGilly-cuddy, demands that Schurz did not feel inclined to take seriously. In 1882, as part of his campaign against the assimilationist policies then prevailing on the reservation, Red Cloud wrote to Washington, D.C., again demanding the agent's removal. S. W. Russell, who was present, describes the ensuing meeting between the agent and the principal chiefs, who were planning to kill the agent if they did not receive some satisfaction:

Dr. McGillycuddy, looking the old man fairly in the eye

said: "Red Cloud for more than three years I have been your agent. I have kept no soldiers here to annoy you. I have never lied to you; I have protected you from those who would have robbed you; I have never made you a promise and then broken it; I have never refused you anything and afterward given it to you. . . . Because you have written this letter, Red Cloud, and because you have been disobedient I now break you of your chieftainship. You are no longer a chief. . . . Red Cloud go to your teepee."[14]

This account is at least a little suspect, and colored perhaps by rhetorical temptations. Red Cloud lived in a government-supplied house by this time, not a tipi, which the agent would have known perfectly well. McGillycuddy's second wife and biographer, Julia McGillycuddy, adds more color to the story with an indignant Red Cloud brandishing a knife, but no one who was actually there remembers the gesture. Red Cloud's demotion by the white agent, however, is not in doubt, and the story tells us what became of the Indians' right to choose their leaders and control their own destinies.

Red Cloud's people didn't necessarily stop thinking of Red Cloud as a chief, and in some sense this split persists today. The Oglala Lakota on the Pine Ridge Reservation have a tribal government with elected representatives and a constitution, developed under the blueprint for tribal government laid out in the Indian Reorganization Act of 1936, by which tribes that had always been governed by democratic consensus were made to be parliamentarians. To this day the Pine Ridge Oglala maintain an alternate system of chieftainship, and Oliver Red Cloud has a liaison office in the Pine Ridge tribal council building.

I once visited with Oliver Red Cloud, now in his eighties. The council was not in session, so we sat in the modern, windowless council chamber among its plastic desks. He spoke of his role in the tribe and of developments relating to the tribe's jealously guarded sovereignty. I was thinking that if he took off his sunglasses and grew his hair longer, he'd look just like his great-grandfather. No, the days when the Lakota ruled the plains were not so long ago.

The Dawes Act was still not the end of the attempts to separate Indians and their land. The trust period of twenty-five years before land could be sold was apparently too long for settlers to wait. The Burke Act of 1906 gave the Secretary of the Interior, rather than Congress, powers to issue full and unrestricted patents to any Indian who was "competent," a status that was interpreted with varying degrees of strictness over the next twenty years but that was often defined by the proportion of white blood and white education possessed by the Indian in question. "Competency commissions" appeared on the reservations. These were cultural road shows. The traveling commissioners were happy to find Indians who fit the bill and treat them to a colorful little ceremony. "Competent" Indians would walk out from a tipi and fire off one last arrow, be addressed by an Indian name one last time. The commissioners would then present each of them with a plow, purse, and an American flag pin, symbolizing the habits and pursuits of "civilization." Often the next white people the newly competent

Indians encountered after the competency commissioners were land agents.

By 1921 the Board of Indian Commissioners, a watchdog agency set up to monitor the BIA and to guard against the graft and corruption that had given the bureau a bad name, reported that "81.5% [of the Indian agents] state that of the patent-in-fee Indians on their reservations, a majority—in some cases all—disposed of their lands and money soon after they were released from Government supervision."[15]

Lest there be too many Indians who didn't want to sell their land, Congress was appropriating it without any niceties about treaties or consent. Between 1904 and 1912 it passed eight land statutes that chipped another five million acres off Lakota lands—more than a third of the reservation lands remaining after 1889. The 1868 treaty had created a Great Sioux Reservation of about twenty-six million acres, with another thirty-four million acres of hunting grounds and "unceded territory" not in the reservation proper; by 1912 total reservation lands amounted to some eight million acres.

During the First World War demand led to higher prices for beef cattle, which presented an opportunity for whites. The Indian agents thought it would be a good thing for the Sioux ranchers to sell their stock and lease their lands for next to nothing to white stock-growers, which they did, using the money to buy consumer goods, mostly second-hand cars and alcohol.

Then years of drought began in 1924. When Calvin Coolidge spoke at Pine Ridge in 1927, he was encountering, if not understanding, the compound effect of various policies that could not be called good for the Indians. The people Coolidge addressed were virtually destitute. There was real, honest-to-God famine in Pine Ridge by 1931.

The Indian schools the president mentioned in his address had a long history. In 1794, the United States made a treaty with the Oneida, Stockbridge, and Tuscarora tribes that included provisions for education. Later treaties tried in various ways to advance the cause of assimilation, offering schools or vocational training. In 1802 Congress appropriated $15,000 for a "civilization fund" to teach Indians farming, spinning, and domestic arts. Education under the treaties was often subcontracted out to missionaries, and in 1818 Congress set up a system of Indian schools in co-operation with religious groups.

The early Indian schools often taught the students how to read their own languages spelled out in English letters, and provided translated textbooks. A few even allowed Indian boys to study medicine or law in addition to the trades; on the recommendation of the BIA this approach was dropped in 1846, and additional missionary-supervised trade schools were developed.

Some government education aid led to Indians developing their own programs. The Choctaws and Cherokees had their own school system by 1841. Cherokee speakers were reading not only in their own language but in their writing system, thanks to the great Cherokee teacher, Sequoyah, who unlocked the secret of the alphabet in a long project starting around 1809. Sequoyah could not read English, but he made the intuitive leap to the understanding that writing conveys the sounds of language. He then invented a system better suited than the English alphabet to the sounds of his native language.

Although Sequoyah was put on trial by the tribal council for witchcraft, he convinced the Cherokee leaders that there was nothing supernatural about his invention, and the tribe officially adopted his system in 1821. Thereafter literacy caught on quickly among the Cherokee. The first Cherokee-language newspaper, the *Cherokee Phoenix*, was published in 1828. In 1841, when the Cherokee and Choctaw took control of their schools, there were thriving newspapers published in the Cherokee language in Cherokee communities wherever they had been scattered by various removal acts. There are books and journals published in Cherokee today. You can download the Cherokee font from the Internet and install it on your computer.

While early Indian education programs may indeed have done some good in preparing Indian students for interactions with the white world, the system as it evolved after the Civil War was a very cruel one. A new concept of special schools to educate Indians was born, symbolically enough, in a prison camp at Fort Marion, Illinois. Captain Richard Pratt (the same who had tried and failed to negotiate the reduced reservations) was in charge of seventy-two Indian prisoners of war there between 1875 and 1878. He decided to educate them. Upon their release some of his charges came with him to the Hampton Institute, founded at Hampton Roads, Virginia, in 1868 as a teacher-training center for newly freed slaves. The institute had a new, segregated Indian department.

Pratt went on to found the Carlisle Industrial Indian School in 1879, at Carlisle, Pennsylvania, at one of the oldest army barracks in the country.[16] The school was deliberately placed far from the families of the attendees, who were recruited from the reservations. As the Indian school system expanded, school and BIA officials made efforts not to place children from the same reservation in the same school. Siblings were usually placed in separate schools and, when in the same school, forbidden to speak to each other. On arrival, students were assigned Christian names and expected to use them exclusively. Discipline was strict. Children at Indian schools wore short haircuts and military uniforms. Corporal punishment was frequent and severe and could be applied for such offenses as speaking an Indian language.

School administrators decided which students could visit their families. If the families objected to sending their children to the schools, they were threatened with loss of the rations provided by treaty, or with forced adoption of their children by whites.

Some Indians, realizing that their children would need white skills to survive in the coming era, and that they would need to read and write and speak English, did voluntarily send them to these schools. Spotted Tail, for example, sent four of his children to Carlisle on condition that his adult daughter and her husband, Charles Tackett, could accompany them. In doing so he convinced other Rosebud and Pine Ridge families to send their children. In 1880 Spotted Tail was greatly disturbed to hear from Tackett that all his children had been baptized into the Episcopal faith and given names such as William, Pollock (after an Indian agent) and Max. Later that year Spotted Tail and several other chiefs were invited east for a ceremony of gratitude for the education their children were receiving. Spotted Tail was courteous to the assembled dignitaries until he was invited to make a speech.

Then he let them have it. He expressed no gratitude for the gift of Christianity. Instead, through his interpreter, he attacked the school as a "soldier place," and he excoriated Pratt for drilling his children in military style and turning them into manual laborers when he had sent them to learn English, to learn to read and write. Spotted Tail announced that he was taking all of the Rosebud and Pine Ridge children home with him. Pratt sent a telegraph to Commissioner Schurz, who forbade him to take the children, but Spotted Tail and the chiefs insisted at least on taking their own.

The scene that followed was very dramatic. The Indians grabbed onto their children and would not let them go; the school administrators sent telegrams flying back and forth to Washington. The Indian Bureau officials threatened, cajoled, blackmailed, but it was no use, and eventually the visitors set off for the train station, still afraid to release their children lest they be stolen from them. Many other Lakota children at the school tried to escape with Spotted Tail and his family. Pratt called out his troops and stopped and searched Spotted Tail's train, and dragged these children back to the school.[17]

From that point on reservation Lakota steadfastly refused to voluntarily send their children to faraway boarding schools. George Hyde writes that "every Indian agent became a professional kidnapper who sent his Indian police out to ambush and drag in weeping Indian boys and girls, to be sent off under guard to one of the big government schools."[18]

Agent McGillycuddy at Pine Ridge was committed to assimilating the Indians, which he saw as the best course for their development. Of all of his "civilizing" innovations he was proudest of the reservation boarding school that he created to remove children from the traditional influence of their parents. But when schoolchildren showed up for the first day of classes, a riot almost ensued. Here is what happened.

> . . . Curious peepers stood close to the windows on the ground floor, deeply regretful of the drawn shades which barred their observation of the activities carried on behind them. There the matron seated a small boy and, taking a lousy braid in one hand, raised the shears hanging by a chain from her waist. A single clip and the filthy braid would have been severed. But unfortunately at that moment a breeze blew back the shade from the window.[19]

The screams of outrage from the watching parents were a sign that they understood the meaning of this act very well. Yet McGillycuddy insisted that the Indians had little choice if they were to make progress; and at that time and place—and granting his definition of "progress"—he was probably right. Within a few weeks he had convinced them to to send their children back to the school.

A sample of Rules for the Indian Schools, published just a few years before Coolidge's visit to the Black Hills, is instructive:

Section 25: The Secretary of the Interior may in his discretion, establish such regulations as will prevent the issuing of rations or the furnishing of subsistence either in money or in kind to the head of any Indian family for [or] on account of any Indian child or children between the ages of 8 and 21 years who shall not have attended school during the preceeding year in accordance with such regulations. [This action, however, requires the approval of the Commissioner of Indian Affairs.]

Section 27: . . . Visits of pupils to their homes are to be permitted only for proper reasons.

Section 28: If any child . . . without permission of the person in charge, leaves a Government school in which he is enrolled, he may be returned to the school by the employees detailed by the superintendent or by the Indian policy acting under orders of the superintendent.[20]

In keeping with the semi-military tradition of these schools, a Bureau of Indian Affairs report on students expelled from the Indian school system in 1931 frequently lists, among many other infractions and examples of moral turpitude, the crime of "Desertion." The choice of a word reveals much about the military aspect of the schools and the loyalty they expected.

The Indian schools produced several generations of confused

children and adults without a strong identity in any culture. Not surprisingly, many of the graduates of these schools lost themselves in the cities, where they became cooks or factory hands (as Coolidge recommended in his address at Pine Ridge), or led lonely lives back on the reservations, where they attempted to reassimilate into Indian culture.

There were exceptions. Henry Standing Bear, who maintained an Indian identity and yet could function in the white world, and who gave the address at Coolidge's tribal induction, was a graduate of Carlisle. So was Ben Black Elk, who played an important role at Rushmore. So was Chauncy Yellow Robe, who performed Coolidge's induction ceremony. Yellow Robe spent six years at Carlisle. Coming back home in his white man's suit, hat, and short hair, he walked right by his mother at the Rushville, Nebraska, train depot. He didn't recognize her in her shawl and blanket. His father had signed the treaty of 1868. Yellow Robe became an athletic director at BIA schools.

At the dedication of the monument the president wore a cowboy hat and boots with his business suit and was honored with a twenty-one-"gun" salute—the sound was made by blasting twenty-one tree stumps with dynamite to make way for the new road to Rushmore. Senator Peter Norbeck served as master of cermonies. As in 1925, the flags of the Bourbons, of Spain, of Napoleon, of George Washington, and of the United States were displayed at the appropriate points. South Dakota political figures gave addresses on the subjects of the sculpture, Washington, Jefferson, Lincoln, and Roosevelt. Borglum scaled the mountain in a hanging chair of his own design, which delighted the crowed, and carved four reference points, presenting three of the four drill bits he used to Coolidge, Doane Robinson, and Senator Norbeck; one he kept for himself.

In his own address Borglum said he was creating a work that would outlast American civilization in its portrayal of the westward course of empire. "There in mammoth letters will be carved where, how and who it was who declared our right to be free and to be happy, who shaped our constitution, through whom, why and when we decided to extend our boundaries westward. . . . Roosevelt completed the dream of Columbus and cut a way to the East, to India."[21]

Coolidge's speech was much the same, with the notable words: "It will be entirely American in its conception, in its magnitude, in its meaning, and altogether worthy of our country. . . . The people of the future will see history and art combined to portray the spirit of patriotism. They will know that the figure of these presidents has been placed here because by following the truth they built for territory."[22]

The next major celebration at Rushmore was during South Dakota's Golden Jubilee on July 2, 1939, at which the Roosevelt head was unveiled.

In 1939 the Nazis were preparing to reincorporate into the Reich the Free City of Danzig (now Gdańsk), a vital outlet on the Baltic Sea. The rest of the world didn't know what to do about it. In editorials and letters to the editor Americans were anxiously, introspectively examining what democracy is and how we should understand it, how Americans could distinguish their country from the totalitarian states of Europe. The British, French, and Russians were discussing a mutual assistance pact. It looked as if war might break out any day, although the British and the French were refusing to make a clear pledge to help Poland over Danzig. The German Ministry of Propaganda had a realistic grasp of the situation. "We are confident of our strength and supremely calm."[23]

For the Rushmore event, Borglum had originally planned a spectacularly irrelevant ceremony, apparently completely unconscious of how little it had to do with Roosevelt, the Black Hills, or anything that was happening in the contemporary world. "The pageant is to be a great drama, for three nights; the first dealing with King John and the Magna Charta; the second with Cromwell and the execution of King Charles; and the third the Revolution in the Western world, establishing the government and then the Unveiling of all the heads at the conclusion of this."[24]

Fortunately for historical sense, very little of this materialized. Yet the actual event did have the distinctive touch of a Borglum production. Governor Harlan Bushfield was, like President Coolidge before him, ritually inducted as a Sioux leader—after making a speech in which he said that Mount Rushmore "typifies in deathless stone" the philosophy of South Dakotan pioneers. "The thing for which they stood—as do these great stone faces above us—is America . . . America with all it stands for of liberty, of free enterprise, free speech and free religion." After Judge Albert Denu responded to the above with "it is comforting to know that South Dakota has demonstrated its Americanism . . . by a steadfast refusal to deviate from the ideals that gave birth to the republic, of which it has become a part," he continued: "America's 'Shrine of Democracy' will proclaim with mute eloquence for unnumbered centuries the basic truth that the individual and not the state is the unit of value by laws of nature and of nature's God."[25]

Of course, both the alternatives offered would seem absurd in many cultures.

Meanwhile, Oglala Sioux were hunting two "renegade" buffalo from the herd in the state game park. The Indians wore buckskins, rode bareback, and used only bows and arrows as they stalked their game for the benefit of newsreel cameras—which just goes to show the organizers' preference for comfortable form over complex substance, since, after all, horses, acquired by Plains Indians through direct or indirect contact with Europeans in the eighteenth century, are no more a part of Lakota "tradition" than rifles are. Acknowledging the recent acquisition of the horse would have meant seeing Indians as part of a living tradition that, by the time of the last real buffalo hunts, had thoroughly absorbed some white technology; but Indians were not supposed to have a viable culture capable of adaptation to the modern world. It was easier to see them as colorful relics.

In an unintended metaphor about where power really lies, the buffalo were eventually shot by Governor Bushfield—with a rifle. The meat was then donated to the Indians.

Borglum gave a speech, not conscious of the way his language echoed that of some of his European contemporaries. "My service to my time has been and is to define accurately what lies at the heart and soul of my race and to record as nearly as possible—without fear or compromise—the truth of our race's secret and sacred dreaming.

We are the spearhead of a mighty world advancement—an awakened force in rebellion against the worn and useless thought of yesterday . . . we are reaching deep into the soul of mankind, and, through democracy, building better than has ever been built before."[26]

Simon Schama has noted that this speech, in its invocation of racial destiny, is suggestive of fascist posturing—and that the reference to democracy renders it somewhat confused.[27]

The aging silent movie star William Hart, who had lived in South Dakota, made a very different kind of speech. He had first come to the state with his father in the early 1880s and had grown up with Indian friends and learned the Lakota language. When he took the stand, he conversed with the Indian leaders present in sign language. Then he started to speak in Lakota, switching to English to rebuke the colonizers. "When we whipped the Indians it was a battle, but when the tables were turned it was a massacre." The nationally broadcast program very quickly ran out of time for his speech, and the producer pulled the plug, which is not mentioned in local reports.

Hart was furious to be cut off. He started shouting at the organizers, at Borglum, at the announcers, demanding to know what was happening to his speech. Louella Jones Borglum, the pretty young wife of Lincoln Borglum, the sculptor's son, rushed forward and began to cover him with theatrical kisses, which, according to eyewitnesses, seemed to mollify or at least confuse the old man.

The highlight of the gathering was a drama of the Black Hills in faux Shakespearean English. The first part presents the Sioux, their proud culture, and their prior possession of the Hills. As the Voice of Prologue proclaims, "Thus these Black Hills do fast unite the brave/Each noble heart the master—none the slave."[28] Later there is a bit of fuss about the white presence, but Red Cloud and Spotted Tail help things along by acknowledging that the time of the Indians is passing. Hart plays a white trapper sympathetic to the Indians.

When gold is discovered in the Hills and the Manypenny Commission comes through with the demand for sale of the land, "a sufficient number of Indian chiefs' signatures have been secured by government agents to a treaty determined upon between the Indians and the White man,"[29] according to the program notes. In fact, the treaty of 1868 did not call for a certain number of chiefs' signatures; it called for a certain number of signatures of all adult male Indians, an important distinction made for good reasons. Nor, of course, were its terms mutually decided on. In valedictory addresses, Red Cloud says, "Since this must be, it is well. The Great Spirit has willed it. The wind blowing from Black Hills has cooled Red man's anger," and Spotted Tail says, "Red man is old. He looks to young white master. Kindness will follow where will is strong."[30]

The pageant concludes with an epilogue:

Nay, not for GOLD alone, ye yearning men
Hath questing led your footsteps to these Hills!
. . . This be your treasure, LIFE and its portent
Wrested from the Rythmed crags and symbolled true

Storied reply to man's eternal search
Flung like a chronicle before his!
Here on the Mount, a carved Beatitude
Imperious commands your quest today
And will command, for aeons infinite.
Gold for the hands in wealth for hands alone;
Gold for the soul is in this sculptured stone.[31]

Didn't Karl Marx say that historical events occur twice—first as tragedy, then as farce? Thus were the sparks that flew when two very different cultures met neutralized in ceremony. When darkness fell on this production, while the world waited for war in Europe, fireworks, including aerial bombs and rockets, burst above the nearly completed faces of four American leaders.

Ben Black Elk, the son of the Lakota mystic Black Elk, said a prayer.

Ben Black Elk represents a whole chapter in the Indian presence at the mountain. He was at Rushmore every summer for more than twenty years, greeting tourists and being photographed in full Lakota ceremonial regalia. The tourists liked him. The various Rushmore superintendents liked him because he gave the tourists a sense of history and added an extra dimension to their visit. He became completely associated with the mountain and was eventually known as the fifth face on Rushmore. In a certain light, cracks in the mountain were seen to trace out his profile, and when this effect could be captured on film, it made the local papers. The lines do seem to sketch out an Indian face.

Black Elk had his own agenda, though, and probably saw his

purpose at Rushmore differently than the superintendents did. He was royalty, insofar as the concept has any meaning in Lakota culture; the Sioux are an egalitarian people whose leaders traditionally led by example rather than command. Still, Black Elk was a cousin of Crazy Horse, whose leadership, strange visions, uncompromising life, and tragic death made him a true hero to his people. Ben Black Elk's father was the man whites knew as Nicholas Black Elk, a boy at the Little Bighorn, a young man at Wounded Knee, a healer, a mystic, the one who tried to explain the spiritual world of the Lakota to John Neihardt in the 1930s, in a series of interviews that resulted in the book *Black Elk Speaks*. The book is astoundingly poetic and tragic; it shimmers with hallucinatory revelation. It takes the reader into an extended vision quest of great power and beauty. It was almost ignored when it first came out, but was rediscovered in the 1960s and became extremely influential as the main (and for a long time the only) point of entry for whites who wanted to understand how the traditional Lakota saw the world.

Ben Black Elk was not assimilated into white culture, although he knew he had to live with it. He grew up near Manderson, a few miles from Wounded Knee. His father had listened to the missionaries and was a practicing Catholic, but saw no conflict between the new religion and the old ways. Father and son were engaged, of necessity and throughout their lives, in discovering the ways of the white world and explaining and defending the ways of the old.

Ben Black Elk hardly spoke English until he was in his teens, when he ran away to the Carlisle Indian School. This was unusual; most of the students who were sent to that faraway place were running in the other direction. But Black Elk wanted to know what a white man's education was, and he knew, at a young age, that he would need such an education in the new world. He was willing to pay the price in isolation from the things he knew. He learned English.

He had to make a living. By the 1930s he and his young family were performing during the summers at Crystal Cave, now known as Sitting Bull's Crystal Cave. There was an open powwow area where Indian dances were demonstrated for tourists—the Omaha dance, the war dance, kettle dance, shield dance. They simulated an Indian scaffold burial, with his daughter Olivia playing the part of the corpse. The sun dance was explained, but it was not performed. Some things are not done for the amusement of outsiders. The sun dance was illegal then, anyway.

He posed for tourists and accepted their tips. When they asked, he explained the meaning of Indian customs. Those who had thought of Indians as savages were surprised to discover that the Lakota were a people of subtlety and depth.

I wanted to know how Ben Black Elk had ended up at Rushmore, so I looked up his daughter Olivia Pourier, who lives near Wounded Knee and runs the Black Elk Museum out of her home. Olivia Pourier is the widow of Hobart Pourier, who was the grandson of Baptiste Pourier, a frontiersman, army scout, and interpreter who was at the Rosebud battle and at Wounded Knee. His nickname was

Big Bat. Today the Texaco station in Pine Ridge, the commercial center of the town, is Big Bat's Texaco.

Talking with me in English while chatting with her sister and nephew in Lakota, she told me that Ben Black Elk's son, her brother, died in 1948. When he died, this is what Ben Black Elk did, a man who had gone to Carlisle and lived in the white world. "He put on his finest clothes, his real Lakota clothes, and took a horse, he had a travois and everything, and went off north to the Hills. Wherever my brother was, that's where he went, he tracked his spirit. He went towards Harney Peak, then through Hill City and Keystone, finally coming down the old Iron Mountain Road. And when he came down that road out towards Rushmore, people would start photographing him, in all his regalia, with his pony and travois. So that's how it all started at Rushmore."

The ritual is translated as "Wandering to Mourn." The concession holder, Carl Burgess, encouraged him to stay at Rushmore because he brought in so many tourists.

Ben Black Elk's mission, as traditional as it could be, had found him a place as an Indian at a monument honoring white achievements. There he stayed every summer except for the last few until his death in 1973. He made good money in tips. It was his summer job, and after all, he had a family to support. "He ended up making a lot more than some of those other people who were up there"—South Dakota is not a high-wage state—and he took the opportunity to point out that the Lakota had a history in the Hills. "My Dad was a strong man. He let everybody know that the Black Hills belonged to the Sioux. He wouldn't have it no other way," said Pourier. "He wanted these tourists to know. But he knew how things were. I remember he told me once, 'That there's the only Black Hills you'll ever have, all the Black Hills you'll ever know in your lifetime'—the Black Hills gold in my ring. He knew the Hills were gone, at least for our time, unless the people could really get together and be strong."

Olivia Pourier and her sister Esther DeSersa remember being at several of Borglum's dedications at which their father and grandfather played a role. The whole family was photographed with President Franklin Roosevelt when he came to Rushmore for the 1936 dedication of the Jefferson head.

A few years later the sisters rode up the mountain in Borglum's old tramway gondola, used during the construction, for the 1939 dedication of the Roosevelt head. They remember their grandfather saying the Four Directions prayer, which echoed through the canyon, and they remember listening as he and their cousin Emma Amiotte sang the Sioux national anthem, which Ben Black Elk wrote. They sang in Lakota.

> The United States flag shall fly forever.
> Beneath it, my people shall live.
> That's why I have done this.

It is an extraordinarily eloquent—and poignant—summary of a life lived between hard choices, an acceptance of the best available way, with a trace of hope, a trace of resignation. The simple words—

although who can tell with translations?—admit of a few subtly different interpretations.

Compare this song with one that Sitting Bull sang in the last years of his life near Fort Yates, in North Dakota, after he had finally submitted to living on a reservation.

My Father has given me this nation
In protecting them I have a hard time[32]

After Amiotte sang in 1939, more rock was blasted off the mountain.

Ben Black Elk appeared in the movie *The Savage*, in which he played a Crow chief opposite Charlton Heston. He was in the movie *How the West Was Won*, in which he played an Arapaho chief, and in the traveling road show of the same name, which took him to Europe, just as Buffalo Bill's Wild West Show had taken his father to Europe. On the road he continued to interpret the Lakota way of life to those who would otherwise have known nothing about it. In the winter he traveled around the West, lecturing on Rushmore and regional history as a representative of the Black Hills and Badlands Association.

On the road and at Rushmore he risked becoming just a colorful character, a decorative item in the picturesque Rushmore landscape. Postcards showing him with the president's heads behind him were sold at the Rushmore bookstore. Sentimental articles about Rushmore refered to him for years as if he were another point of interest that tourists shouldn't miss, and praised his pride in America in a way that made it a less complicated matter than it probably was.

In 1962, the very first commercial television satellite broadcast included a section on Rushmore. One of the featured participants was Ben Black Elk, who earned a place in broadcast history next to President Kennedy, an honor of which Black Elk was very proud.

Modern pageants have considerably less Indian participation, a matter of some embarrassment for Park Service impresarios. The militant Indian protests of the 1970s, though opposed by a considerable number of Lakota, did have the effect of forcing a reexamination of the benefits of assimilation and prompting a focus on real sovereignty. By the time of the Fiftieth Anniversary celebration in 1991 (an odd date—actually the anniversary of when work stopped on the mountain) the shift was complete. When President George Bush the elder led the ceremonies, only one mixed-blood Lakota could be found who would take part: White Eagle, an opera singer who had also performed at Bush's presidential inauguration. The presidents and chairmen of all nine North and South Dakota reservations were invited; all declined. White Eagle, who said that he "saw both sides" because his father was Sioux and his mother of German descent, felt obliged to add, "I can feel the dignity and the pain of my father's ancestors as we stand on this sacred land we call the Paha Sapa. I stand with my mother's ancestors and feel the pride that inspired the sculpting of this magnificent monument. I lift my voice, a point of light, to help heal all the people of the planet in the hope that the ideal behind the words I sing becomes a reality for everyone."[33]

White Eagle seems to have mastered the political and cultural vocabulary today, a vocabulary that pushes away historical pain even while acknowledging it. Still, his lone presence was a long way from the paid Indian pageants, collaborative vindication of a fantasy history, that marked Indian participation when Borglum was on the scene.

10

INDIANS TAKE CHARGE

O n August 21, 1970, Richard Hansen gave a speech inau-
gurating the first Mount Rushmore Presidential Institute, a series of lectures and classes held at the original
visitors' center at the monument under the sponsorship of the University of South Dakota. In his introductory remarks, Hansen commented that the Shrine of Democracy combined "the genius of man
with the wonders of nature."[1]

The purpose of the five-day workshop was to teach political science students more about the role and responsibilities of the president. Classes were scheduled on such topics as "the president as
world leader," "the president and the quality of American life," "the
Presidential library and researchers," and, ironically, "the president
and civil disorders."

A troop of Boy Scouts making their thirty-second annual "pilgrimage" to the monument were also on the scene. In light of what

soon occured, this was particularly apt. The Boy Scout organization was one of many youth organizations of the early twentieth century set up to confront the problems of an urbanizing America and what was seen as the corrupting, feminizing influence of cities on a generation of boys, boys whose character and patriotism had no exposure to the character-building qualities of rural life. In the earliest days of the Boy Scouts there was an ideological split between administrators who found the best model of youthful virtue in the white frontiersmen—cowboys, soldiers—and those who found it in nature, pastoralism, conservation—Indians—or at least, popular ideas about Indians.

Ernest Thompson Seton, an author, naturalist, and teacher, had developed his ideas about the restorative powers of nature study in a youth group he called the Woodcraft Indians in 1902. The group created a fake tribe, the Sinaways, who camped on Thompson's estate in Connecticut. They wore Indian costumes, performed rituals, and conducted meetings according to a tribal structure of putative Indian origin that in fact mimicked the cooperative challenges of modern American life; where earlier writers had seen anarchy in Indian customs, Thompson emphasized obedience and submission to the will of the group. Thompson was later a cofounder of the American version of Robert Baden-Powell's Boy Scout movement.

In the Boy Scouts he had to struggle against the soldier model of a youth organization and also against the "pioneer" values brought into the Boy Scouts by Daniel Carter Beard, who founded the Sons of Daniel Boone in 1905. The Sons' mandated fraternal meeting place was not the council fire of the Sinaways but a frontier stockade of the imagination, and their role-playing often involved mock-deadly fights with the Indians that Thompson posed as models for his Woodcraft boys. Beard was suspicious of Thompson's program of nativist virtue and made much of Thompson's English birth and his onetime description of the white pioneers as "scalawags and low types." Beard insisted on a patriotic, truly "American" program, and as the First World War approached, his ideas won out, forcing Thompson out of the Boy Scouts in 1915.

At Rushmore in 1970 the assembled Boy Scouts, students, and professors had a front-row seat from which to observe civic action taking place under the noses of four presidents. The Boy Scouts saw real Indians expressing ideas about democracy, responsibility, and governance: as Hansen spoke, a protest was going on at the Rushmore grounds.

Indians from the Pine Ridge reservation had been protesting in the Badlands National Park since July. The Department of the Interior had planned to expand the park onto land that had been part of the Sheep Mountain Gunnery Range; but this land, more than 265,000 acres, had belonged to Pine Ridge before the war, when it was part of an even larger parcel that was expropriated for wartime target practice. The whole parcel was supposed to revert to the reservation when the war ended. Many Pine Ridge Lakota suspected that should the land become part of a national park, their claim to it would be forgotten entirely. A complication was the presence (then and now) of still-unexploded ordnance on the range, making much of it unsafe for civilian use.

On August 24, 1970, Leo Wilcox moved the protest to Mount

Rushmore. Wilcox was a Pine Ridge Tribal Council member. As a young man he had studied to be a medicine man and had served in the U.S. Marines. A few days before his death in 1973 he reminisced with Stanley Lyman, the Bureau of Indian Affairs administrator at Pine Ridge, about mystical experiences at Rushmore, about being lifted up by a giant figure at the top of the mountain and walking off with him into the air, about becoming invisible. Wilcox was undergoing treatment at the Fort Meade Veterans' Hospital then, and Lyman thought he rambled a bit.

At the time of Wilcox's death, the village of Wounded Knee was occupied by AIM militants, who were expressing their opposition to the U.S. government and to the Pine Ridge tribal council. Wilcox was one of the council members who were allied with Pine Ridge tribal chairman Dick Wilson, whom AIM saw as a corrupt enforcer for the white power structure. Wilcox died in a flaming car wreck on the road to Scenic, South Dakota, near the northern entrance to the reservation. There were rumors that AIM people were responsible, but nothing was ever proven.

Taking the 1970 protest to Rushmore was a logical way to focus national attention on an Indian land claim. Wilcox asked for and received a permit to perform traditional dance and music on the Rushmore grounds. The performances turned into statements about history, with hand-lettered signs claiming the land for the Lakota and demanding payment for the Hills.

In Sioux country, a protest against the loss of the Sheep Mountain range became a platform to launch a discussion of rights under the 1868 Fort Laramie treaty. What better place to do this than at

Rushmore? At any rate, that is where the Badlands protesters ended up, around the same time as the Boy Scouts and the group of professors studying democracy.

Wilcox's group was soon joined by some of the most focused of the Indian rights groups: the United Native Americans led by Lehman Brightman; the Minneapolis and Cleveland chapters of AIM; and Indians of All Tribes, the pan-Indian group that had been founded during the 1969 occupation of Alcatraz. The All Tribes leader, John Trudell, was there, as were Russell Means and Dennis Banks of AIM. Many smaller tribal and political groups were also represented at Rushmore.

When Banks and Means arrived from Minneapolis at the invitation of the Lakota elders Lizzie Fast Horse and Muriel Waukazo, their group scouted the visitors' center bookstore, where they found that the concessionaires were selling postcards of photographs taken at Wounded Knee. There were scenes of the mass burial, and of soldiers posing next to bodies frozen on the field and in the ravines where the killings took place. The AIM Indians wrecked the display stands.

The first day at Rushmore, Brightman gave a speech in the monument amphitheater in which he went over some of the less well known, unsavory facts about the four presidents on the mountain: Washington's career as an Indian killer, Jefferson's advocacy of the "annihilation" of the Indians, Lincoln's order to execute Indians who attacked civilians in the 1862 Minnesota Sioux Uprising, Teddy Roosevelt's violation of numerous Indian treaties in creating his system of national parks and forests.

Responding to Brightman's charges, Superintendent Wallace McCaw defended the presidents' historical records by saying that all of them had assumed that their policies would eventuate in the quick assimilation of Indians into the mainstream of American society, which, they assumed, would solve all the Indians' problems. However sincerely McCaw may have offered this defense, it was not one that was likely to find favor with the militants, and his apparent belief that it would calm things down was a measure of how out of touch he was with a changing world.

The demonstrators invited President Nixon, Governor Frank Farrar of South Dakota, Senator George McGovern, Commissioner of Indian Affairs Louis Bruce—and Johnny Cash—to attend their vigil at the mountain, all of whom declined. But a certain number of visitors to Rushmore stopped and listened to Dennis Banks tell the story of Black Hills treaty violations and heard him describe the monument as a "Hoax of Democracy." A few of them signed petitions to the president and Congress asking that Indian treaty claims be reexamined.

By this time the protesters had added the demand that all concessions at the monument be run by Indians. Oddly enough, representatives of the United Sioux Tribes, an organization dedicated to advancing Sioux self-governance, treaty rights, and general well-being through the official tribal leaderships, were at that very moment meeting with Interior Secretary Walter Hickel in Washington, D.C. They were presenting a detailed and thoroughly researched argument for tribal control of the concessions at Rushmore, an idea originally suggested by Ben Black Elk. Webster Two

Hawk, president of the United Sioux Tribes, and Clarence Skye, the executive director, found Hickel to be receptive and supportive. Then the photographs of Means, Trudell, Brightman, and their followers appeared in the newspapers. "That just about did us in," says Two Hawk. "We lost Hickel's attention. Ben Reifel [congressman for South Dakota, the first Sioux ever elected to Congress] wasn't going to support our claim on the concessions in a situation where this occupation was going on." Two Hawk believes that the confrontation destroyed a useful, professional relationship with the Department of the Interior and its secretary, who oversees the Bureau of Indian Affairs as well as the National Park Service and therefore Mount Rushmore.

More than anything else, the occupation was about the 1868 treaty and the Sioux Black Hills claim. The issue was pressing and topical.

In 1923 the Sioux, represented by Ralph Case, filed a claim demanding payment for their Black Hills. They sued on the grounds that the Black Hills had been improperly assessed for its confirmed value in 1877 and that the obligations the government had taken on at that time had never been satisfactorily carried out. The case had been in the courts ever since, in a variety of incarnations and jurisdictions, a measure of the tenacity of several different sets of lawyers and the tremendously complex nature of Indian law. Politics, precedent, bureaucracy, patronage, sentiment, and populism all played a part.

At the time of the Rushmore protests, the Court of Claims—a

judicial body set up specifically to hear and clear Indian land claims—was preparing to issue judgments on the complicated questions of the mineral and surface value of the Sioux lands when they were taken. Value discovered subsequent to their appropriation, including the billions of dollars in gold taken out by the Homestake and smaller mines, would not count, even if the gold was thought but not proven to be there in 1877.

So the Rushmore protesters pressed a demand for payment according to the 1877 agreement. A joint statement issued by Brightman, Banks, and Means explicitly addressed the basis of their claim. "This protest is part of [the] fight to awaken the U.S. government to the fact that the Sioux Indians have been wronged. The government illegally seized the Black Hills and has not paid for them."[2] Brightman, asserting that the Indians were not going to leave the monument until they met with Interior Secretary Hickel, also remarked during the protest: "This is land illegally taken by the government. It rightfully belongs to the Indians until it is paid for."[3]

Although such statements did not seem controversial at the Indian encampment, a few years later they were heresy in the Indian movement, as we shall see. But in 1970 demands for correct and legal payment for the Hills were very much on the Indian public agenda. This demand, whether they realized it or not, weakened their rhetoric about the 1868 treaty. If 1868 was the guiding law, then taking any part of the act of 1877 seriously would be to accept that the 1877 rules superseded those of 1868.

Such subtleties were not part of the protesters' agenda at the base of the mountain. As night fell after Brightman's amphitheater speech, several dozen protesters climbed up to occupy the mountain, eventually camping in a small depression behind Roosevelt's head. The park administration, aware that the rangers were outnumbered and unsure of how to deal with the demonstration, decided to wait it out.

When it became apparent that the Indians weren't going home anytime soon, the NPS and Superintendent McCaw began an ambivalent strategy of sometimes appeasing the protesters, sometimes threatening them with arrest and legal action. While insisting that they had to come down off the mountain and that the NPS had no authority to grant any of their demands, the rangers more or less ignored supporters going up the mountain with groceries; indeed, the rangers occasionally delivered groceries themselves. When Lizzie Fast Horse, who was not in good health, wanted to go up to the camp above the faces, a ranger carried her. The NPS turned a blind eye as the camping protesters cut trees and built fires at night, very much against park regulations.

The occupiers hung a huge banner above Lincoln's forehead that read, "Crazy Horse Monument Indian Power," and named their group the Crazy Horse Movement and the Teton Nation Indian Movement, neither of which seems to have lasted much beyond the events of that fall. The Park Service, though not wanting to risk a violent confrontation during the height of the tourist season, was worried by the speeches of excited young people who spoke of blowing up the mountain or bombing it symbolically with paint.

While Means was on the mountain, he was able to bring the

treaty to the forefront of Rushmore visitors' consciousness in a dramatic way. He found a small ledge running between the heads of Lincoln and Roosevelt. When he sat there to speak, his voice was amplified by the bowl of the mountain, and at night he yelled out the Ten Commandments to the assembled crowds, dwelling long and loud on "Thou shalt not steal." And he gave an eleventh commandment: "THOU SHALT HONOR THY TREATIES. I forgot that one in my last message."[4]

Means also indulged himself in another piece of theater, highly expressive of his view of the monument, when he urinated on Washington's face. Talking to participants in the Rushmore protest, I found that this was a not-uncommon way for Indians to express their feelings about the Great Fathers. Washington was generally the first choice for the honor, but among those militants who were Sioux, Lincoln was also a popular target, in remembrance of the thirty-eight leaders of the Minnesota Uprising of 1862 whom he ordered hanged at Mankato, Minnesota. It is true that the local authorities had wanted to hang more than three hundred, and it was only because Lincoln insisted on an investigation that the penalty was limited to those who had killed civilians; it is true that the Sioux had killed more than six hundred whites in 1862. To the militants of the 1970s and of today, the leaders of the revolt were patriots defending their land from foreign invasion, and Lincoln's act was one of judicial murder.

While the Indians were on the mountain, the Lakota medicine man Frank Fools Crow visited them and performed a sanctification ceremony, a symbolic claiming of the land. The patch of ground where he did this is remembered and annually marked by Indian pilgrims, who return to the spot with the permission of the Park Service.

Most of the protesters were down from the mountain by the end of September, although some stayed until the bitter cold of December.

Despite Russell Means's contention that Indian reaction was universally positive—"we were heroes"—support among South Dakota Indians was far from solid. Many traditional reservation Indians were upset by the act of confrontation, and many of those who were involved in the tribal government structures felt directly threatened. The *Rapid City Journal* lectured Indians on their political bickering[5] and printed letters from outraged tribal officers, one of which said that the protesters "have done more harm to the Indians of this state than all the communistic movement across the country has done in the last 10 years."[6]

Overall, however, the media coverage was more amused than alarmed. Many of the editorials and even news articles seemed to accept the basic premise of the Indian action—they use phrases like "white thievery of the Hills"—yet also seemed to regard the protests as irritating and pointless. What, after all, do these Indians want?

Less than a year later, there was another protest at the monument, this time shorter and less organized but taken a little more seriously by the authorities. This protest was more strictly an AIM affair. Russell Means, his brothers Ted and Bill, their cousin Madonna Gilbert from Eagle Butte, Dennis Banks, and Clyde Bellecourt and his brothers Vernon, George, and Charlie were there.

They had come specifically to take possession of the mountain this time, in order to once again dramatize their claims under the treaty of 1868 and to emphasize their right to perform religious ceremonies in the Black Hills. They came prepared with a blessing from Leonard Crow Dog and with precise instructions from him regarding rituals to sanctify their protest. Upon climbing the mountain they set up an altar and arranged sacred tobacco ties that indicated their spiritual orientation.

Banks and the Bellecourts had been under FBI surveillance since leaving Minneapolis. With advance knowledge of Indian intentions to do something at Rushmore, the Pennington County Sheriff prepared a military line of defense, arranging for support from the South Dakota Highway Patrol, the state Game, Fish, and Parks Division, the Rapid City and Custer Police Departments, and Custer and Meade County deputies. He also requested that the governor activate the National Guard, fifty of whom were sent but who were used only for establishing a perimeter of operations. By the time the Indians had set up camp, they were under helicopter surveillance.

Superintendent McCaw had authorized force to remove the protesters, but the authorities were nervous. The group had vowed to resist removal in a press release issued on the day of the occupation.

The smallness of the group and the lack of any significant support from the large Indian community in Rapid City were measures of how the confrontational tactics of AIM continued to alienate some among those whom AIM would have liked to claim as a solid bloc of supporters. Pine Ridge tribal judge Hobart Keith suggested a different course of action: "In my opinion we need to go to the federal courts, all the way to the Supreme Court, with the world and the United Nations watching, devoid of any encumbrances by the capricious Indian Court of Claims. . . . I want to keep the conscience of Christianity guilty for transgressions against the true aristocrats of the land." He disavowed any connection with AIM, however. "Our position here is based purely on legal and moral grounds. We don't want anything to do with a militant group coming from out of state and don't recognize it."[7]

The protest was quickly cut short. National Guard troops and NPS rangers dragged most of the group off the mountain within ten hours, arresting twenty-one all together; the rest of the group, not wanting, as the hard-core activists did, to be arrested, had escaped down the back of the mountain. There was no fooling around this time. The Indians were shackled. When they refused to cooperate in leaving the mountain, many of them were dragged down the steep, rough trails by the cursing Guardsmen, even sometimes deliberately pushed down sharp drops, until they finally agreed to walk down. Means says that the arrested Indians agreed only to prevent the Guardsmen from sexually harassing the women in the group as they carried them down.

At press conferences and public meetings in Rapid City after the event, the militants demanded a full reexamination of the 1868 treaty in federal court; the return of Sheep Mountain; and, somewhat tamely by comparison, that Rushmore concessions be handled by Indians. Then the protest faded out.

In the years after the Rushmore occupation, fears of violence at the site would surge and subside, reaching a peak in the mid 1970s and gradually ebbing in the early 1980s. On June 27, 1975, a bomb exploded on the terrace outside the visitor center at Rushmore. The date is significant. Just the day before, two FBI agents and an AIM supporter had been killed during a shootout in the Pine Ridge Reservation town of Oglala when the agents drove into an AIM encampment, supposedly searching for a petty thief. Sixteen suspects in that incident were fugitives, including Leonard Peltier, who is in jail to this day after a trial that made a mockery of the American justice system. Pine Ridge was crawling with FBI agents, state police, and BIA SWAT teams; and within the next few weeks, bombs were set at a half-dozen BIA offices all over the nation, including the BIA offices at Pine Ridge Village. It was a low point in Indian-white relations in the region.

Jury selection was in progress for the trial of Dennis Banks in Custer, on charges stemming from the Custer courthouse riot of 1973. The court proceedings were taking place with extraordinary security precautions, including, for the first time in that jurisdiction, the use of metal detectors and searches. Jurors and court employees had to wear prominent badges at all times.

It was only two years after the three-month occupation of Wounded Knee. The last of the Wounded Knee trials were in progress in Cedar Rapids, Iowa.

The bomb at Rushmore injured no one, and the shattered glass at the visitors' center was repaired within hours. There was a great deal of fear about what might follow, however. There were rumors—unsubstantiated, and many of them found to be fed by FBI wires—that AIM was planning to blow the faces off the mountainside on July 4th. The rumors detailed the method: the group was going to distract security personnel and, while their backs were turned, quickly dig a big trench using an earthmover and fill it with three hundred cases of dynamite. There were descriptions, reported by state law-enforcement authorities, of three AIM demolition experts staying at motels in Rapid City, one white, one black, and one mysterious figure "about whom no other facts are available."[8]

In the midst of all this, Ted Means came up to the mountain and filed a formal request for a demonstration permit on July Fourth. The park staff debated over whether granting such a permit, under the circumstances, would be wise. To their credit, Superintendent Harvey Wickware, his aides, the NPS, and the governor decided that the First Amendment had to be respected. Means and AIM got their march and demonstration permit, although extremely elaborate preparations were going on behind the scenes to prepare for an emergency while at the same time allaying, as much as possible, the fears and suspicions of the Indians. This part of the plan almost went awry when, while Means and the park staff were inspecting the proposed site of the demonstration, an FBI helicopter made an unauthorized landing on the spot and sat there for several minutes, observing the group as rangers frantically signaled it to leave. Wickware was quite worried about the effect this incident might have on the attitude of his guests. The Indians were inscrutable.

Before the big day Wickware prepared emergency evacuation announcements: "Ladies and Gentlemen, it is necessary to clear the visitor area . . . " Bomb search plans were prepared, as well as standby plans for law-enforcement strike forces, riot control, arrests, prisoner detention, helicopter landings for emergency evacuations, perimeter defenses. Yet a protest march from Keystone and a rally of only a few hours duration came off quite peacefully. A few tourists got to see a religious ceremony honoring what Means called "our war dead," Indians of all generations who had fallen in the fight against colonialism and specifically the two who died at Wounded Knee '73, Buddy Lamont and Frank Clearwater, and Joe Stuntz, the AIM supporter who had been killed at Oglala the week before.

Those Independence Day celebrants who were interested could also hear a short speech by Dennis Banks, free on bail pending the outcome of his trial (he later skipped bail on the Custer charges and fled to California, whence governor Jerry Brown refused to extradite him to South Dakota, much to the fury of South Dakota governor Bill Janklow.) Under the circumstances, it is not surprising that Banks used a courthouse metaphor. "For 199 years we've been on trial, and for 199 years we've been found guilty. The next two hundred years will not be like the last. All this year the United States of America will be on trial by Indian people. How white America handles the next year will determine its punishment."[9] Speaking to tourists, Clyde Bellecourt repeated a long-standing AIM call for a tourist boycott of South Dakota, and made a threat that terrified many precisely because it was so ambiguous: "When July 4th, 1976, comes, unless [whites] honor their treaties and commitments, we will be back here to blow out the candles on their birthday cake"[10]— a threat that the FBI took very seriously.

The Rushmore protests received some press and public attention, but not much—certainly nowhere near as much as the AIM-led occupation of the Bureau of Indian Affairs offices in Washington D.C., in 1972, or as much as the Wounded Knee occupation in 1973. But there were repercussions in the American consciousness, both short-term and long-term.

To the extent that modern pro-Rushmore authors look at Indian issues at all, they have to be defensive about Indian claims to the Hills. Writing in 1976, the bicentennial of the nation and the centennial of the Little Bighorn and the Manypenny Commission, a time when AIM was pointing out Indian claims with a series of dramatic actions, June Culp Zeitner and Lincoln Borglum commented on the Rushmore protests:

An ever present problem in Western South Dakota is the Indian problem, which is sometimes dramatized by events such as the occupation of Wounded Knee or a powwow at Rushmore. There is a large Sioux population in Rapid City and three large reservations are close. The whole of the Black Hills area is claimed by the Sioux, and to publicize their cause, a group of Indians camped on Mount Rushmore one summer. . . . The claim to the Hills seems mostly for the purpose of treaty renegotiation and

monetary reimbursement. Most of the Sioux prefer the
Reservation system, and they regard any threats to terminate this system with intense hatred and fear. The
Sioux did not live in the Hills, so the Hills were not really
theirs, no more than Lake Superior could be considered
as the homeland of the tribes who lived near it.

It was not, of course, renegotiation that the protesters wanted,
but rather adherence to the original treaty as it had been negotiated.
They were against unilateral renegotiation by the other contracting
party—as who wouldn't be?

When Zeitner and Borglum talk of the reservation system, it is
possible that they are referring to the "termination" policy of the
1950s. Saying that the Sioux object to termination is a very different
thing, however, from saying that they "prefer the Reservation
system."

And somehow the United States manages to claim half of Lake
Superior as its territory, although no one lives there. By this stan-
dard most of Alaska and large tracts of the Midwest could be said to
not really belong to the United States. Only the southern tier of
Canada would be under the sovereignty of its central government.
The Russians would lose most of Siberia.

The authors go on to laud the notoriously substandard free
health care that the reservation Indians receive—Russell Means
himself lost his hearing in one ear as a child owing to the incompetence of Indian Service doctors—and to blame any expressions of

Indian discontent on "out-of-state agitators, many of them neither Sioux nor Indian." They note the pride that the white community takes in Indian achievements. "Bias is more on the basis of drunkenness versus sobriety, industry versus laziness, violence versus peace, than on the basis of red versus white." From their point of view, "radical groups accuse some predominantly white towns of prejudice, but this has not been proven."[11]

When I asked Zeitner, now retired from her primary career as a gemologist and lapidary, about the historical background of the Indian protests at Rushmore that she and Lincoln Borglum so harshly criticized, her expression became a little cold. "The Indians are American citizens, too," she said, taking up the assumption of a shared nationhood. "They have no right to vandalize or interfere with a national park."

The sense of nationhood was not and is not lost on many Indian activists, although sometimes their arguments are more ethically than practically relevant. As the Sioux lawyer, intellectual, and author Vine Deloria, Jr. points out, the American record of treaties with Indian peoples has implications for America's foreign policy. After all, how much trust and faith can other foreign nations have in U.S. treaties when such treaties are not honored with those who have signed the longest-running ones?[12] The record does seem to show that America's good faith toward Indians has rarely been a concern of other foreign-treaty partners, except when they wanted to score ideological points—which is to say, when they were not interested in warm relations with the United States anyway.

The Rapid City attorney Charles Abourezk has his own take on

Zeitner and Borglum's comments. Abourezk, a warm and soft-spoken man who still wears his graying hair in the long ponytail he favored as a young AIM sympathizer, grew up in Mission, on the Rosebud reservation, where Zeitner lived for many years and taught school. He knows the environment she came from.

"You have to understand this white clique in Mission. These guys acted like they weren't even on a reservation, it was like South Africa almost. They created their own city government there, a white mayor, an island of white jurisdiction on the reservation. Those guys really reacted strongly when the American Indian Movement came along, because they were the most threatened. They were used to a relationship of superior to inferior, and as long as Indians were 'good,' which meant that they knew their place, everything was just fine; it was only when Indians started articulating that they had rights and ideas and political thoughts of their own, that they were human beings, it started to disturb the fabric of things as they existed around here; so that passage doesn't surprise me at all. There was total denial of the meaning of the protests at Rushmore; they will never admit that, although some of the protests ended up being violent, they created change around the area.

"After the protests that began with the Yellow Thunder case, and especially after the Custer courthouse—that was a real wake-up call—it was a lot harder for Indians to be victimized by non-Indians around here. A lot of that was the fear factor; you hate to see change occur like that, but it did. People backed away from Indians, and that gave Indians room to breathe and change, and grow into a feeling of greater power, which was a wonderful thing."

Abourezk and his family have a long history with Indian civil rights. He grew up watching his father, James Abourezk, support Indian causes as a lawyer, congressman, and eventually U.S. senator and chair of the Subcommittee on Indian Affairs. James Abourezk generally aided the Sioux Black Hills claim as much as he could, several times in the 1970s intervening in the progress of the case through the courts by sponsoring bills that altered the underlying law in the Indians' favor—at that time something that the majority of his Indian constituents wanted him to do. Abourezk was instrumental in closing down the Indian Health Service's program of sterilization of Indian women without their informed consent, a practice that can only be called a tool of genocide and one that continued well into the 1970s. So much for the program of free health care that Zeitner and Borglum held up as a measure of Indian privilege.

James Abourezk, incidentally, also employed Russell Means three times, in roles that mirror the evolution of Means's militant Indian consciousness: in 1965, as an Indian show dancer dancing for tourists outside Abourezk's Gaslight Tavern in Rockerville, South Dakota; in 1970, as a campaign worker touring the South Dakota reservations during Abourezk's first bid for Congress; and in 1978, when Means worked for his Sioux Falls office on a work-release program while serving prison time on charges stemming from a "riot to obstruct justice" in 1974. This riot had begun when AIM supporters, during a hearing related to the Custer events, refused to stand for Judge Joseph Bottum and were attacked by police.

Charles Abourezk was friendly with many of the leaders of AIM and traditionalist movements on the Rosebud and Pine Ridge reservations in the 1970s, and he saw the lengths to which the corrupt tribal governments would go to preserve their privileges; his friend Byron DeSersa, a great-grandson of Black Elk and a tribal attorney, was killed in January 1976 in an ambush on the road near Wanblee, a town on Pine Ridge whose inhabitants had defied the administration of tribal chairman Dick Wilson. Wilson, who ruled through his armed "goon squad"—the name was given by opponents, although Wilson tried to neutralize it by calling his thugs the "Guardians of the Oglala Nation"—was supported by the BIA and the FBI, who hardly bothered to investigate the killing nor the bullets fired into Abourezk's house later that night, just missing his head.

In addition to his troubles with Wilson's tribal administration, Charles Abourezk's sympathies for AIM also brought him under the suspicion of the FBI. In 1976 the organization wrote a memo that named him as an arms supplier to a training camp for AIM militants, so-called "Dog Soldiers" who were sworn to die fighting and who were planning to bomb Rushmore and various other national monuments as the bicentennial approached. Strangely, this memo, not intended for public release, was left lying out on a desk at a West Coast BIA office. It found its way onto the news service wires, causing a great deal of fear in the plains states, already stirred up by several high-profile incidents of violence between Indians and civil authorities. None of the details of this memo were ever proved to be more than the fantasy of an informer who knew what the FBI wanted to hear, and, indeed, the memo turned out to be an embarrassment for the bureau. When James Abourezk filed papers under the Freedom of Information Act to determine how the FBI had developed this information and how the memo had reached the press, the FBI was forced to concede, somewhat stiffly, that "The teletype contained information pertaining to the American Indian Movement (AIM) furnished by a source with whom, as the teletype stated, insufficient contact had been had to determine his reliability, but who was in a position to furnish reliable information."[13] James Abourezk believes that the report was designed to discredit him and his son, a political attack on them for their sympathies with the Indian civil rights movement.[14] Russell Means, commenting on this incident, found it ridiculous but also listed some ambiguous benefits:

> We found the FBI's absurd accusations quite amusing. AIM couldn't afford to buy even one gun, let alone ship thousands or get two thousand "warriors" together. We thanked the FBI for its good PR. By dining on the same propaganda they relentlessly dished out, the feds had built AIM into a vast subversive organization with outlaws and renegades lurking behind every tree. The white man's fear of Indians had increased dramatically as a result. South Dakotans were just as worried about Indians as their great-grandfathers had been.[15]

If Zeitner and Lincoln Borglum reacted with hostility, many Indians, of many tribes, all over the country, were inspired by the occupiers' bold statement. Cultural ripples spread in other directions as well and kept the actions alive in art and in political memory. In a rather odd but passionate 1996 novel, *Sun Dancer*, David London wrote of a loose-knit traditionalist movement on the Pine Ridge Reservation that takes over Rushmore in 1990. Having learned from the 1971 experience, the activists are heavily armed. They even have antitank missiles stolen from Fort Benning and provided by a defrocked Catholic priest, a social-justice romantic. Their plan is to chain down hunger strikers on top of the stone heads in the old Lakota tradition of the *Napesni*, the No-Flights—warriors who staked themselves to the ground in battle so that they would have to prevail or die—while the armed militants hold off the feds so that their points about the Black Hills and the treaty can finally be told to the world via the media interest that the occupation draws.

London's novel is clunky and obvious in some ways. The narrator, Joey Moves Camp, is a cynical Lakota-speaking mixed-blood who both wants and doesn't want to believe in the old ways. Although he scoffs a bit, the mysticism of the "traditionals" is presented with a wide-eyed reverence that is a bit cloying. He has a privileged white girlfriend who means well but is ultimately feckless. All the other non-Indian characters are pure evil, except the rebel priest, who is pure good. The narrator's half brother, Clement Blue Chest, is a despairing drunk who finds the right path and sees a vision of the Black Hills returned to the Lakota through an extraordinarily punishing sun dance. He just may be the Messiah.

When FBI gunships and sharpshooters move in for the kill, Clem performs a suicidal sun dance, piercing his pectorals down to the rib cage and throwing himself off the top of Lincoln's head, his staked chain attached to the sharpened railroad spikes—symbolic of the iron roads that destroyed the buffalo and the plains Indian way of life—thrust through his chest. He insists that this act of sacrifice will get the Black Hills back for the Lakota, that it will serve as a powerful statement of what the Hills mean to his people, even if the only audience is made up of FBI and military men. Unsurprisingly it does not, at least by the time the novel ends in 1996, after the narrator serves his jailtime and comes home.

However labored the references, London does a good job of working the facts of the treaties into his story. He's done a fair amount of research on Rushmore itself. There's an interesting plot twist: although the press does show up to publicize the event, the Indians eventually realize that the reporters are all fakes, special agents brought in to distract the occupiers while the evil feds cordon off the area using the excuse of a chemical spill on a Black Hills rail line. They impose a news blackout so that they can shoot the Indians and keep the world in the dark about their treaty claims. Hey, it might've happened! For all we know.

Another novel, by Dan O'Brien, was inspired in small part by the Indian occupations of 1970 and 1971. His *Spirit of the Hills* is subtler and more far-ranging than *Sun Dancer*, capturing the beauty and power of the diverse South Dakota landscape, as well as the banality of much of the modern approach to the land. The central character is Bill Egan, an old man who is the world's greatest wolf tracker and trapper. He is called out of retirement to fight a duel with what may be a lone surviving gray buffalo wolf, a renegade like himself, a creature thought to have been extinct for more than fifty years.

The destinies of Egan, the wolf, several local officials, and Tom McVay, a Vietnam veteran from Toledo who has come west to avenge himself on a local drug dealer who is responsible for his little brother's death, all intertwine.

Spirit of the Hills also features an Indian encampment in the Black Hills modeled after Camp Yellow Thunder, an occupation of federal land in the Hills led by AIM militants that lasted for almost six years, from 1981 to 1987. Although the encampment is generally peaceful, there is a small splinter group, inspired by stories of AIM's Rushmore actions, that wants to blow up the monument.

This group has stockpiled explosives in a cache near the secret marijuana farm of P. J. Billion, the drug dealer that McVay has come to South Dakota to kill. When McVay and Billion are interrupted in their final struggle by the militants coming to collect their hidden explosives, McVay grabs a rocket launcher that Billion happens to have handy in his *own* Vietnam-era weapons stash, and unknowingly fires it right into the radicals' dynamite stockpile. The resulting massive explosion and fire neatly tie up several practical and symbolic plot threads: the Rushmore plan is foiled, as is the white man's anti-ecological fire prevention policy in the Hills, a symbol of the disastrous taming of what should be wild. All this happens as Egan kills his wolf and dies trying to prevent the wolf's body from being hung from a lamppost by rednecks who have read of, but do not understand, frontier traditions. Egan respects the wild even as he knows he must fight it, and although he kills the wolf, he does not want its dignity taken away. He protests in vain: nature is humiliated by thoughtless yokels. Fire rages in the Hills, a warning to all.

An explosion set off by a character named Tom McVay may seem like a cultural reference, but this book was published in 1988, seven years before Tim McVeigh, driving a Mercury Marquis with no license plates and carrying a .45-calibre Glock semiautomatic pistol, was stopped by Oklahoma Highway Patrolman Charles Hanger as he sped away from downtown Oklahoma City and into the national consciousness.

Some leeway must be granted a work of fiction when it describes real-life events, but O'Brien seriously overarms the AIM occupiers of the 1970s. In his book the Rushmore rangers speak of them having had explosives and of planning to blow up Rushmore as a last resort, which certainly was never the case—they did have some red paint, and some of them may have intended to use it on the faces. Still, the really interesting point about works like *Sun Dancer* and *Spirit of the Hills* is that they show how events echo not only in history but in imagination. In reworking Indian actions at Rushmore, these novelists both help to keep treaty issues on the national agenda and help to mythologize the occupation.

As a platform for presenting treaty grievances, the national monument, like Plymouth Rock—where AIM protested between the two Rushmore actions—has tremendous symbolism. In disputing the official meaning of Rushmore, perhaps the activists triggered some reflection among whites that the official story the monument tells about the majesty and justice of American leaders, institutions, and history has an alternative version. Even the most irony-deficient non-Indians might note that a monument to leaders who built a nation founded in part on respect for property rights was carved on a mountain that was stolen.

$$\boxed{11}$$

MORE POLITICS

C onceived as a tourist attraction but executed as a political statement, Rushmore has been put to many political uses, although its creator probably would not have imagined the range of opinion on the matter, nor the tools that would become available to Rushmore partisans of every political stripe, tools that would make his local pageants seem decidedly amateurish. When Gutzon Borglum died in 1941, television was a theoretical possibility, an experiment in laboratories in the United States and the Soviet Union. Given his wide-ranging technical and social interests and his voracious reading, it is not at all unlikely that Borglum had heard of and knew something about television technology. It is unlikely that he could have guessed how it would transform American society.

Television marked, in fact, a dramatic shift in the way cultural touchstones were presented and experienced, as well as a new way of

thinking about permanence and factuality. Rushmore looks impos-
ingly permanent, static, unchanging. It intentionally marks an idea
for the ages, yet it is also personal. To get the full effect, you have to
make an effort to get there, to stand in front of it. Television is tran-
sient, vulnerable to the whims of fashion, and does not invite a personal response. You can view television from just about anywhere in
the world nowadays. Film and video footage are easily fabricated.

Borglum thought of Rushmore as an intimately public experience, if that is not a contradiction, as a reaffirmation of the individual's faith in democracy and in American culture—Borglum
assumed that his audience had his own cultural perspective. Television, impersonal as it may be, is equally concerned with the rein-
forcement of cultural identity. Perhaps it is not so strange that
Rushmore and television were combined at a very important
moment in world broadcasting history.

It was a moment when national identity was of the utmost concern. Today, a decade or so into the post-Soviet period, it is already
hard to remember the paramount importance of the superpower
struggle only a few years ago. One has only to listen to presidential
debates from as recently as 1984, long after the peak of Cold War
hostility, to be reminded that the conflict shaped political discourse.
In the summer of 1962, with a hostile Soviet Union bristling with
hydrogen bombs, after the Cuban missile crisis, after recurring
Berlin crises, after Khrushchev had very recently pounded his shoe
on his U.N. podium and promised to "bury" the West, it was the
backdrop of all political and cultural life.

Given the technological obsessions of both nations, ideological competition automatically became technological competition, and in more than H-bombs, although these were naturally foremost in the thoughts of many. Kennedy had defeated Nixon partly on the strength of his 1960 debate statement about the missile gap being more important than the color television gap. Still, the color television gap mattered, especially after the Soviets launched Sputnik, the first man-made satellite, in 1957—a terrifying event that made Americans suddenly feel both outdone and naked, exposed to the prying eyes of our enemies. President Eisenhower and Congress immediately mandated an emergency national science curriculum, financed in part by cutting federal subsidies for teaching art in the public schools.

So the first commercial, international, American-satellite-bounced television broadcast was a bigger deal even than it seemed, although it was not generally presented as a major engagement in the Cold War. July 23, 1962, saw the inaugural of America's Telstar satellite, and the content chosen for the event had a political as well as a cultural significance. There were two 20-minute segments, one delivering American images to Europe, one European images to America. The European segment focused on iconic elements of the Old Culture: the Louvre, Big Ben, etc. The American segment was no less distinctive. We sent the Europeans a baseball game (Cubs versus Phillies), a presidential press conference, and Mount Rushmore, including a lingering pan on the face of Ben Black Elk. A Lakota Sioux was thus one of the very first people in the world to have his image broadcast by satellite across the Atlantic.

We hailed the Europeans (and the Soviets, whose leader we knew would be watching, even if the proletariat were forbidden to do so) with the full Mormon Tabernacle Choir, three hundred and twelve voices belting out "A Mighty Fortress Is My God" and "The Battle Hymn of the Republic." Subtlety was not the keynote of the era.

As the camera panned over the faces on the mountain, an announcer solemnly spoke of the presidents and their contributions to our nation's history. It was a powerful way to bring American values to the world, and the Soviets huffily took the hint. Though offered the broadcast for their networks, they declined, with Moscow radio indignantly noting that President Kennedy was using the hookup "in the same Cold War spirit as before."[1] Yugoslavia's Marshal Tito, who liked the Soviet Union as little as Kennedy did, eagerly accepted the broadcast. In the American media there was speculation that a majority of East German viewers had clandestinely tuned their televisions to the West German channels for the broadcast, which is impossible to verify but seems quite likely.

Borglum the visionary might have predicted the world of superpower satellite competition of that day, just twenty-one years after his death. Yet there is no question that it was a far different world than any of his subjects on the mountain could have imagined.

Like those who would enforce reverence for other symbols of nationhood, such as the flag, the proponents of a single meaning for Rushmore neglect an important danger of public iconography: the power that an official symbolism conveys, and the potential for turning that power to the service of a cause of the moment, no matter how dangerous or bizarre.

Ten years before the Telstar broadcast, in a radio address marking the twenty-fifth anniversary of the beginning of work on the monument, South Dakota Senator Karl Mundt reflected on what advice the figures on the mountain might have given to the modern world. Mundt seems to have had a bit of a one-track mind. He decided that all of them would have warned of the Soviet Union and of the communist threat, and especially of the traitors in our midst. Thus, Mundt's Lincoln:

> When a colossal danger such as global Communism threatens our country, let there evolve cooperation and support behind such common course of action as is necessary to the preservation of the last best hope on earth for human happiness and individual freedom. . . . Once more it is clearly indicated that if this country is ever to be destroyed, it will not be from without but from within.

And his Jefferson:

> Fellow Americans, in these days when Communists and foreign agents, Fascists and fairweather friends of freedom, urge you in the mis-named cause of Liberalism to forsake your individual rights, your freedoms, and your powers of self-decision for some foreign political pattern by which absolute power comes to be exercised by dissolute men of politics, may I remind you that the

Constitution of the United States remains the greatest liberal instrument of Government that the hand of man has ever written. Keep your Government as your servant. Keep yourselves as the masters of your destiny. Keep the miracle of Americanism as the most priceless heritage of future generations. Again may I remind you that Government is best which governs least.

And his Teddy Roosevelt:

As the opening of the Panama Canal fulfilled the dream of Columbus by opening a seaway westward from Europe to Asia, and as it knit closer together the East Coast with our West Coast, so today the radio, the airplane, television and atomic energy have fashioned our country into a tight little company of interdependent people and our World into a steadily diminishing globe of civilized and uncivilized communities. In this swift race of modern life, we must courageously assert our position in the world and confidently pursue our American success formula in increasing and maintaining our position of world leadership.[2]

The Roosevelt he presents is plausible; after all Roosevelt was closest to the world that Mundt knew. Roosevelt lived to see the early days of the Bolshevik revolution, and he might have guessed at

Mundt's intended political context, although the scope and the stakes would have been beyond even Roosevelt's considerable imagination. What could Lincoln have made of the Cold War? He must have known of the European revolutions of 1848, so decisive in forming Marx's political philosophy; but of Marx himself or of any modern doctrine of socialism he was probably entirely unaware. As to what Jefferson might have thought of the state of international affairs in 1952—but it doesn't matter. They all made an appearance in the Cold War.

Mundt never seems to have doubted his right to speak for these dead men, to play the medium who could convey their thoughts (which happened to align with his own and those of the more single-mindedly anticommunist wing of his Republican Party, as well as, admittedly, the mainstream American mood of the 1950s). The use of Rushmore and the borrowing of its authority in the service of contemporary political ideas and positions are an important aspect of the story of the monument.

Rushmore made a more entertaining appearance in the fight against global communism in 1959, when the mountain served as the backdrop for the defeat of Soviet spies in Alfred Hitchcock's *North by Northwest.*

Rushmore, with its power to evoke the grandeur of American democracy, appears on the cover of a decidedly odd document, a 1945 pamphlet that is an invitation from the governors of South Dakota, Nebraska, and Wyoming to the newly formed United Nations to make its home in the Black Hills. This was before the U.N. became associated in the minds of militia types in the West with socialistic plottings and crushing collectivism. The times were more optimistic in many ways, with the war just over, U.S. power unchallenged—the Soviets didn't have the Bomb until 1949—and the postwar world order not too distressing to those Americans who might nowadays obsess about national sovereignty and spend their weekends in camouflage outfits. The governors' reasoning is hopeful, if somewhat strained. They present maps to show that the Black Hills are equidistant from all the world's continents, and point out that

> no large city will absorb your capital's identity. Build your own capital on [a] natural location with its own individuality, in your own time, in your own way, adaptable to your own purposes. . . . Build in the Black Hills Country a United Nations Capital for World Peace where the last frontier of the world still remains in natural condition, free from embarrassing historical influences, awaiting the United Nations Charter to free the world of war.

The lack of "embarrassing historical influences" is interesting. The governors go on to say that "no racial, religious or nationalistic controversies exist. Complete freedom of religion and equality of persons before the law have always existed here"[3]—and perhaps there is no greater lesson to be learned from this than a reaffirmation of the healthy mistrust of the diplomatic maneuverings that all modern nations engage in. Still, it is worth saying that the sun dance and many other vital aspects of Lakota religion were explicitly against the law in 1945, and had been for some time. At Pine Ridge, Agent Valentine McGillycuddy announced in 1881 that the sun dance was interfering with the progress of civilizing the Indians, and that it was to cease in the following year. "The day of the Indian as an Indian [was] passing."[4]

Although McGuillicuddy found the sun dance—the "torture dance," he called it—appalling, it had some interest for him as a quaint curiosity, and when a lady ethnographer from Washington came to visit he saw no harm in appropriating for her a fertility symbol, the rawhide figure of an Indian with an enormous erection, that hung at the top of the last sun dance pole that the Lakota were to know for a very long time. While the Governors wished to present Rushmore as a symbol of freedom for the United Nations, it is important to remember that the sun dance was a ritual at the heart of who the Sioux were as a people. McGillycuddy was not being disingenuous in his belief that he was helping them to "progress" as a people, but he was a shrewd agent who knew the Sioux well, and banning the dance was a frankly political act.

It was not until the 1950s that the Lakota, after years of lobbying by the spiritual leader Frank Fools Crow, were to openly perform the sun dance again—and even then they could not hang from the ceremonial cottonwood tree or drag buffalo skulls attached by skewers in pierced flesh; they had to use harnesses that simulated piercing. It took another decade before they won back the right to practice their religious rituals as they defined them, and then only in closely supervised ceremonies.[5] Right up until 1978, when the

American Indian Freedom of Religion Act became law, government interference with the practice of Indian religion was legal.

The most directly political arguments over Rushmore have been about who should be on the mountain, and these arguments have been around for as long as the project itself has. Since Borglum's rejection of Doane Robinson's idea about western figures, candidates have included Woodrow Wilson, Franklin Roosevelt, Eleanor Roosevelt, John F. Kennedy, and Ronald Reagan. In the 1930s the feminist Rose Arnold Powell spent years lobbying tenaciously for Susan B. Anthony, struggling against Borglum's indifference and condescension.

The conservative writer William F. Buckley suggests that Ronald Reagan should be on Rushmore whenever he talks about Reagan's legacy, and the former president's actions toward indigenous people surely qualify him. To take just one example, Reagan gave political and military support to the tiny, European-descended Guatemalan elite that, in order to maintain its feudal privilege, had virtually enslaved the indigenous majority of the country. This elite—the two percent of the population that owned eighty percent of the land—used murder and torture as weapons of terror against Mayan Indians who were struggling for the most basic human rights. Among other things, the Guatemalan death squads were known to torture children as a way of getting their parents to confess to political activity. Reagan said often that American aid was intended to help those who were struggling for liberty in Central America. This monstrous doublethink is truly worthy of Rushmore.

Right-wing activist R. Emmett Tyrrell, former publisher of *The American Spectator* and longtime foe of liberal thought, also proposed Reagan for Rushmore. Tyrrell knows something about Presidents. *The American Spectator*, of course, was the magazine that launched the secret, so-called Arkansas Project, a plan to dig up dirt on President Clinton. The project was bankrolled by the reactionary businessman Richard Mellon Scaife to the tune of several million dollars. We all know the result of this project.

Tyrell is fun to talk to. He enjoys stirring things up. In 1989 he announced a plan to put Reagan on the mountain, "We plan to fly in a concrete nose and possibly two concrete ears, depending on the President's setting on Rushmore. The concrete appendages will be constructed in co-operation with Soviet industry, a leader in the field . . . "[6]

Tyrrell, the perennial bad boy of the American radical right, was having a little fun while making a larger point. "Reagan was the most effective President since Roosevelt," he told me, "the man who brought the Cold War to an end. He profoundly effected both foreign and domestic policy. Reagan was a very great President; but by the 1990s he also set off sirens in the minds of the politically correct, and I thought it would be amusing to see how they responded. In calling for this I found that it set off the sirens I expected, they went berserk . . . Any time life was getting boring for me, all I had to do was let fall in some public forum that I was revving up a campaign to put Reagan on Mount Rushmore, and the press would all be at my door. It was the kind of thing they took very, very seriously . . .

The media seemed to assume that this was what the editor of *The American Spectator*, notwithstanding the fact that he's written four or five books and edited several more, this is the kind of thing that really drives him, running around the country putting monuments up to right-wing presidents . . . The politically correct were mightily offended, and scared to death that we were on our way up there with the chisels."

There were no geologists and no money was actually raised by the committee itself, and Tyrrell did his best to prevent others from making money on the idea. But he did make an impression.

When I asked about the implications of the abrogated treaty of 1868 for the meaning of Rushmore, about the Indian protests at the mountain, about Borglum's associations with the Klan, Tyrrell didn't seem to know quite what to do with the questions. "Well I don't know about that. Frankly, I think these disgruntled groups— one would be the people who want to raise money—they're all out for their own self-advertisement. It's a meretricious impulse . . . "

When I asked him who else might deserve to be on the mountain, he suggested "Geronimo!" taking for granted that this is a way to honor the American Indian, and seemed quite confused that there is some Indian opposition to the Crazy Horse monument that is now under way in the Black Hills, about twenty-five miles from Rushmore.

The anger that liberals felt at Tyrrell's plans, that he knew they would feel, does show the power that has been invested in this mountain, the degree to which it confers influence on those who control the faces it presents to the nation. It's a purely rhetorical argument, since there isn't going to be any new carving on Rushmore. The NPS rangers will explain to all who suggest presidential additions that it's Borglum's work and it can't be changed, and that anyway there's no room on the mountain. Mountain monuments are out of touch with the modern mood. It's hard to imagine that Rushmore would get anywhere if it were proposed nowadays.

Regardless of who is on it, Rushmore as a symbol has taken on an almost religious sheen over the years. Indeed, it was always Borglum's explicit intention that the work have a somewhat religious aspect. Whether he was thinking in terms of a civil religion of democracy or truly along the lines of a Christian shrine is hard to say—these ideas are frequently muddled up together in his writings.

When Indian people criticize Rushmore, they frequently describe it as idolatrous. The word seems funny at first, something from a different age, but then so is Rushmore. The mountain carving may be dedicated to the nation, an expression of the personality cults of the various leaders and, secondarily, to the secular ideal of democracy, but it does have an air of religiosity. It is, after all, our Shrine of Democracy. In his 1927 dedicatory address, Calvin Coolidge spoke an odd phrase that was little remarked at the time but which seems to give sanction to this idea of the religious. Speaking of the apparent incongruity of such a massive undertaking in a relatively undeveloped state, he said: "The American spirit still goes where our people go, still dominates their lives, still inspires them to deeds of devotion and sacrifice. It is but another illustration of the determination of our people to use their material resources to minister to their spiritual life."[7]

Maybe the sense of a place is more powerful than the way its occupiers interpret it. The Black Hills had a religious significance for the Sioux and for the Crow and Cheyenne whom they displaced, who came to the Hills for hunts, for visions, ceremonies, and spiritual renewal, rarely staying for very long. The power of this land was heard in strange, thunderlike rumblings from the Hills. Mystery lived here.

Often in history, after conquest old ideas of worship appear in familiar forms acceptable to the conquerors. The transformation works both ways: it is how the conquered survive as the people they know themselves to be, and it is how the conquerors orient themselves in a land that is not theirs. The people of the Inca culture of Peru carried the mummified bodies of their rulers through the streets on feast days. The Spaniards put a stop to this idolatry, but allowed the processions to continue, replacing the mummies with life-size statues of saints. These modified processions continued for hundreds of years, until the day the wooden statues were taken for repair, at which time the workmen found that the Inca mummies were hidden inside the saints' images. There is a deep truth about cultural syncretism here, no less important for the fact that the Spanish rulers never knew what they had absorbed.[8]

The presidents on the mountain have consistently been described allegorically as objects of worship by those most closely associated with the project. Borglum himself, making the case for a presidential monument rather than one commemorating heroes of the West, wrote: "We believe the dimensions of national heartbeats are greater than village impulses, greater than city demands, greater than state dreams or ambitions. Therefore, we believe a nation's monument should, like Washington, Jefferson, Lincoln and Roosevelt, have a serenity, a nobility, a power that reflects the gods who inspired them and suggests the gods they have become."9

No Baptist or Pentecostal challenged Borglum on these words, which, however eloquent, do smell of the Golden Calf. The deification is startling, and when combined with Borglum's statements on scale and purity in art, it is hard to avoid the impression of a cult in the making—a cult at the service of the nation. The ascendance of "national heartbeats" over "village impulses" is the outcome of the story, in which the right of local people to have their own values and their own history is denied, subsumed by the national destiny, which is in turn a concept directed by a national secular religion.

It was around 1936, after Franklin Roosevelt spoke at the Jefferson unveiling—when Borglum specifically asked him to use the term—that Rushmore started to be commonly called America's Shrine of Democracy, although J. S. Cullinan of the Mount Rushmore Memorial Association had referred to it as "America's shrine to political democracy" as early as the Washington dedication in 1930. In the early days it had carried the working titles of the Empire Memorial, the Northwestern Memorial, or the Northern Memorial—in contrast to Stone Mountain, the Southern Memorial.

While FDR may well have been sincerely moved by the monument, he had a pragmatic reason for praising it in 1936. Against the backdrop of Rushmore, the father of the New Deal would certainly have wanted to emphasize both the abstract beneficent qualities of government and its ability to create jobs; Rushmore was by this time receiving some Depression-era funding from the Civilian Conservation Corps.

Near the end of Borglum's life, when it was plain that the faces were going to be finished, he wrote, "It is the hope that when completed it will be protected as a shrine, as Franklin Roosevelt so dedicated it, somewhat religious in character and not cheapened by concessions or other commercial agencies that abuse and destroy the sanctity of nearly all our places of interest."[10]

Calling the monument a "shrine" and invoking ideas about spiritualism and sanctity are rhetorical touches; but these kinds of references were used suspiciously frequently when it came to promoting and explaining Rushmore in those years, and popular opinion followed and resonated to these suggestions. And what are we to make of a 1941 article by Doane Robinson in which he compares Lincoln to Jesus of Nazareth?[11]

By 1958, when the new Rushmore amphitheater was fully in service and various local groups were trying to get permission to use it for functions, the meetings that the monument administration felt appropriate for the site included Flag Day celebrations and "any other patriotic ceremonies that are national in scope," the concluding ceremonies for the annual Boy Scout "pilgrimage"—and Easter Sunday rites.[12]

When I suggested to Charlotte Black Elk, the granddaughter of

Ben Black Elk and the great-granddaughter of the Lakota mystic Black Elk—she is a Lakota activist who has long been involved in Black Hills claims issues—that Rushmore has taken on a religious quality in mainstream American life, she responded, "There's a need in Western society to have a being or a person to worship at a specific place. The United States being a country and European-Americans being people without a long tradition here, and having structured a government that really secularized itself, there is a notion that we will come up with these [points of worship] in a different way. 'This is our pyramid or our Parthenon, our Notre Dame, Sistine Chapel ceiling, or whatever; we're going to create something that shows that we have heroes, that we have a tradition.' Most of the people from the immigrant society that by and large makes up the United States are not people who brought their cultural traditions with them in totality, so they tried to replace them where they could."

The Black Hills have for now been lost to the Lakota as a focus of spiritual life, and prayer groups would not get permission from the NPS to clamber around on Rushmore for religious services—not that, in its present, tourist-oriented form, it is a spot where it is particularly easy to feel the pulse of the natural world. Throughout the Black Hills area, a sort of uneasy and fluctuating truce prevails between the spiritual practices of Indians and the recreational demands of tourists.

Rushmore has been invested with an official reverence, and visitors are constrained to treat it with respect; yet Indians are often reduced to bargaining and suing for the right to carry on religious practices in their own land, the land that Rushmore looks out over like some inscrutable fetish. Any conclusions about the meaning of Rushmore would be incomplete without looking at the local politics of Indian religious observance and the contrast with the politics of the officially unacknowledged, semi-religious veneration of Rushmore.

Non-Indians in this country have usually been able to take for granted that their religious rights will be respected. They can find some security in the First Amendment. This has never been the case for American Indians, and since Indian/white politics almost always involve land and resources, and Indian religion by its nature is bound to the land, there is an entwinement of religion, land and politics.

Take the case of Mato Tipi-la—Bear Lodge—or Devil's Tower, as the town of Hulett, Wyoming, voted in 1996 to continue calling it, even though that name is offensive to those who follow traditional religions in which the site is important. There is no Devil, no figure of absolute evil in Indian lore, although the Trickster figure, who teaches through mischief, is ubiquitous in American Indian cultures. They share him with virtually every indigenous culture in the world, where he appears as Loki of the pre-Christian Norse, Bamapana of the Northern Australian Murnging, the Chinese Monkey King, the Polynesian Kaulu, a thousand others. While those who know the Trickster may fear his power, they know they can learn from him. The Lakota, like the West Africans, know him as a spider, and they call him Iktomi.

Devil's Tower National Monument is the oldest park in the National Park system, inaugurated by Teddy Roosevelt in 1906. The tower itself rises out of the earth in a cracked and grooved column hundreds of feet into the clear blue Wyoming sky, a landmark from some violent younger age of the planet; it prompts the viewer to imagine it surrounded by primeval volcanoes, exotic ferns. No wonder the aliens of Hollywood's *Close Encounters of the Third Kind* chose to land here.

The tower is visible from twenty miles away on a clear day. The guideposts say that the hard granite was exposed as the Belle Fourche River eroded away the surrounding softer alluvial deposits over the passage of forty million years. The small post office and KOA campground near its base seem trivial, the feeble attempts of humans to impose their presence on this strange landscape; their transience is plain next to the tower.

When geologists look at the tower, they see rock that hardened underground from volcanic magma and is therefore plutonic rather than igneous. During the cooling process, the rock contracted and split, acquiring its characteristic grooves. The traditionalists see the marks left by a bear who pulled the tower up into the sky, dragging his claws along its length. Bear Lodge.

The difference in viewpoint is as profound as the differing ideas on the use of the land; it is a difference in the way people think about the seen and the unseen which has been a continuing argument within rationalized, pragmatic Western civilization, not just between that civilization and others. Take this description of the tower, for instance, from a pamphlet published for tourists in Sundance,

Wyoming, in the 1940s: "The weight of the tower proper without the broken off material at its base is estimated at about four hundred million tons. It has also been estimated that a single column with an average diameter of ten feet and length of five hundred fifty feet would, if crushed, provide enough material to surface more than four miles of sixteen foot highway. The entire mass of the Tower would provide sufficient surfacing for a sixteen foot roadway nine times around the world."[13] Contrast these words with the climbing policy expressed by the NPS a few years earlier, in 1937: "As we view it resting in silent solemnity upon its imposing throne, we sense that it bespeaks a commemorative message from the directing force of all nature,"[14] a statement that many Lakota traditionalists could accept. Are these views opposed? Many of those involved in present-day politics at the tower insist that they are not and that dual-use can be a psychological as well as a utilitarian concept.

There is a long approach to the tower by road, then a parking lot high in the thin, cold Wyoming air. When the light hits the tower on the "rough" side, it glows pink; around on the "smooth" side, where I took a walk along a carefully managed NPS trail, it is darker and colder. An air of reflection, almost of brooding, set in as dusk found me alone there.

On the road from the parking lot signs for the visitor read: "The Tower Is Sacred to American Indians—Please Stay on Path." "Please Do Not Disturb Prayer Cloths and Prayer Bundles." There are many of these, multicolored flags of material hanging from trees, waving slowly in the afternoon breeze.

The traditionalists come to the tower each year to perform such ceremonies as the sun dance, sweat lodge rites, and vision quests and make prayer offerings, but they never climb it. The sun dances and sweat lodges are on the banks of the Belle Fourche.

In recent years these observances have been increasingly disturbed by recreational rock climbers. Pressured by Indian religious practitioners, the NPS responded in 1995 with a compromise plan: a voluntary ban on climbing the tower during the month of June, when most of the Indian ceremonies take place, accompanied by aggressive educational efforts on its spiritual significance to the Indians; a discontinuation of commercial climbing licenses for that month, starting in 1996; no additional placements of climbing bolts and pitons; and a ban on climbing routes that disturb the nesting sites of the falcons that live on the cliff face. Of the Indians and climbers who responded to NPS polls in the first year the ban was in effect, most appeared to at least accept the compromise.

Not all climbers, and not all Indians. Many Indians would prefer that there be no climbing at all, and some climbers and those who profit from climbing were outraged at the restrictions on their right to public land. Andy Petefish, director of Tower Guides, and several other climbers, under the rubric of the Bear Lodge Multiple Use Association, sued the NPS for unlimited climbing access all year round. They were represented by the Mountain States Legal Foundation.

The foundation likes to present itself as a populist defender of constitutional rights, but it has some funding sources that are pretty far from ordinary people—virtually all the major oil companies

(Amoco, Chevron, Exxon, Marathon Oil, Phillips 66, Texaco), the Ford Motor Company, the Coors Foundation and Company—a regional power—and timber and gas interests. Founded in 1977, it has long been associated with the "wise use" movement, a loose coalition of anticonservation groups that seek relaxation of environmental protection and endangered species laws in the name of fighting "arbitrary and capricious" regulation. In keeping with the right-wing view of nature as a pest to be subdued, the foundation has sued to prevent the Department of the Interior from reintroducing wolves into Idaho, Wyoming, and Montana and condors into Arizona, Utah, and Nevada. It also supports reactionary causes outside the strictly environmental arena, working against gun control, unions, and affirmative action, helping to win a major Supreme Court case in *Adarand v. Pena*, which severely limited minority set-asides in federal contracting. Former Idaho representative Helen Chenoweth, one of the most extremist, anticonservation, antifederal politicians in the country, someone who has spoken approvingly of the paranoid "militia" movement that spawned Timothy McVeigh, has called the foundation "one of America's finest litigating organizations."[5]

The foundation has consistently claimed that Indians have no aboriginal or treaty rights that are inherently different from those of other American citizens—and that any assertion to the contrary is merely a ploy by the federal government to further erode individual freedom.

The foundation is certainly not responsible for the more radical beliefs and actions of fringe groups in the Pacific Northwest. Its agenda, however, is very topical in a part of the country where there has been persistent—and often violent—opposition to government restrictions on federal and private land in the name of conservation, where land-use issues are political minefields, and the activities of the Forest Service, Fish and Game Service, and the Environmental Protection Agency are frequently read as an apocalyptic conspiracy, the end of freedom; and where employees of these agencies often have to operate under armed protection.

The foundation presented the Devil's Tower issue as a matter of taxpayer rights and the nonestablishment of religion governed by the First Amendment. After all, the climbers and guides don't want to force anyone to climb the tower, and they don't object to Indian religious practices there; they just want the freedom to do their thing.

William Perry Pendley, president and chief legal officer of the foundation, tries to keep his opposition to the NPS policy in First Amendment terms, although at times a hint of a larger agenda showed through as he explained the issue to me. "If the NPS is able to restrict access to a particular part of the federal lands, lands that are open to logging, snowmobiling, whatever, because some Americans believe that a particular site is sacred, other federal land managers, the Forest Service, the Bureau of Land Management, or any other agency that regulates federal lands, would be able to do the same thing. . . . The Forest Service up in Medicine Wheel, in Sheridan County, Wyoming, is planning to make a decision that a certain amount of timber will not be harvested because that timber is visible from Medicine Wheel. The Forest Service has made a decision in New Mexico that a Santa Fe ski area cannot expand because some Native Americans regard the area of the expansion as sacred. These decisions have economic consequences, and that's disturbing."

When I pointed out to him that Devil's Tower is within territory covered by the 1868 treaty, which has never been legally superseded, he doesn't want to go there. "That was then; this is now. We all have to live under the U.S. Constitution. I'm not going to fight that fight." He suggested that there were more serious offenses against Indians to discuss than anything that is happening at Devil's Tower, which is true enough. And yet by his own admission his organization aims at the larger issue of preserving economic access to lands that were in many cases illegally expropriated from Indians—while he refuses to talk about treaty issues. The conversation is both interesting and frustrating, for Pendley cannot accept any way of doing things that would involve giving up any of the economic and legal privileges to which he and his sponsors feel entitled. It is a most basic form of tribalism.

The Multiple Use Association plaintiffs were opposed by the NPS and by elders of the Cheyenne River Sioux Tribe, as well as by the tribe itself as a formal entity. The NPS and the tribe were at first rebuffed by Judge William Downes in Casper, Wyoming, who accepted the plaintiff's First Amendment argument; but the NPS responded with a version of the policy in which commercial licenses would be issued but climbing would be "discouraged"; Indian

employees would be responsible for explaining the spiritual importance of the tower and the ceremonies, with the goal of turning away
climbers.

The Mountain States Legal Foundation, which opposed both
the voluntary ban and the cultural education program—which it
called "proselytizing"—in its original brief, continued to fight the
revised policy. Pendley told me that a voluntary restriction at the
tower would amount to intimidation of those who wanted to climb
in June, because no climbers, regardless of how they felt about
Indian religious practices, would want to end up as a statistic
proving the NPS's case for an involuntary ban. The foundation has
even litigated, on the basis of the establishment clause and the
assumption of intimidation, against the placement of the signs
advising visitors of the tower's significance to American Indians.
This argument has so far been without success in the courts.

If Pendley is diplomatic in his appeals to constitutional interpretation and to larger issues of managing public resources, his client
Andy Petefish is frightening in the intensity of his anger against
anyone who would limit his own gratification.

We had a rather odd conversation.

I asked him if, in spite of his legal position, he had any sympathy
for the Indians' needs. This is the point at which most people say
something like "I understand how they feel, but . . . "

"Sympathy?" he asked, injecting an amazing amount of scorn into
the word. "I don't really understand the question."

When I asked again, he said, "I respect their right to practice their religion, but I respect my right to practice my religion too, and part of my religion is climbing. I don't respect the fact that they don't respect my religious freedom."

When I asked him how climbing qualifies as a religion, he said, "Who are you to decide? . . . Climbing is a spiritual pathway, it opens your mind to awareness, makes you a better person from my point of view. . . . We don't really have a God or anything, but it doesn't really matter. Who are you to say?"

Speaking of prior claims, he said "The Indians may have been there before we were, but they were all running around killing each other because that was their way of savage, tribal life. So maybe we should just go back to that and throw away all of our civilization and our law and equal rights and equal treatment . . . maybe we should just go back to the savage way of life that they used to live."

Few Americans nowadays, even in the West, are quite this unabashed.

I knew, of course, that the issue is more complicated than the question of the persistent legality of the 1868 treaty; yet Petefish defended his case so self-righteously on the basis of the Constitution that I could not resist pointing out that the treaty is in fact the only legitimate law here, that it was negotiated with a sovereign nation and has never been legally superseded. Here his legal scholarship seemed to run out of steam. He was even more casual about the treaty than Pendley was. "Oh, treaties are broken all the time," he said. "That doesn't apply now."

"You can't hide behind the law as long as it does what you want it to do and then say that it's irrelevant when it comes to treaties," I said.

"That's just the way things happen," he replied. "Laws can be changed. The treaty law is no longer applicable."

He then used the classic line of the historically privileged. "I think equal rights is where it's at. It doesn't matter what treaty law or whatever happened back then, because that's outdated; it's ancient history. We're talking about today and we're talking about equal rights, and everyone should have the equal right to practice their religion the way they see it. . . . Allowing climbing does not prohibit their free exercise. I have a paper right here that says so."

When I asked whether it was not simply a matter of money for him, because his own climbing was not affected by a voluntary restriction on climbing, so his definition of climbing as his religion was a moot point, he said that being a teacher and a guide was part of his religion, too.

Bear Butte—Mato Paha (bear mountain)—has dual-use problems, too. It rises up near the town of Sturgis, South Dakota, the home of Fort Meade and the U.S. Cavalry Museum. This is perhaps the most sacred Indian site in the Black Hills, a place for the vision quest, that ancient ritual of self-denial and enlightenment. The mountain is a startling shape on the surrounding prairie; it really does look like a bear resting on its side, its head on its paws. The pine growth on its steep ridges is thick and dark. Wild buffalo graze in the parkland around it. Here in 1857 the Sioux tribes in their largest-ever gathering, met and agreed to resist further white invasions.

The first government representative to come through the area, in 1855, apparently started no trouble, although his mission was ominous: Dr. F. V. Hayden was involved in a geological survey. He was followed in 1859 by Captain William F. Raynolds, who presided over the first known Christian services in the Black Hills. Most famously, Custer came through in 1874 on his way out of the Hills after finding that gold.

Bear Butte has been a state park since 1961. At the visitors' center at its base is a small bust of Frank Fools Crow with an inscription declaring him a man of peace and wisdom. Ceremonial offerings of tobacco are set upon the pedestal. Along the paths winding up the sides of the butte, some paved and some not, multitudes of prayer cloths flutter in the breeze; some are tied to small trees and bushes, and others cover the ground, held down with rocks. There are also long strips of offering cloths, tied in any number of knots from a few to hundreds, each knot a measure of pain and devotion containing a tiny piece of flesh cut from the devotee's body. Christians are redeemed through the suffering of Christ; the Sioux traditionalists, a tough lot, take their responsibilities personally.

At Bear Butte, as at Devil's Tower, there have been conflicts relating to whether tourism and religious ceremonies can coexist, made somewhat more difficult by the fact that the vision quest can take up to four days to complete and requires complete isolation. Enrolled tribal members are not subject to the park use fees that are required of others, but permits are required to conduct religious ceremonies, a most odd restriction on religious activity in this country. In 1982, when the state required religious practitioners to camp several miles away while construction went on at the park, Frank Fools Crow filed a federal suit under the First Amendment, the Indian Religious Freedom Act, and the International Covenant on Civil and Political Rights, asking for complete and unrestricted access to the park. U.S. District Court Judge Andrew Bogue ruled against the petitioners; his judgment, like that of Judge Downes in Wyoming, was rendered on the grounds that the relief sought from the state actually violated the anti-establishment clause of the First Amendment; the distractions of multiple-use tourism did not constitute religious restraint.

As the Indians see it, the noise of vehicles and hikers is a problem, as is the intrusion of those who photograph ceremonies and sometimes even take home, for souvenirs, offerings left on the mountain. It is hard to imagine the NPS enforcing the Lakota prohibition on menstruating women in the area during the sacred ceremonies. The prospect of even asking female tourists and hikers about that condition, much less enforcing the ban, raises such a nightmarish prospect of litigation for the NPS that it would probably be simpler to close the park altogether or give it back to the tribes as strictly tribal land. It is unlikely that any of these alternatives will come to pass.

Beyond any specific contrast in the attitude toward religious affairs in the Black Hills when Indian and non-Indian practitioners are involved, religion plays a role in the unique politics of Indian land. Religious rights can be expressed in political terms; political rights can be secured through the invocation of religion. Lest this seem too abstract, the point is this: The Mount Rushmore area will continue to be treated as a semi-religious shrine and a political focus for some whites without much government objection. Indians will continue to have to beg, ask, demonstrate, and sue for reasonable access to their own religious areas—on their own land, ceded to them by treaty.

12

THE BLACK HILLS SETTLEMENT

T he taking of the Black Hills is a story with some surprising twists. In 1980 the various Sioux tribes and their lawyers, Arthur Lazarus and Marvin Sonosky of Washington, D.C, won a settlement of seventeen million dollars plus interest from 1877 from the Indian Claims Commission, a body set up specifically to allot monetary compensation for Indian claims. The judgment, along with several smaller related settlements, amounted to $117 million, the largest judgment ever in an Indian claims case. By that time the issue of taking money for land had become such a symbol of cultural sellout that tribal representatives could not accept anything less than the return of the Black Hills, with the ultimate goal of getting back other land that had been in the Great Sioux Reservation of 1868. The Pine Ridge tribal council attempted to sever its ties with the lawyers, who had fought the case for more than twenty years and who during much of that time had

had the support and encouragement of many of the traditional people and elders on the reservation.

Mario Gonzalez, who grew up in the northeast part of the Pine Ridge reservation and who was the first Oglala Sioux tribal member to become a licensed attorney, was the general counsel of the Oglala Sioux Tribe. On July 18, 1980, he filed a motion in U.S. district court for an injunction to prevent disbursement of the money to the 1868 treaty tribes. The simple transfer of the money from an account belonging to the General Accounting Office to one belonging to the Department of Interior, which includes the BIA, would have constituted "payment" for the Black Hills and an extinguishment of Sioux title. There was a time limit on disbursement, and once it expired any release of the money would require authorization from Congress to distribute the funds.

Gonzalez had a better idea for a settlement. He sued the United States for return of the Black Hills and an $11 billion settlement, $1 billion of which was to be compensation for suffering and loss of life resulting from the destruction of the Indians' economy, and the remainder for the resources taken out of the Black Hills since 1877—all that timber, coal, tin, and Homestake silver and gold. He based his case on the fundamentally unconstitutional nature of the confiscation under the Act of 1877, an apparent abrogation of the Fifth Amendment, for it was done not to accomplish any strictly public purpose, but rather in order to take the land for the private economic endeavors of miners, mining corporations, homesteaders and railroad companies.

The federal courts dismissed the case on the grounds that only the Indian Claims Commission had jurisdiction to hear Indian treaty cases, and the Indian Claims Commission was authorized only to dispense monetary judgments.

The courts may have considered the case closed, but the courts are only one branch of the government. A few years after the Supreme Court upheld the Black Hills settlement, traditionalists and political activists from several of the South Dakota reservations formed the Black Hills Steering Committee, organized to submit new Black Hills legislation to Congress and to lobby for its passage. To oversee the legislative effort the committee appointed Gerald Clifford, a mixed-blood Oglala traditionalist (by way of a stint in a Catholic monastery) and the husband of the traditionalist and activist Charlotte Black Elk. The bill that the council eventually drafted included some of the things that Gonzalez had sought in his lawsuit and indeed was greatly influenced by his efforts. It was an attempt to invoke the terms of the 1868 treaty in a way as nearly compatible as possible with conditions in the modern world.

What eventually became the Sioux Nation Black Hills Act described an area of tribal jurisdiction somewhat reduced from the 1868 area and including the existing reservations. The "re-established area" of the bill was to be more or less the Black Hills segment of South Dakota, about 1.3 million acres. The bill set up a timetable for the return of all land, water, and mineral rights and all federal property in this area to the Sioux Nation, with some exemptions for particular vital uses; it mandated the renegotiation, with the Indian authorities, of all private timber, grazing, and other resource leases on the returned land after two years or the expiration of the lease, whichever came first; it set up tribal administrative structures for the land in question and set aside a Sioux National Park and National Forest, under Indian jurisdiction, for the protection of religious sites, where the Indians would have the final say about who could be on the land and for what purpose. It adhered to the terms of 1868 in that non-Indian lawbreakers on the returned lands were to be extradited to U.S. jurisdictions, although it left open the possibility that the tribes could negotiate for prosecutorial authority in the future.

The bill specifically did not return land held by private individuals or by the state of South Dakota, although it required the tribes to be offered the right of first refusal when private or state land was sold. It required the federal government to acquire certain lands in the Black Hills in order to return them to the tribes. And it gave the Indians an acceptable option for claiming their Black Hills money, by defining it as compensation for confiscated resources rather than as settlement of a land claim. The bill included a formula for the investment and conservation of this money for purposes that would benefit the tribes as a whole.

It exempted Mount Rushmore from the lands to be returned, although it specified that the tribes should be given preference in concessions contracts.

In 1985 the Black Hills Steering Committee persuaded Senator Bill Bradley of New Jersey to introduce the legislation in the Senate, and it then became known as the Bradley bill.

Bradley had some connection with the Lakota people. In the early 1970s he had run summer basketball clinics on the Pine Ridge

Reservation. Standing by the marker at Wounded Knee and looking out over the prairie landscape, he had felt something of the tragedy of the patchwork reservations, the small and resource-poor parcels of the Indians' patrimony.

Bradley, always something of a maverick in national politics, was willing to take an extraordinary political gamble on behalf of people who were not even his constituents. His bill earned the complete hostility of the two South Dakota senators and the single representative, as well as that of many other western congressmen. South Dakota governor George Mickelson, who had been to some extent an ally of the Lakota, bombarded Bradley with legal defenses of the status quo and historical arguments against any Lakota claim to the Hills.

The arch-conservative senator from South Dakota, Larry Pressler, insisted that returning the land had no moral or legal basis and that the Indians of New Jersey might have a better claim. His friend Senator Malcolm Wallop of Wyoming obligingly threatened to introduce legislation that would return a million acres of New Jersey land—including the Statue of Liberty—to the Leni-Lenape. Indeed, New Jersey Indians who still exist as distinct groups might well have a just claim, which may explain why many senators and many Americans felt threatened by the bill. If Congress were to start returning land to its owners by treaty, where would the business stop?

The bill was just as fervently opposed by Jim Abdnor, the other senator from South Dakota. Although Abdnor was defeated in the 1986 election, his replacement, Tom Daschle, who, unlike Pressler, had campaigned as a friend of the Indians, fought the Bradley bill with more than just rhetoric. He set up the Open Hills Council, an organization dedicated to blocking any attempt at returning land or offering monetary compensation to the Lakota. Amid distractions from a competing land-return bill backed by tribal factions opposed to the work of the Black Hills Steering Committee—a bill that had no chance of passage in Congress because it involved a $3.1 billion cash award for damages and virtual Lakota secession from the United States—the Bradley bill died a quiet death in committee.

The Sioux Nation Black Hills Act was big news in South Dakota, although the actual terms of the bill were not widely understood. Many non-Indian property owners in the Hills felt that their rights were threatened and seemed not to realize that the bill did not affect private property.

In one sense, however, the bill was truly cataclysmic, and perhaps this was at the root of much of the panic it inspired. The legislation was an attempt to understand and fulfill some of the most important assumptions that the Indians had held about the treaty they signed in 1868—that is, that it was a treaty between sovereign nations who were trying to work out rules for following separate destinies in mutual respect. In acknowledging not only property claims but also limited legal jurisdiction and religious rights—the bill refers to religious sites and traditional Lakota values without condescension and in the Lakota language—it was again treating the Lakota as a separate and to some extent sovereign nation. To Americans who were used to an assumption of loyalty to a single national state, the recognition of an Indian nation within the United States could be highly disturbing. Why should the Indians be treated differently from anyone else? Aren't we all Americans? The likelihood that the bill would have just a small impact on the actual day-to-day lives of non-Indians in the Hills was easy to overlook.

Pervading all the property and legal issues, some aspects of history and culture won't go away so easily, either. Charles Abourezk, the Rapid City attorney who has long worked on Indian civil rights issues, put it to me like this:

"The Black Hills is an easy issue if you address racism. It's sort of a code word for racism. Racism is all about maintaining privilege and control over the institutions that matter. If you've been raised like many whites around here, with the idea that Indians are on the bottom, the idea that Indians could be managing the forests, running the concessions at Mount Rushmore, selling hunting and fishing licenses, all that is appalling—and also frightening. And there's fear of oppression. Whites who own property in the Hills are afraid that they'll be treated like they treated the Indians. If you take away racism, it's just a change of land management. But the battles—the competition for land resources—are still going on. There are many who want to complete the process that started with military actions, continued with treaty making, and is now being fought in the policy arena."

With congressional action to restore the Black Hills now a very remote possibility, there remains the question of what to do with the Black Hills money, if anything. So far the Sioux tribes have been unanimous in their rejection of the claims money. This may be changing. Since the mid-1990s some cracks have appeared in the wall of Sioux solidarity against accepting the money. In June 1996,

Representative Bill Barrett of Nebraska formally gave his support to a petition by the Santee Sioux tribe of Nebraska to claim money held by the government, not under the Black Hills claim itself but a related Sioux claim that concerns land both east and west of the Missouri. The Sioux had held this land under an 1851 treaty and by aboriginal title, and the government claimed they had voluntarily ceded it by the treaty of 1868. Money for this claim and the Black Hills claim has now been merged into interest-bearing accounts maintained by the Secretary of the Interior.

The Santee settlement, like the Black Hills settlement, had been politically untouchable. This particular action was beaten back by Mario Gonzalez, who showed the Indian Affairs Committee that the Santee Sioux tribe was not a legitimate signatory to the 1851 treaty, and by the eight modern-day Sioux tribes who have an interest in the claim. The presidents of the Pine Ridge, Rosebud and Cheyenne River tribes all testified against the Santee claim at the congressional hearing.

In 1997 the tiny Fort Peck Assiniboine Sioux tribe in Montana voted to accept their share of the settlement, which would come to about two and a half million dollars. There is some ambiguity about their claim, however, because the Fort Peck tribe was created in 1888 by an executive order, and the tribe has to prove that its members are lineal descendants of the parties to the treaty of 1868. The Fort Peck tribe does not have the support of the Great Sioux Nation Treaty Council, the pan-Sioux organization made up of representatives from the tribal councils. It is these tribal councils that would, under treaty law, be responsible for securing the assent of three-quarters of the adult tribal members and then requesting that Congress draft legislation to release the money.

It is easy to see that a per capita distribution of this money would be a disaster, a birthright quickly squandered. At first glance it is less easy to see the political objection to, for example, setting up a tribal endowment with the money—with compound interest the settlement is now worth $500 million—and using the interest to buy back public and private land in the Black Hills. It's hard for an outsider to even express this idea; most Lakota people will be all over the speaker as fast as he can say "Why not accept the money and then . . . ?"

Accepting the money, even with the specific understanding that it would be used to buy back Black Hills land, would cause both practical and ideological problems. In practical terms—not the most important part of the argument for many Lakota—buying back land and incorporating it into the tribal domain would be more difficult than it seems. A tribal attorney explained it to me like this. "So the Lakota have a half-billion dollars in an endowment. What's the interest on that? We'll make it easy, say 10 percent. So the tribes have fifty million a year to spend on land, and everyone in the Black Hills who wants to sell knows it. How much do they inflate their prices for these rich Indians? Three times? Four times the market price?

"The only way for the tribe to acquire land at a reasonable price would be to use a non-Indian as a front. But then what happens? To get the land into trust status, which has to be done if tribal sovereignty and tribal property tax exemptions are to apply, the land must officially belong to the tribe. It's not so simple as having the front sell it back to the tribe for a dollar. Any county, any township, that feels it would lose tax revenue on the deal could object to the sale. That would make acquiring land for the tribe almost impossible."

The whole question of accepting the money on any terms would open up a very risky and divisive debate. Some would want it distributed per capita, and some would propose worthwhile tribal projects. Some would wrangle about who was entitled to recover the money—only full-bloods? Only the direct descendants of those who signed the treaty? Only—who? Some non-Indians would be delighted to see this divisive debate take place among the Sioux. During his Senate tenure, Larry Pressler, always an enemy of tribal sovereignty, often pressed for a referendum among the Sioux tribes on whether to accept the Black Hills money; he knew that the forms of democracy could be used as a weapon against them.

For many Lakota, such issues are moot. The position that the land was never sold and therefore cannot be bought back is an article of almost religious faith. Raymond Ogle, chair of the Fort Peck tribal council may argue that by accepting the money "the only thing you are giving up is your right to say you never sold the land,"[1] but that statement remains an impossible barrier to settlement for many. Beyond that lies the matter of what the treaty really meant and means, the same matter of perception that proved so problematic for Red Cloud and the politicians who dealt with him: Was it essentially a treaty of peace or a treaty of cession?

There is a matter of political identity. Although the argument is not explicitly made that the government has an interest in "terminating" the special rights of the Sioux tribes with a onetime monetary payment, there is a great fear on the reservations that settlement would result in termination by another name, that accepting the money would mean the end of a legal status based on treaty relations and the end of all government support for tribal programs and tribal sovereignty—which would spell the end of any sort of recognition, no matter how ambiguous, of the Sioux as a distinct national unit, a separate cultural and political identity.

This fear is not paranoid. Much of U.S. Indian law is still governed by the precedent set in 1823, when Supreme Court Justice John Marshall laid out his "doctrine of discovery." He ruled in *Johnson v. McIntosh* that the Christian discovery of "heathens" gave Christians ultimate dominion over non-Christians. In Marshall's view, by the same token, the authority of the United States superseded sovereignty of the tribes.

The decision is a strange mixture of brutal candor, regard for the civil rights of potential citizens, and a rather modern faith in the idea of racial integration. It is worth quoting at length.

On the discovery of this immense continent, the great nations of Europe were eager to appropriate to themselves so much of it as they could respectively acquire. Its vast extent offered an ample field to the ambition and enterprise of all; and the character and religion of its inhabitants afforded an apology for considering them as a people over whom the superior genius of Europe might claim an ascendancy. The potentates of the old world found no difficulty in convincing themselves that they made ample compensation to the inhabitants of the new, by bestowing on them civilization and Christianity, in exchange for unlimited independence. But, as they were all in pursuit of nearly the same object, it was necessary, in order to avoid conflicting settlements, and consequent war with each other, to establish a principle, which all should acknowledge as the law by which the right of acquisition, which they all asserted, should be regulated as between themselves. This principle was, that discovery gave title to the government by whose subjects, or by whose authority, it was made, against all other European governments, which title might be consummated by possession.

The exclusion of all other Europeans, necessarily gave to the nation making the discovery the sole right of acquiring the soil from the natives, and establishing settlements upon it. It was a right with which no Europeans could interfere. It was a right which all asserted for themselves, and to the assertion of which, by others, all assented.

Those relations which were to exist between the discoverer and the natives, were to be regulated by themselves. The rights thus acquired being exclusive, no other power could interpose between them.

In the establishment of these relations, the rights of the original inhabitants were, in no instance, entirely disregarded; but were necessarily, to a considerable extent, impaired. They were admitted to be the rightful occupants of the soil, with a legal as well as just claim to retain possession of it, and to use it according to their own discretion; but their rights to complete sovereignty, as independent nations, were necessarily diminished, and their power to dispose of the soil at their own will, to whomsoever they pleased, was denied by the original fundamental principle, that discovery gave exclusive title to those who made it. Although we do not mean to engage in the defence of those principles which Europeans have applied to Indian title, they may, we think, find some excuse, if not justification, in the character and habits of the people whose rights have been wrested from them. . . .

The title by conquest is acquired and maintained by force. The conqueror prescribes its limits. Humanity, however, acting on public opinion, has established, as a general rule, that the conquered shall not be wantonly oppressed, and that their condition shall remain as eligible as is compatible with the objects of the conquest. Most usually, they are incorporated with the victorious nation, and become subjects or citizens of the government with which they are connected. The new and old members of the society mingle with each other; the distinction between them is gradually lost, and they make one people. Where this incorporation is practicable, humanity demands, and a wise policy requires, that the rights of the conquered to property should remain unimpaired; that the new subjects should be governed as equitably as the old, and that confidence in their security should gradually banish the painful sense of being separated from their ancient connexions, and united by force to strangers.

When the conquest is complete, and the conquered inhabitants can be blended with the conquerors, or safely governed as a distinct people, public opinion, which not even the conqueror can disregard, imposes these restraints upon him; and he cannot neglect them without injury to his fame, and hazard to his power.[2]

Although Marshall waved the banner of conquest, he waved it with some subtlety. I spoke with Mario Gonzalez, who added some historical dimension to the decision. "John Marshall described the tribes as conquered nations, although in the case of the Sioux bands this is not how they saw themselves—the Sioux have never been conquered militarily and ended the war of 1866-67 by entering into a treaty of friendship and peace with the United States. But Marshall wrote that the property of the tribes should be protected, and that they should not be forced to give allegiance to the conquering government. He believed it more desirable to let the younger generation come to identify with the new culture over time, as the generations that had a strong allegiance to the old culture died off. He saw an eventual merger of peoples, an assimilation of Indian people into the conquering culture.

"This has in fact been the government's long-term policy: that the reservations and Indian cultures are temporary fixtures, eventually to be integrated into 'mainstream' American life. The conquest of North America will then be complete, when the two cultures merge as one people. From the government's point of view, land issues like the Sioux land claims need to be resolved so that assimilation can take place. Indian people are diametrically opposed to this; it is exactly what they are fighting against. They want to maintain their cultures, their land base, their sovereignty, and their reservations."

Gonzalez also pointed out that the payment of both annuities and the tools of "civilization" promised to the Indians in the Act of 1877 are not seen by the Sioux as a handout, as gratuitous government largesse. The annual payments of goods, now transformed into BIA grants, are compensation for the real loss of a way of life that would ensue when the buffalo no longer "range . . . in sufficient numbers to justify the chase."[3] This meant that the government had and has a continuing obligation to make payment for the vital resources it took away. The obligation became all the more profound after the 1868 treaty reservation was truncated by the congressional enactments of 1877 and 1889, since these remaining reservation lands are not adequate to support a population density far higher than in the surrounding non-reservation counties.

Contrast this idea of continuing obligation with the goal of the Indian Claims Commission, which heard the case that resulted in the proffered Black Hills settlement. Its goal, in the language that established the commission, is the "full discharge of the United

States of all claims and demands touching any of the matters involved [in Indian claims]."[4]

The prospect of a monetary resolution to Indian land claims, which would involve a final extinguishment of title, leaves many Sioux wondering what a postsettlement future would be like, a great unknown without a trial identity that has recognized claims rooted in prior occupancy of the land. Today, the reservation Sioux of North and South Dakota are among the poorest people in North America, with desperate medical, educational, and economic development needs. Sitting in a bank in Washington, D.C., is a settlement now worth $500 million. It is truly remarkable, and truly a measure of the combined fears, wisdom, stubbornness, political shrewdness, and spiritual striving of the Sioux, that they have collectively resisted this tempting Faustian bargain for more than twenty years.

13

TWILIGHT OF EMPIRE

O ne day in the summer of 1997 I drove to Pierre—in South Dakota you say "Peer"—to see a painting, one that tells a strange little story about the present state of Indian-white relations in South Dakota, the power of symbols in the work of history, and the political cost-benefit calculations those symbols provoke.

The South Dakota Capitol, recently restored, is lovely, reminding the visitor of a time when Americans knew the importance of public space and invested it with grandeur. You can see the dark dome of the building on the west side of the Missouri as you approach the city on South Dakota 44. It sits in a little park by an artificial lake, with a grand front staircase leading up to a doorway guarded by veined white marble Corinthian columns. Inside, offices and legislative halls are arranged along two crossing lines, suggesting the design of a church. A high curved arcade has a roof of stained glass. The water fountains are of white marble with sensuous curved brass fittings. In the men's room the chrome pipes gleam, leading up above the toilets and urinals to shiny wooden water tanks. The floors are mosaic tile and glass brick.

The building, like Rushmore, tells a story about identity—no less a story than the epic of Western settlement and the shock of cultural confrontation, a story told in a layering of images from several generations. On the ceiling under the dome are paintings of pioneer women dressed in togas and tending their farms—a claim to both Western traditions. Above the doorway at the end of the second-floor arcade is a large painting of an Indian submissively spreading a buffalo robe at the feet of a young white pioneer in buckskin. The ceiling of the senate chamber features a mural on the theme of the Louisiana Purchase: a half-nude Indian woman drops a Fleur-de-Lis as she is covered with the Stars and Stripes by a winged figure representing America.

Around the rotunda mezzanine fly the flags not only of the United States and of South Dakota but of the United Sioux Tribes and of Mount Rushmore (I hadn't known it had its own flag). Hanging with the flags is a Sioux ceremonial staff, trimmed with eagle feathers.

In the hallway outside the governor's office, painted near the ceiling in shallow niches, are scenes of Indian, pioneer, and farm life: *Buffalo Hunt, Prairie Schooner* (a covered wagon), *Breaking the Soil, Indian Camp, Wagon Train.*

A glass case near the entranceway tells the story of how former Governor George Mickelson proclaimed 1990 a Year of Reconciliation. He later proclaimed a Century of Reconciliation and staked a considerable amount of political capital on improving race relations in his state, and it wasn't just talk; he began the process by taking on some really hard issues, like tribal rights in the Black Hills.

The painting that I came to see hung in the governor's reception room, where those who have come to see the governor sit and chat with his secretary while they wait for their appointments. It's a large piece by Edwin Blashfield, a famous muralist whose works decorate the government buildings of many Western states, including the statehouses of Minnesota and Iowa.

The central figure is a white woman in a white robe, her eyes cast heavenward, her hands clasping a book across her chest (the title of the book is not visible, but it's not hard to guess what book it is). She seems to simultaneously abhor and approve what is happening around her, a nasty but necessary piece of business. Two handsome men, one on each side of her, one with a pistol, one with a rifle, are pushing dark, sinister Indians to the ground and trampling them into the mud. One Indian, of indeterminate gender, face covered by a sort of scarf so that only the evil-looking eyes are showing, is being expelled from the scene off stage right. A settlers' wagon train is visible behind this tableau, obviously awaiting the outcome. A bosomy angel hovers overhead, looking down with tender, sisterly solicitude at the white woman and pointing the way forward—westward. The tones of the painting are dark and subdued, except for the two female figures, who are shining with an internal light.

The painting bears a plaque: "Painted in 1910 by Edwin Blashfield, this mural, 'Spirit of the People,' symbolized the history of the period. To appropriately reflect the change in the times and the attitudes of the people, it has been retitled 'Only By Remembering Our Mistakes Can We Learn.' " The new title seems well intentioned, yet quite Orwellian. Although a work may acquire new meanings through time, the intended meaning can't be retroactively changed.

The painting has a tangential and serendipitous connection with Rushmore: it was Doane Robinson, as Superintendent of the Legislative Reference Division, who corresponded with Blashfield in 1908 and 1909 and eventually recruited him to paint this panel in the new statehouse, just as, sixteen years later, he recruited Borglum for another grand and symbolic project. It is doubtful that Robinson, who was close to the genesis of the piece, would have been susceptible to this rather bizarre reinterpretation. He told Blashfield in November 1908 that "Mr. Andrews, who has the decorations of the new capital in charge, is here and he has shown me your suggestion for the panel which you are to fill in the building. I like it very much. Its simplicity particularly appeals to me. Frankly, I was fearful that you would give us an allegory so involved that it would require a 'set of directions for operating,' but this scheme is so lucid that with a mere key word everyone will comprehend its significance."[1] Indeed, the message is clear as a bell.

Like symbols of the Confederacy throughout the South, the painting has been causing embarrassment and defensive reactions for some time, and as with the Confederate flag, attempts to neutralize it have led to legislative logjams. The story of the painting is one of those little tragicomedies of modern politics that would almost be funny if it didn't reveal so much about the tenacity and the nastiness of identity myths.

The piece is affixed to the plaster of the wall. This either makes it difficult to remove or offers a good excuse not to remove it, depending on your point of view. It has a very specific iconography: the central female figure represents South Dakota itself, the white man on her right the civilian militia, the man on her left the cavalry. The angel blessing the scene represents the Spirit of Progress, and the settlers in the background are, well, settlers, the bearers of "civilization." The Indian with the partially hidden face is Evil or, in some interpretations, Ignorance, on the run. This explanation was, until recently, part of the official Capitol tour.

The mural was on display continuously from 1910 until 1971, when the newly elected governor, Richard Kneip, ordered that it be hidden from public view by a curtain. Kneip commissioned a busy and rather kitschy piece by Paul War Cloud Grant, a narrative pictorial history of South Dakota from the dinosaurs to Wounded Knee to the college graduations of modern youth. Nowadays it hangs in the South Dakota Cultural Heritage Center near the Capitol. It is not a very good painting, in my opinion, but it has the virtue of not being the Blashfield.

Kneip stepped down in 1978; he was appointed ambassador to Singapore by Jimmy Carter, and the lieutenant governor served out his term. In 1978, William Janklow was elected governor.

Janklow is an interesting political study. When he was in law school he spent his summers working for James Abourezk, then an innkeeper near Rapid City, and became a good friend of the family—and of Russell Means, who was also working for Abourezk. As a young lawyer serving the Rosebud Sioux tribe in the late 1960s, he was known as a dedicated, hard-working advocate for his poor clients.

When a resurgent Indian nationalism and a more confrontational Indian politics began to sweep South Dakota in the 1970s, inspired by but not limited to AIM, Janklow built a career by playing on white fears and not-so-latent racism.

As a South Dakota prosecutor, he vigorously pursued charges against the Custer courthouse rioters, getting a one to five year prison term for Sarah Bad Heart Bull. Soon afterward, as attorney general, he pursued a legal vendetta against AIM leaders, personally directing the prosecution of Dennis Banks on charges stemming from the 1973 occupation of Wounded Knee and from the Custer courthouse riot.

In 1975 two FBI agents were killed at Oglala, on the Pine Ridge reservation. The murders were the crime for which Leonard Peltier was later given two life sentences, although there are serious doubts about both the evidence and the conduct of his trial and appeals.[2] Janklow, an ex-Marine, grabbed his AR-15, threw a bulletproof vest over his business suit, and joined the massive FBI manhunt. How useful he was to the FBI is questionable, but the political astuteness of this piece of theater is not.

Janklow has opposed virtually every move by South Dakota tribes to reclaim treaty land, most recently in a three-sided dispute between tribal governments, militants claiming 1851 and 1868 treaty rights, and the South Dakota government over a stretch of

Missouri shoreline that the federal government transferred to the state. He opposed the Bradley bill. He recently boasted that it was his intervention that prevented Bill Clinton from granting a pardon to Leonard Peltier on his way out of office.[3] His consistent opposition on Indian land and tribal sovereignty issues—as well as his evidently personal vendetta against the militant leaders—has led many Indians in South Dakota to call him Wild Bill Janklow, the Indian Fighter.

Janklow's first term as governor ran from 1979 to 1983; he served again from 1987 to 1991, and in 1995 he took office yet again; his present term expires in 2003. He is a popular Republican governor, good at getting federal subsidies for his state, a strong supporter of George W. Bush (he was an elector from South Dakota in 2000) but relatively moderate in affairs not involving Indians.

In 1994 the South Dakota legislature, led by Rosebud legislator Paul Valandra and under unceasing pressure from tribal groups and the South Dakota Peace and Justice Center, passed a law requiring that the Blashfield painting be removed or covered up. At some point, perhaps during the caretaker administration of Harvey Wollman, perhaps in the early days of the Janklow administration, the Blashfield had gone back on display. I cannot find out exactly when this happened; no one involved in either administration will own up to uncovering it. However it happened, until 1997 Janklow was steadfast in his opposition to either removing or draping the painting. He took the line (which is taken by several South Dakota newspapers that want to keep the painting as it is) that the painting is simply an acknowledgment of history and has an important educational function; those who say this never seem to ask what it is doing in the governor's office. If education is intended, it doesn't seem particularly effective. In 1997 the governor's receptionist seemed surprised that anyone could be offended by the piece, remarking, "Most people really like it. They say it's art and it's just a part of history."

When it became clear, several years after the law was passed, that Janklow and the committee in charge of Capitol renovations intended to continue to find ways to allow the painting to remain on display, there were several protests in the governor's office. It must surely have become an annoyance to him. It was probably something of a surprise that a symbolic issue could retain such vitality.

Perhaps the governor wanted to avoid the lawsuit on the issue that was about to be filed by the South Dakota Peace and Justice Center; perhaps he needed to find a way to withdraw with honor. At any rate, after several phone conversations with an elderly Pine Ridge woman, Marie Randall, he did seem to come around to the idea that the painting was hurtful and not conducive to the state's business. He decided to have it covered with an internal wall.

In keeping with the human urge to record, to explain the workings of human belief, a note has been sealed up with the painting explaining what it is and why it has been covered. In its place will hang a star quilt presented to the governor by Marie Randall.

Having seen the piece on display, I wanted to see how the government had dealt with covering it. On my second visit to the governor's office his receptionist pointed to the wall where it was; the covering wall is so cleverly matched to the other walls that you'd never know it wasn't the original. The receptionist assured me with a great big smile, "It's been preserved, so if they ever want to put it on display again, they sure can do that."

Why can't Americans simply agree to see Rushmore and other artifacts of conquest as symbols of our common heritage and agree to interpret the details as individuals? Perhaps we could, if the past were behind us. If neutralizing a painting that threatens and demeans particular citizens of South Dakota required such a struggle, if a racial myth cherished by the majority group could foster such opposition to removing it, how dead is Manifest Destiny?

If the past didn't matter, 1868 and 1877 and 1889 and 1890 wouldn't matter—and they do matter. The reservations wouldn't matter—and they do matter.

Homestake can't turn a deep open cut back into a mountaintop again.

Despite generations of treaty-mandated payments in various forms, non-Indians have won the the struggle for resources. Indians remain among the poorest people in America.

The racial ideas at the heart of the sculptor's political ideology are not going to be addressed at his monument.

Nor is Rushmore's more disturbing history available to the broad popular culture. One particularly important example is children's literature about Rushmore. There has been quite a lot of this over the years. Of course, they all tell the story in the ritualized, standard manner: Borglum's drive, his art, his charming eccentricity, the greatness of the presidents he chose, the technical challenges he faced. Some of these books mention Red Cloud or the treaty in passing, as ancient history. Judith St. George, in her *The Mount Rushmore Story*, is one of the few children's writers who mention the treaty at all. If the children's books mention Stone Mountain, they typically resolve it much as do most of the general interest books about Rushmore. Lynn Curlee, in his 1999 work, *"Rushmore,"* for example, states: " . . . the aristocratic Atlantans who considered Stone Mountain their project treated Borglum as an employee—an impossible situation for the headstrong artist. In 1925, he destroyed his working models and abandoned the job rather than submit to interference with his ideas."[4]

Is this really a responsible way to teach our children? Surely, if Rushmore and our true national history are to be treated with respect, they deserve better than this. Curlee's book is recommended for nine- to twelve- year olds. They may not be ready for the full truth, but can such a truncated truth be called truth at all?

What is to be done?

When I lived in Rapid City, I became friendly with a group of young, politically active college students. They were idealistic, and their ideas were decidedly out of the mainstream for South Dakota, although often their idealism was fed by an insular naïveté: of about a dozen in this group, who had all grown up in the area, only one had ever set foot on an Indian reservation. When I asked them what ought to be done with Mount Rushmore, I got a simple and direct answer: "Blow it up."

I thought about this. My first response was that it showed both the arrogance and the perception of youth, which recklessly despises all lies, recognizes the damage that they do, and is willing to do more damage in combating them.

I remembered a newsreel I saw when I was about fourteen. It was shot soon after the Allied victory in Europe, with themes of devastation, redemption, justice. One scene was from liberated Nuremberg. A swastika sat above a huge triumphal arch, built as part of the staging for Hitler's massive 1934 rallies. The camera zoomed in on the swastika and held there, motionless, for a good ten seconds—a long time in a newsreel. And then—boom!—the swastika disintegrated.

Why blow it up? Soldiers had to be taken from other duties to climb the arch and wire the swastika. Surely dynamite was needed for other purposes. The Nazis were already decisively defeated; eliminating a design served no tactical necessity.

Yet the gesture mattered.

No, I am not comparing the Indian wars, the dispossession of the Plains Indians, and their subsequent relations with the U.S. government with the Nazi era, although the comparison is not quite so far-fetched as it might strike some people. Given the politically subordinate status of a whole people, the arguments based on need and superior civilization that were used to acquire their resources, certain parallels are easy to draw. What I am saying, however, is that the truth matters, and sometimes truth involves the conquest of lies.

So do I agree with my young friends' prescription? No. Politics doesn't work like that, and symbolically violent warfare would do no one in South Dakota any good.

Nor would it offer the clean, hard truth of blowing up a swastika. However misleading Rushmore may be as a national symbol, idealistic people of sterling character worked on it, fought for it, and believed in it. Borglum's ego may have driven the project, it may have been infected with ideas of conquest, but Rushmore would not have happened without many Depression-era miners who came to believe in what their labor was creating. Carving Rushmore required the quiet political support of men like South Dakota Congressman William Williamson and Senator Peter Norbeck, hard working sons of Norwegian immigrants with strong and selfless values who indeed embodied the best of the tradition of the homesteaders who struggled with a difficult land to make a life for themselves. Whatever it was meant to mean, it has over the years brought out a feeling for the best of America in millions of visitors who know nothing about treaties or the Ku Klux Klan. Consider George Moses, eldest son of immigrants, graduate of the American Gentlemen's School for Tailors and fifty years a tailor in the Black Hills area. He was inspired to write his own book about Rushmore and Borglum, about the example that Borglum set in terms of overcoming obstacles. Moses saw a metaphorical dimension to the task. He described the blasting that revealed the Rushmore heads in terms of the responsibility of discovering one's own truest, most profound character and capabilities. It is a belief about Rushmore and a reaction to it that is worthy of admiration and respect.[5]

Perhaps, in the fullness of time, Rushmore will become a purely commercial playground, like Stone Mountain, bereft of ideology. There has been some movement towards this with the commercialization of Keystone and the kitsch aura of the mountain. We are not there yet—Mount Rushmore means something to the nation that Stone Mountain no longer means to Confederate sentimentalists— and it's no real solution anyway, for without any historical grounding, the truth is not served.

Maybe Rushmore will go the way of the Little Bighorn Battlefield, where a conscious effort has been made to bring in other elements of the story, other perspectives, and to give it a meaning more profound and useful than that of the expansionist imperative. This can't happen so long as the Lakota have outstanding land claims in the Black Hills—without a resolution of these claims there is no way to come to an agreement about history. As far as the government is concerned these claims were settled with an offer of money more than twenty years ago.

What if the government were to restore federal land in the Black Hills to the Lakota and let them decide what to do with Rushmore, how to interpret it? A radical notion; a fantasy.

If the Lakota are not to get the land back, they have the option of endorsing a challenge to Rushmore on its own terms. This approach is underway at Crazy Horse Mountain, where the family of sculptor Korczak Ziolkowski—an erstwhile apprentice at Rushmore—is continuing the work that occupied him from 1947 until his death in 1982: carving an entire mountain into an equestrian sculpture of Crazy Horse. This project, although it was instigated at the request of Henry Standing Bear, a relative of Crazy Horse, is subject to all the reservations about the individual as an object of worship expressed by another Crazy Horse relative, Charlotte Black Elk, in relation to Rushmore.

There are several other problems with a Crazy Horse mountain sculpture that do not apply to Rushmore. Crazy Horse was one of the very few Indian leaders who never allowed his image to be captured. In his political roles he was passionately dutiful rather than personally ambitious. He was not particularly sociable. His own contemporaries, in fact, considered him rather odd, and he did not seek out fame. Would he have wanted to see a mountain blasted in his memory? Or not in his memory, since no one really knows what he looks like; in the memory of an imagined leader. Opinion among the Lakota people is divided.[6] The writers Ian Frazier and Larry McMurtry both noticed that Crazy Horse mountain is one of the few places where a visitor sees many smiling Indians. Yes; but the visitor only sees the Indians who choose to be there.

Monuments are built to stop unauthorized historical interpretation. Their purpose is to seal up meaning at a particular time, set it in stone, end debate. That doesn't mean that debate actually ends. Time does funny things to ideas as well as stone, in spite of Borglum's conviction that both can remain unchanged for millions of years. Less than sixty years after the sculpture was completed, the sculptor's ideas about the history of the United States and of the white race are so out of the mainstream that they cannot be discussed at the monument he built.

There are lots of historically problematical structures in a world strewn with monuments to empire. Many of them commemorate the forward movement of settlers claiming land. That land was usually taken from other people. It seems to me inevitable that, at some time not very far in the future, Rushmore will have to confront this fact, and the racial ideology that justified it. It will have to do better than a small display that mentions 1868. Until that happens, it will be a monument not to truth but to a part of a truth, not to America's greatness but to the capacity for self-deception that a strong and successful people have developed out of necessity.

Notes: Chapter 1

1. See Chapter 1 in Edward L. Widmer, *Young America: The Flowering of Democracy in New York City.*

2. *United States Magazine and Democratic Review*, 10/1837, pp.7-8.

3. Ibid, 7-8/1845, p. 9.

4. *New York Morning News*, 2/7/1845.

5. Ibid, 12/27/1845.

6. Display notes, Mount Rushmore National Memorial.

7. Ibid.

8. MR archives; plan written by Russell A. Apple, park historian, and Merrill Mattes, regional historian

9. Loren E. Pedersen to the *Rapid City Journal*, 3/27/1998.

Notes: Chapter 2

1. Figures for 2000, courtesy of the Rapid City Chamber of Commerce.

2. *American Guide Series of the Federal Writers' Project: South Dakota.* p. 140.

3. Figures for 2000. U.S. Department of Labor, Bureau of Labor Statistics.

4. Figures for 1997. U.S. Bureau of Indian Affairs, *Population and Labor Force Estimate Report.*

5. American Indian relief Council, 2001.

6. U.S. Department of Justice. *American Indians and Crime*, 1999.

7. I have changed both of these names to protect "Ajax's" privacy. The reader may rest assured that his real Indian name is at least as poetic as the one I made up.

8. It is not unprecedented for the Congressional Medal of Honor to be rescinded. For example, Congress felt that merely guarding Lincoln's body was not a sufficiently heroic act, and after the nation's sorrow passed, stripped the medals from the soldiers who accompanied his casket on its way west to Illinois.

9. For details, see Paul Chaat Smith, "Big Movie." 1992.

10. A reproduction of Riggs' Dakota primer, published in 1851, can be seen at the Treaty Museum, Travois de Sioux, Minnesota.

11. In Virginia A. Armstrong, *I Have Spoken: American History Through the Voices of the Indians*. pp. 128-9.

12. E. Black Elk DeSersa, O. Black Elk Pourier et al, *Black Elk Lives*, p. 137.

13. Charles Larpenteur, *Forty Years A Fur Trader*, p. 430.

Notes: Chapter 3

1. *Rapid City Journal*, 7/28/1927

2. *High Country Herald*, Gold Discovery Days 1997 Souvenir Edition.

3. Larpenteur, p. 133.

4. There are some exceptions to the pattern of settlement density.

Aztec Tenochtitlan—today's Mexico City—was one of the largest and densest cities in the world when Cortes came across it in 1519, a development dependent on agriculture and the ability that it gave to the Aztecs to become an Imperial culture. But while the Aztecs and their subordinate peoples grew crops, nowhere in the New World was there anything like the number and diversity of domesticated animals that there was in the Old. This may well have been simply the luck of the draw in terms of the paucity of viable candidate creatures for domestication, coupled with a geography that, unlike the broad flat European plain, discouraged the diffusion of domesticated animals and techniques of domestication. For a thorough discussion of this fascinating subject, see Jared Diamond, *Guns, Germs and Steel*, and Alfred Crosby, *Ecological Imperialism: The Expansion of Europe 900-1900*.

5. Northwest Ordinance, Article 3. July 13, 1787.

6. Shephard Krech III, *The Ecological Indian*, p. 147.

7. Nathaniel West, *The Ancestry, Life and Times of Hon. Henry Hastings Sibley, LLD*, p. 263.

8. Proceedings of the Military Commission, Senate Executive Document 26, 39th Congress 2nd Session, p. 129-130.

9. *Rocky Mountain News*, 12/29/1864

10. Proceedings of the Military Commission, p. 47.

11. Ibid, p. 117.

12. Evan S. Connell, *Son of the Morning Star*, p. 132.

13. Secretary of the Interior Columbus Delano, 3/28/1872.

14. Annie Tallent, *The Black Hills, Or the Last Hunting Ground of the Dakotahs*, p. 10.

15. Ibid.

16. *Bismarck Tribune*, 6/17/1874.

17. *Chicago Inter-Ocean*, 8/27/1874.

18. *Yankton Press & Dakotaian*, 8/13/1874.

19. William Blackburn, *History of North and South Dakota*, SD Historical Collections v. 1, 1902, p. 65.

20. Sheridan to Terry, in the *Yankton Press and Dakotaian*, 9/3/1874.

21. *Yankton Press & Dakotaian*, 9/10/1874.

22. Sheridan to Terry, as quoted in Arthur Lazarus, *Black Hills, White Justice*, p. 343.

23. Nicholas Black Elk, *Black Elk Speaks*, p. 79.

24. Ibid, p. 127.

Notes: Chapter 4

1. Gutzon Borglum, "I Molded A Mountain," *Coronet* magazine, 1941.

2. Doane Robinson to the *Pioneer Times*, 2/6/1924.

3. "The Woman On Mount Rushmore," in Simon Schama, *Landscape And Memory*.

4. Rushmore chapter in Albert Boime, *The Unveiling Of The National Icons: A Plea For Patriotic Iconoclasm In A Nationalist Era*.

5. June Culp Zeitner and Lincoln Borglum, *Borglum's Unfinished Dream*, p. 92.

6. LOC, Gutzon Borglum collection; notes for autobiography; and as quoted in Mary Borglum and Robert Casey, *Give The Man Room*, p. 28.

7. SDSHS, Frank Hughes collection; Mary Borglum to Mrs. Frank Hughes.

8. LOC, Gutzon Borglum collection; August [Borglum] Williams to Mary Borglum, 10/17/1947.

9. LOC, Gutzon Borglum collection;.Borglum radio speech broadcast from Washington, DC, 2/28/1934.

10. Leonard Crow Dog, *Crow Dog: Four Generations of Sioux Medicine Men*, p. 37.

11. In the original Seven Major Crimes Act of 1885, these were: murder, manslaughter, rape, assault with intent to kill, arson, burglary, larceny.

12. Schama, p. 397.

13. I am indebted to Ann Marie Wood for an interesting discussion of this experiment.

14. William Gilpin, *The Mission of the North American People*, p. 69.

15. Gilpin, p. 109-110.

16. Thomas L. Karnes, *William Gilpin, Western Nationalist*, p. 350.

17. Gilpin, p. 56.

18. Gilpin, p. 63.

19. LOC, Gutzon Borglum collection.

20. See, for example, Borglum's correspondence with President Hoover, LOC, Gutzon Borglum Collection.

21. LOC, Gutzon Borglum collection; Borglum telegram to Karl Mundt, 2/7/1941.

22. Felix Frankfurter, *Felix Frankfurter Reminisces*, p. 55.

23. LOC, Gutzon Borglum collection; draft of Czech Declaration of Independence.

24. Gutzon Borglum, "Art that is Real and American," *The World's Work*, June 1914.

25. LOC Gutzon Borglum collection; Gutzon Borglum, undated draft of an article on George Washington.

26. Gutzon Borglum, "Art that is Real and American."

27. Michael Crawford, *The Origins of Native Americans*, p. 39.

28. *San Francisco Examiner*, 2/22/1934.

29. All submissions in LOC, Gutzon Borglum collection.

30. Gutzon Borglum, letter to the *Sioux Falls Argus-Leader*, 8/25/1938.

31. Gutzon Borglum, *South Dakota Hiway Magazine*, June 1939.

32. E. Black Elk DeSersa and O. Black Elk Pourier et al, pp. 99-100.

33. Gutzon Borglum, "The Political Import and the Art Character of the National Memorial at Mount Rushmore," in *The Black Hills Engineer*, Vol. XVIII No. 4, 1930.

Notes: Chapter 5

1. SDSU, undated pamphlet, from FBI AIM files, Reel 7.

2. Mary Crow Dog, *Lakota Woman*, p. 119.

3. Details of the riot are from *State v. Bad Heart Bull, Nos. 11531, 11573, Supreme Court of South Dakota*. The South Dakota Supreme Court combined two cross cases; Sarah Bad Heart Bull, Robert High Eagle, and the State of South Dakota are all both plaintiffs and defendants. I have relied primarily on this case record and on Means and Mary Crow Dog, who were present.

4. *Rapid City Journal*, 2/9/1973.

5. E.W. Martin, quoted in the *Hot Springs Star*, 8/20/1925.

6. *Chicago Inter-Ocean*, 8/27/1874.

7. Tallent, pp. 3, 12.

8. Narration from Custer City Gold Discovery Days Pageant of Paha Sapa.

9. Millie Heidepriem explanatory text, Custer Courthouse Museum.

Notes: Chapter 6

1. George Hearst, 5/23/1878; quoted in Mildred Fielder, *The Treasure of Homestake Gold*, p. 57-58.

2. *American Guide Series of the Federal Writers' Project: South Dakota.* p. 116.

3. "Butte and Lead Compared." *Engineering and Mining Journal*, 8/29/1914, p. 378. Quoted in Jopseph Cash, *Working the Homestake*, p. 98.

4. See, for example, *Homestake Mining Company v. Board of Environmental Protection And The Department of Environmental Protec-*

tion, State of South Dakota, Nos. 12705, 12706 Supreme Court of South Dakota 289 N.W.2d 561; 1980 S.D; United States of America v. Homestake Mining Company No. 78-1728, 595 F.2d 421; 1979 U.S. App; Homestake Mining Company v. United States Environmental Protection Agency, 584 F.2d 862; 1978 U.S. and 477 F. Supp. 1279; 1979 U.S. Dist.

5. Homestake Mining Company, *Homestake Centennial*, p. 1. 1976.

6. *The New York Journal*, 10/10/1897.

7. Ibid, 10/11/1897.

8. Ibid, 10/17/1897.

9. Ibid, 2/19/1898.

10. Ibid, 3/25/1898.

11. Ibid, 2/17/1898.

12. Theodore Roosevelt, *The Rough Riders*, p. 75.

13. Ibid, p. 133.

Notes: Chapter 7

1. Email from Gerard Baker, 7/13/1998.

2. George A. Custer, *My Life on the Plains*, p. 80.

3. Ibid, p. 22.

4. It is interesting although probably not in any way significant that Chivington, Custer, Grant, Sherman and Sheridan were all from Ohio. Something in the water.

5. Custer, in comments printed in the *Sioux Falls Independent*, 3/9/1876.

6. As reported in the *New York Times*, 6/26/1976. In his autobiography, Means recalls a slightly more bellicose version of this speech.

7. The recently completed FDR and Korean War monuments—unlike Mt. Rushmore—were entirely funded by private donations.

Notes: Chapter 8

1. LOC, Gutzon Borglum collection; Gutzon Borglum, unpublished article.

2. Shaff and Karl Shaff, introduction, p. ix.

3. LOC, Gutzon Borglum collection; Borglum to D.C. Stephenson, undated draft of telegram.

4. David Chalmers, *Hooded Americanism*, p. 27.

5. For details of the meetings with Wilson and White, see Eric Goldman, *Rendezvous with Destiny*, p. 228-229.

6. *Atlanta Journal*, 11/22/1915.

7. Ibid, 11/21/1915.

8. Ibid, 12/7/1915.

9. Ibid, 12/15/1915.

10. Ibid, 12/7/1915.

11. Ibid, 12/7/1915.

12. Ibid, 12/19/1915.

13. Ibid, 11/20/1915.

14. Ibid, 11/20/1923.

15. William G. Shepherd, "The Fiery Double Cross." *Collier's Magazine*, 7/28/1928.

16. LOC, Gutzon Borglum collection; short unpublished article, "Suggestions for Immigration," Borglum to D. C. Stephenson, 9/5/1923.

17. LOC, Gutzon Borglum collection; Borglum to D. C. Stephenson, 9/20/1923.

18. LOC, Gutzon Borglum collection; Borglum to D. C. Stephenson, 6/2/1923.

19. LOC, Gutzon Borglum collection; Borglum to D. C. Stephenson, 12/20/1923.

20. LOC, Gutzon Borglum collection; Borglum to D. C. Stephenson, 7/19/1924.

21. LOC, Gutzon Borglum collection; Henry S. Johnston to Hollins Randolph, 2/10/1928.

22. LOC, Gutzon Borglum collection; Sam Venable to Borglum, undated handwritten note.

23. From Silver Dollar City's corporate web site, www.silverdollarcity.com.

Notes: Chapter 9

1. LOC, Gutzon Borglum collection; Henry Standing Bear to Borglum, 6/3/1938.

2. SDSHS Doane Robinson collection; Frank J. Hughes papers.

3. *Rapid City Daily Journal*, 10/10/1925.

4. Rex Alan Smith, *The Carving of Mount Rushmore*, p. 111.

5. *The Black Hills Engineer*, Vol. XV, #1, 1927.

6. Ibid.

7. Ibid.

8. Ibid.

9. Ibid.

10. BIA Report of 1838, quoted in James Officer, "The American Indian and Federal Policy," in Waddell and Watson, *The American Indian in Urban Society*, p. 25.

11. This should not be read as saying that he actually did collect enough legitimate signatures. There is some evidence that many of the signatures were those of women, children, or non-Lakota traders. See Mario Gonzalez & Elizabeth Cook-Lynn, *The Politics of Hallowed Ground*, Appendix D.

12. Leupp, F. E. *The Indian and His Problem*, p. 85.

13. Edward Lazarus, *Black Hills, White Justice*, pp. 96-98.

14. SDSHS, Doane Robinson papers; Doane Robinson account of interview with Russell, confirmed by McGillycuddy.

15. Annual Report of the Board of Indian Commissioners for 1921.

16. The combination of military and educational use continues at the site, which is now the U.S. Army War College.

17. See George E. Hyde, *Spotted Tail's Folk: A History of the Brulé Sioux*, p. 292-293, and *A Sioux Chronicle*, pp. 53-57.

18. Hyde, *A Sioux Chronicle*, p. 57.

19. Julia McGillycuddy, *McGillycuddy, Agent*, pp. 205-206.

20. U.S. government, *Rules for the Indian School Service*, 1931.

21. *Rapid City Journal*, 8/10/1927.

22. Ibid.

23. *New York Times*, 7/2/1939.

24. LOC, Gutzon Borglum collection; Borglum to Alvin Waggoner, 11/16/1938.

25. Quotes from the *Rapid City Journal*, 7/3/1939

26. Ibid.

27. Simon Schama, *Landscape and Memory*, p. 394.

28. Ibid.

29. RM; program of 1939 dedicatory pageant.

30. Ibid.

31. Ibid.

32. Stanley Vestal, *Sitting Bull, Champion of the Sioux*, p. 276.

33. *Rapid City Journal*, 7/5/1991.

Notes: Chapter 10

1. *Rapid City Journal*, 8/22/1970.

2. *Rapid City Journal*, 9/12/1970.

3. Ibid.

4. Means, p. 170.

5. *Rapid City Journal*, 9/1/1970.

6. Ibid, 9/3/1970; letter from Joseph Dudley, Chairman, Yankton Sioux Tribe.

7. *Rapid City Journal*, 6/10/1971.

8. RM; Rushmore report.

9. *Rapid City Journal*, 7/5/1975.

10. Ibid.

11. June Culp Zeitner and Lincoln Borglum, *Borglum's Unfinished Dream*, pp. 153-155.

12. See Vine Deloria, Jr. *Custer Died For Your Sins.*

13. Memo prepared by the FBI for Director Clarence Kelley, FBI Files on the American Indian Movement, Microfilm collections, USD.

14. Interview with James Abourezk, 8/31/2001.

15. Means, p. 348-9.

Notes: Chapter 11

1. *Rapid City Journal*, 7/24/1962.

2. SDSHS, Doane Robinson papers; transcript of Karl Mundt, Rushmore anniversary radio broadcast, 1952.

3. RM; plan for United Nations headquarters.

4. SDSHS, Doane Robinson papers; account by McGillycuddy, in letter to Doane Robinson.

5. Means, p. 189.

6. *Rapid City Journal*, 5/18/1989.

7. Calvin Coolidge, as quoted in *The Black Hills Engineer*, Vol. XVIII No. 4, 1930.

8. Ronald Wright, *Stolen Continents*, p. 179.

9. LOC, Gutzon Borglum collection.

10. Gutzon Borglum, "I Molded A Mountain."

11. Mount Rushmore National Memorial Committee brochure, 1941.

12. SDSHS; Superintendent's Annual Report to the Mount Rushmore National Memorial Society, 1958.

13. USD, found in Peter Norbeck papers.

14. USD, found in Peter Norbeck papers.

15. Statement to the U.S. House of Representatives on a proposal of the U.S. Fish And Wildlife Service to introduce grizzly bears into Idaho, July 28, 1997.

Notes: Chapter 12

1. *Indian Country Today*, December 1-8 1997.

2. From John Marshall, writing for the Supreme Court in *Johnson v. McIntosh*, 1823.

3. Treaty of 1868, Article 11.

4. Indian Claims Commission Act, Section 22.

Notes: Chapter 13

1. SDSHS, Doane Robinson collection; Robinson to Blashfield, 11/16/1908.

2. For an exhaustive survey of the case, see Peter Matthiessen's *In The Spirit Of Crazy Horse*, Viking Press.

3. *South Dakota governor says he persuaded Clinton not to pardon Peltier*, Associated Press State & Local Wire, 2/2/2001.

4. Lynn Curlee, *Rushmore*, p. 14.

5. George Moses, *The Mount Rushmore Story: Carve Your Own Mountain*.

6. For a survey of Lakota views on Crazy Horse Mountain, see the special series in *Indian Country Today*, 6/25/1996 to 7/22/1996.

SOURCES

For sources directly relating to Mount Rushmore and Gutzon Borglum I have made extensive use of primary materials in the archives at Mount Rushmore; in the South Dakota State Historical Society Archives at Pierre (Doane Robinson papers, Frank Hughes Papers); at the University of South Dakota at Vermillion, SD (Peter Norbeck Papers); and in the archives of the Library of Congress (Gutzon Borglum Collection.)

FOOTNOTE KEY:

RM—Rushmore archives

SDSHS—South Dakota State Historical Society Archives at Pierre, SD.

USD—University of South Dakota Archives at Vermillion, SD.

LOC—Library of Congress Archives at Washington, DC.

BOOKS AND ARTICLES

Althearn, Robert G. *Forts Of The Upper Missouri.* Englewood Cliffs, NJ: Prentice-Hall, 1967.

Armstrong, Virginia I. *I Have Spoken: American History Through The Voices Of The Indians.* Chicago, IL: Sage Books, 1971.

Billington, Ray Allen. *The Far Western Frontier, 1830-1860.* Albuquerque, NM: University of New Mexico Press, 1995.

Blackburn, William M. *A History of Dakota.* Aberdeen, SD: News Printing Co., 1902.

Black Elk, Nicholas (with John Neihardt). *Black Elk Speaks*. Lincoln, NE: University of Nebraska Press, 1988.

Boime, Albert. *The Unveiling Of The National Icons: A Plea For Patriotic Iconoclasm In A Nationalist Era*. Cambridge, UK: Cambridge University Press, 1998.

Borglum, Lincoln (with Gweneth Reed DenDooven). *Mount Rushmore: Heritage of America*. Las Vegas, NV: KC Publications, 1977.

Borglum, Mary and Casey, Robert. *Give The Man Room*. New York: Bobbs-Merrill Co. Inc., 1952.

Borglum, Gutzon. "Art that is Real and American," *The World's Work*, June 1914.

—"I Molded A Mountain", *Coronet* magazine, 1941.

—"The Political Import and Art Character Of The National Memorial At Mount Rushmore." In *The Black Hills Engineer*, Vol. XVIII No. 4, 1930. Rapid City, SD: South Dakota School of Mines and Technology, 1930.

Bradley, Bill. *Time Present, Time Past*. New York: Alfred A. Knopf, 1996.

Brands, H. W. *T. R.: The Last Romantic*. New York: Basic Books, 1997.

Brown, Dee. *Hear That Lonesome Whistle Blow: Railroads In The West*. New York: Holt, Rinehart & Winston, 1977.

—*Bury My Heart at Wounded Knee*. New York: Henry Holt, 1971.

Bryan, Jerry. *An Illinois Gold Hunter In The Black Hills*. Springfield, IL: Illinois State Historical Society, 1960.

Carrington, Frances. *My Army Life And The Fort Phil Kearny Massacre*. Freeport, NY: Books for Libraries Press, 1971.

Cash, Joseph. *Working the Homestake*. Des Moines, IA: Iowa State University Press, 1973.

Chalmers, David. *Hooded Americanism: The History of the Ku Klux Klan*. New York: Franklin Watts, 1981.

Connell, Evan S. *Son of the Morning Star: Custer and the Little Bighorn,* New York: Harper & Row, 1984.

Craig, Reginald S. *The Fighting Parson; the Biography of Colonel John M. Chivington.* Tucson, AZ: Westernlore Press, 1959.

Crawford, Michael. *The Origins of Native Americans: Evidence from Anthropological Genetics.* Cambridge, UK: Cambridge University Press, 1998.

Crosby, Alfred W. *Ecological Imperialism: The Biological Expansion Of Europe, 900-1900.* Cambridge, UK: Cambridge University Press, 1986.

Crow Dog, Leonard (with Richard Erdoes). *Crow Dog: Four Generations of Sioux Medicine Men.* New York: HarperPerennial, 1995.

Crow Dog, Mary (with Richard Erdoes). *Lakota Woman.* New York: HarperPerennial, 1990.

Custer, George Armstrong. *My Life on the Plains.* Oklahoma City, OK: University of Oklahoma Press, 1962.

DeLand, Charles E. *The Sioux Wars.* Pierre, SD: South Dakota Historical Society, 1930.

Deloria, Philip J. *Playing Indian.* New Haven, CT: Yale University Press, 1998.

Deloria, Vine Jr. *Custer Died for Your Sins.* New York: Macmillan, 1969.

DeSersa, Esther Black Elk; DeSersa, Aaron; DeSersa, Clifton; Pourier, Olivia Black Elk. Neihardt, Hilda, and Utecht, Lori, eds. *Black Elk Lives. Conversations with the Black Elk Family* Lincoln, NE: University of Nebraska Press, 2000.

Dewing, Rolland. *Wounded Knee II.* Chadron, NE: Great Plains Network, 1995.

Diamond, Jared. *Guns, Germs and Steel: The Fates of Human Societies.* New York: W. W. Norton, 1997.

Dixon, Thomas Jr. *The Clansman.* Lexington, KY: University Press of Kentucky, 1970.

Dobyns, Henry F. "Estimating aboriginal American populations:

An appraisal of techniques with a new hemispheric estimate." In *Current Anthropology*, n. 7, 1966.

Federal Writers' Project (Lisle M. Reese, ed.). *South Dakota: The American Guide Series*. New York: Hastings House, 1952.

Fielder, Mildred. *The Treasure of Homestake Gold*. Aberdeen, SD: North Plains Press, 1970.

Fite, Gilbert. *Mount Rushmore*. Norman, OK: University of Oklahoma Press, 1952.

Fixico, Donald L. *The Urban Indian Experience in America*. Albuquerque, NM: University of New Mexico Press, 2000.

Frankfurter, Felix (recorded in talks with Harlan B. Phillips). *Felix Frankfurter Reminisces*. New York: Reynal Press, 1960.

Frazier, Ian. *Great Plains*. New York: Penguin Books, 1989.

— *On The Rez*. New York: Farrar, Straus, Giroux, 1999.

Gilpin, William. *The Mission of the North American People: Geographical, Social and Political*. Philadelphia: J. B. Lippincott, 1873.

Glass, Matthew. "Producing Patriotic Inspiration at Mount Rushmore." In *Journal of the American Academy of Religion*, v. LXII, n. 2. 1994.

Goldman, Eric. *Rendezvous with Destiny*. Chicago: Ivan R. Dee, 2001.

Gonzalez, Mario. "The Black Hills: The Sacred Land Of The Lakota And Tsistsistas." In *Cultural Survival Quarterly*, Winter 1996.

Gonzalez, Mario, and Cook-Lynn, Elizabeth. *The Politics of Hallowed Ground: Wounded Knee and the Struggle for Indian Sovereignty*. Chicago: University of Illinois Press, 1999.

Griffith, T. D. *America's Shrine to Democracy*. Rapid City, SD: Mount Rushmore National Memorial Society, 1990.

Hagan, William T. *Theodore Roosevelt and Six Friends of the Indian*. Norman, OK: University of Oklahoma Press, 1997.

Hayes, Robert E. "The Rape of Mount Rushmore." Unpublished paper presented at the Dakota History Conference, Augustana College, Sioux Falls, SD, 1997.

Hess, Milton Jerome. *The Origin and Implementation of the Dawes Act in the Dakotas, 1865-1914*. New York: Columbia doctoral dissertation, 1982.

Homestake Mining Co. *Homestake Centennial 1876-1976*. Deadwood, SD: Homestake Mining Co., 1976.

Hyde, George E. *A Sioux Chronicle*. Norman, OK: University of Oklahoma Press, 1956.

—*Red Cloud's Folk: A History of the Oglala Sioux Indians*. Norman, OK: University of Oklahoma Press, 1937.

—*Spotted Tail's Folk: A History of the Brule Sioux*. Norman, OK: University of Oklahoma Press, 1974.

Jackson, Donald. *Custer's Gold*. Lincoln, NE. University of Nebraska Press, 1972.

Jensen, Richard E. *Eyewitness at Wounded Knee*. Lincoln, NE. University of Nebraska Press, 1991.

Karnes, Thomas L. *William Gilpin: Western Nationalist*. Austin, TX: University of Texas Press, 1970.

Kentfield, Calvin. "A Letter From Rapid City." *New York Times Magazine*. New York, 1970.

Krech, Shephard III. *The Ecological Indian*. New York: W. W. Norton & Co., 1999.

Larpenteur, Charles. *Forty Years a Fur Trader on the Upper Missouri*. Minneapolis, MN: Ross, & Haines, 1962.

Lazarus, Edward. *Black Hills, White Justice: The Sioux Nation vs. the United States, 1775 to the Present*. New York: HarperCollins, 1991.

Leupp, Francis E. *The Indian and His Problem*. New York: Arno Press, 1971.

Limerick, Patricia Nelson. *The Legacy of Conquest: The Unbroken Past of the American West*. New York: W. W. Norton and Company, 1987.

London, David. *Sun Dancer*. New York: Simon & Schuster, 1996.

Lutholtz, M. William. *Grand Dragon: D. C. Stephenson and the Ku*

Klux Klan in Indiana. West Lafayette, IN: Purdue University Press, 1991.

Lyman, Stanley. *Wounded Knee 1973: A Personal Account.* Lincoln, NE: University of Nebraska Press, 1991.

Matthiessen, Peter. *In the Spirit of Crazy Horse.* New York: Viking Press, 1991.

Mayo, James M. *War Memorials As Political Landscape: The American Experience And Beyond.* New York: Praeger Publishers, 1988.

McGillycuddy, Julia. *McGillycuddy, Agent.* Stanford, CA: Stanford University Press, 1941.

McLaughlin, James. *My Friend the Indian.* Boston and New York: Houghton Mifflin company, 1926

McMurtry, Larry. *Crazy Horse.* New York: Penguin Putnam, Inc. 1999.

Means, Russell (with Marvin J. Wolf). *Where White Men Fear To Tread.* New York: St. Martin's Press, 1995.

Melbo, Irving R. *Our America.* New York: Bobbs-Merrill Co., Inc., 1937.

Mooney, James. *The Ghost Dance Religion and the Sioux Outbreak of 1890.* Lincoln, NE: University of Nebraska Press, 1991.

—"Population." In F. W. Hodge (Ed.). *Handbook of American Indians North of Mexico.* Washington, DC: Bureau of American Ethnology, 1910.

Morgan, Kathleen O'Leary and Morgan, Scott (eds.). *South Dakota In Perspective 2001.* Lawrence, KS: Morgan Quitno Corporation, 2001.

Morris, Roy Jr. *Sheridan: The Life and Wars of General Phil Sheridan.* New York: Crown Publishers, 1992.

Moses, George. *The Mount Rushmore Story: Carve Your Own Mountain.* Rapid City: 1993.

O'Brien, Dan. *Spirit of the Hills.* New York: Crown Publishers, 1988.

Officer, James E. "The American Indian and Federal Policy." In

Waddell, Jack O. and Watson, O. Michael (eds.), *The American Indian in an Urbanizing America*. Boston, MA: Little, Brown & Co., 1971.

Price, Willadene. *Gutzon Borglum: Artist and Patriot*. New York: Rand McNally & Co., 1962.

Price, Catherine. *The Oglala People: A Political History 1841-1879*. Lincoln, NE: University of Nebraska Press, 1996.

Ricker, Eli and Danker, Donald. *The Wounded Knee Interviews of Eli S. Ricker*. Lincoln, NE: Nebraska State Historical Society, 1981.

Roosevelt, Theodore. *The Rough Riders*. New York: Random House, 1999.

Samuels, Peggy and Samuels, Harold. *Teddy Roosevelt at San Juan*. College Station, TX: Texas A&M University Press, 1997.

Schell, Herbert. *History of South Dakota*. Lincoln, NE: University of Nebraska Press, 1968.

Shaff, Howard and Shaff, Audrey Karl. *Six Wars at a Time: The Life and Times of Gutzon Borglum, Sculptor of Mount Rushmore*. Sioux Falls, SD: The Center for Western Studies, 1985.

Shepherd, William G. "How I Put Over The Klan." In *Collier's Magazine*, 7/14/1928.

—"Ku Klux Koin." In *Collier's Magazine*, 7/21/1928

—"The Fiery Double Cross." In *Collier's Magazine*, 7/28/1928.

Smith, Paul Chaat. "Big Movie." Catalogue essay written for the Dunlop Art Gallery's film series "Story of Our Lives," October 1992, Regina, Saskatchewan.

Smith, Paul Chaat, and Warrior, Robert. *Like A Hurricane: The Indian Movement From Alcatraz To Wounded Knee*. New York: The New Press, 1996.

Smith, Rex Alan. *The Carving of Mount Rushmore*. New York: Abbeville Press Publishers, 1985.

Swanberg, W. A. *Citizen Hearst*. New York: Bantam Books, 1963.

Sweeney, Marian Hopkins. *Indian Land Policy Since 1887 With*

Special Reference To South Dakota. Pierre, SD: South Dakota
State University Press, 1926.

Tallent, Annie D. *The Black Hills; Or, the Last Hunting Ground of the
Dakotahs.* Saint Louis, MO: Nixon-Jones Printing Company,
1899.

Traxel, David. *1898: The Birth of the American Century.* New York:
Vintage Books, 1998.

United States Government. *Proceedings of the Military Commission*
(Chivington investigation). Senate Executive Document 26,
39th Congress 2nd Session, 1867.

—*Annual Report of the Board of Indian Commissioners for 1921.*
Washington, DC: Government Printing Office, 1921.

—Rules for the Indian School Service. Washington, DC: Government Printing Office, 1931.

Utley, Robert M. *The Lance and the Shield: The Life and Times of
Sitting Bull.* New York: Henry Holt & Co., 1993.

—*The Last Days of the Sioux Nation.* New Haven, CT: Yale
University Press, 1963.

Vestal, Stanley. *Sitting Bull, Champion of the Sioux.* Norman, OK:
University of Oklahoma Press, 1989.

Welch, James and Stekler, Paul. *Killing Custer: The Battle Of The
Little Bighorn And The Fate Of The Plains Indians.* New York:
Penguin Books, 1994.

West, Nathaniel. *The Ancestry, Life and Times of Hon. Henry Hastings
Sibley, LLD.* St. Paul, MN: Pioneer Press Publishing Co., 1889.

Widmer, Edward L. *Young America: The Flowering of Democracy in
New York City.* New York: Oxford University Press, 1999.

Williamson, William. *A Biography of William Williamson.* Chicago:
The Lakeside Press, 1964.

Wright, Ronald. *Stolen Continents: The Americas Through Indian
Eyes Since 1492.* Boston: Houghton Mifflin, 1992.

Zeitner, June Culp, and Borglum, Lincoln. *Borglum's Unfinished
Dream.* Aberdeen, SD: North Plains Press, 1976.

CHILDREN'S BOOKS ON RUSHMORE:

Curlee, Lynn. *Mount Rushmore*. New York: Scholastic Press, 1999.

Gabriel, Luke S. *Mount Rushmore: From Mountain to Monument*. The Child's World, Inc. 2000.

Prolman, Marilyn. *The Story of Mount Rushmore*. Chicago, IL: Children's Press (Cornerstones of Freedom series), 1969.

St. George, Judith. *The Mount Rushmore Story*. New York: G. P. Putnam, 1985.

Santella, Andrew. *Mount Rushmore*. New York: Children's Press (Cornerstones of Freedom Series), 1999.

Wilkes, Mary and Morrison, Barbara. *They Said It Couldn't Be Done: A Life Story of the Sculptor of Mount Rushmore, Gutzon Borglum*. Aberdeen, SD: North Plains Press, 1976.

TREATY DOCUMENTS

Northwest Ordinance of 1787

Great Sioux Treaty of 1868

Sioux Act of 1877

General Allotment Act of 1887 (Dawes Act)

Burke Act of 1906

Sioux Nation Black Hills Act (Bradley bill) S.705 (not enacted)

PRESS

Exact citations are given in the relevant footnotes.

Atlanta Constitution

Atlanta Journal

Associated Press

Bismarck Tribune

Black Hills Engineer

Chicago Inter-Ocean

Coronet Magazine

Custer Weekly

Gordon Journal

High Country Herald

Indian Country Today

Los Angeles Times

New York Journal

New York Times

New York Morning News

Pioneer Times

Rapid City Journal

Rocky Mountain News

San Francisco Examiner

South Dakota Hiway Magazine

Sioux Falls Argus-Leader

Sioux Falls Independent

United States Magazine and Democratic Review

World's Work

Yankton Press & Dakotaian